OPEN

YOUR

HEART

LATINO PERSPECTIVES

José Limón, Timothy Matovina, and Luis Ricardo Fraga,
series editors

INSTITUTE *for*

Latino Studies

UNIVERSITY OF NOTRE DAME

The Institute for Latino Studies, in keeping with the distinctive mission, values, and traditions of the University of Notre Dame, promotes understanding and appreciation of the social, cultural, and religious life of U.S. Latinos through advancing research, expanding knowledge, and strengthening community.

OPEN

Religion and Cultural Poetics

YOUR

of Greater Mexico

HEART

DAVID P. SANDELL

UNIVERSITY OF NOTRE DAME PRESS

NOTRE DAME, INDIANA

Library of Congress Cataloging-in-Publication Data

Sandell, David P.
Open your heart : religion and cultural poetics of greater Mexico /
David P. Sandell.
pages   cm
Includes bibliographical references and index.
ISBN 978-0-268-04146-5 (pbk. : alk. paper)
ISBN 0-268-04146-6 (pbk. : alk. paper)
1. Mexican American Catholics—California—Fresno—Religious life.
2. Catholic Church—Customs and practices.   I. Title.
BX1407.M48S26   2015
263.0972—dc23
2014049367

FOR GABRIELA, CLAUDIA, AND ALEJANDRO

CONTENTS

ACKNOWLEDGMENTS

This book comes by way of encouragement and guidance from research participants, colleagues, mentors, friends, and family members. They have been a part of a journey that began long before my first visit to the parish of Saint Anthony Mary Claret in southeast Fresno, California, and my role as a student in Austin, Texas, among other events that mark the passage of time. Their presence on the journey accounts for a collective effort, as does the journey's outcome in this book. Any errors or faults, however, I claim as my own.

Gracie Romana Adame taught me to think of life as a journey. Gracie also taught me to make this journey with trust in fellow travelers. She trusted me with her name, asking that I use it. She introduced me to parishioners. On one occasion, she declined to sign a document that asked research participants if they understood the research and were, indeed, willing to participate. "We don't need these things," Gracie said, indicating that we were to continue according to the terms of the parish and its people. These accounts of trust make Gracie a representative of all the people featured in this book. I thank Gracie for her help. And in doing so, I thank all participants for their generous contributions.

Material support came from several libraries and staff members. They include the University of Texas at Austin's Benson Latin American Collection, Dolph Briscoe Center for American History, and Perry-Castañeda Library; Fresno State University's Henry Madden Library; Fresno County Library; and Texas Christian University's Mary Couts Burnett Library. I am particularly indebted to the Diocese of Fresno Pastoral Center and archivists Adrienne Alston and Scott Alston for their attention to my research needs.

Chapter 3 was originally published in *Anthropology of Consciousness*, and chapter 4 in *Aztlán: A Journal of Chicano Studies*. I thank reviewers and editors for their guidance.

Contributions also came in the form of conversations with mentors and colleagues, each playing a role in different stages of progress. John Hartigan, Ricardo C. Ainslie, Kathleen C. Stewart, Pauline Strong, José E. Limón, and Richard R. Flores inspired me early on and in many ways continue to do so to this day. At the University of Guanajuato, Luis Miguel Rionda introduced me to a different area of research that created distance from this project and allowed time for reflection, leading, I believe, to a better, refined work. Douglas E. Foley has been an ever-present voice since my Mexico stay, also offering an ear and a good dose of humor.

My colleagues at Texas Christian University deserve special mention. Shawn Keane brought ease to the day. Morrison Wong, Nowell Donovan, and others in administrative positions gave me time to write. Michael A. Katovich and Miguel C. Leatham were always available for conversation, acting as consultants under the auspice of friendship.

Ken R. Crane, Anthony M. Stevens-Arroyo, Ana María Díaz-Stevens, and other members of the Paral Study heard, read, and/or endured parts of this project, always providing feedback and support.

The University of Notre Dame Press's editorial team and reviewers provided direction that enabled me to bring this project to an end. I thank Acquisitions Editor Stephen Little for reaching out to me at a time when I thought the project was on indefinite hold.

William Scott Howard at University of Denver has been a wonderful friend and conversationalist, often tipping the scale of reciprocity far in his favor.

Marilyn Brown, a family friend and Fresno resident, gave me a place to stay and delightful evening conversation during an exploratory phase of research.

My aunt, Sister Patricia Celeste Pagliarulo, read the manuscript in different stages with the eye and patience of a copy editor.

Diego Gándara and Florencia Gándara Sáenz, my in-laws, have encouraged me for years, particularly in relation to unconventional choices. I am most thankful.

As indicated in the pages that follow, the writing responds to the loss of my parents, Carol Sandell and Harold David Sandell. I am forever grateful to them for just being who they were. I also thank my siblings, Mary, John, and Katy—my family.

And my wife, Gabriela, and our children, Claudia and Alejandro, have traveled along my side, helping to make a remarkably beautiful life.

INTRODUCTION

Many questions drive this work about Latino people of faith in Fresno, California. One addresses history and the way history impresses itself upon the present. Another addresses the application of theory—in particular, historicism and psychoanalysis—to what people say and experience. And another addresses my role as a writer and my ability to represent the lives of people whom readers might perceive as different from themselves and, moreover, to compel readers to empathize with those people. These questions constitute the theoretical baggage that I took to the field. I realized very shortly, however, that I couldn't begin to answer them, much less consider their relevance, until I addressed two other interrelated questions. These other questions were much more immediate and fundamental. They came up every time I participated in such activities as attending Mass, prayer groups, and processions: Why do these people practice religion? What is the role of rituals that define their religion?

The answers to these questions involve a paradox. This paradox is similar to Sister Mary Tiziana's comments about locating the center of a sacred circle (which I discuss in chapter 4).[1] My efforts to find answers entailed frustration and thoughts of wasting time. But they also involved an underlying conviction that I was never far from answers—that they were everywhere but with no special designation, enabling me to craft responses that readers could understand.

1

Then, in January 2001, after seven months in Fresno, I attended a monthly parish council meeting at Saint Anthony Mary Claret Church,[2] where I spent most of my time. About eight or nine of us sat around a table in the back room of the parish social hall. We clasped hands in preparation for a "live rosary," a ritual prayer consisting usually of five decades of the Hail Mary, each initiated with the Our Father and an implicit recollection of a biblical mystery about Mary and her son Jesus. At a live rosary, each participant takes a turn saying the Our Father, with another saying the first half of the Hail Mary and the entire group saying the second half. On this occasion, however, there was a change in the format. Before saying the Our Father, participants took turns expressing a special intention with respect to an event or condition—an upcoming retreat, an economic hardship, a friend's battle with cancer. This moment reminded me of what James Fernandez (1986) has said about metaphors: they link semantic domains, and in doing so, link the lives of the people affected by those domains.

This summary explanation of the ritual was, of course, simplistic, not capturing nearly what was at stake; nevertheless, it provided me with direction. At my next meeting with my friend and consultant Gracie Romana Adame, I asked, "Gracie, can you tell me about the rosary?"

Gracie said, "Ah, the rosary is a journey that tells how Mary followed her heart. Mary loved, Mary obeyed. Mary got involved. So a journey of her life, today, brings me to this journey that I am so involved with. . . . The rosary is a journey about following your heart."[3]

Each time I met with Gracie, I asked the same question: can you tell me about the rosary? She always responded in the same way. She would say, "The rosary is a journey," and proceed to tell me stories about her grandfather who had escaped assassination under Porfirio Díaz's regime, about her grandmother who'd tell a little girl that somebody loved her, about the mothers of incarcerated children, about the youth group, about going places and the way those places would affect other places and times. She told her stories for hours. They often came with tears, laughter, and long pauses that broached new images about love, strife, fear, abjection, and hope, always ending with same comment: "You see; the rosary is a journey."

Gracie provided insight into the rosary's poetics and suggested the ritual's ability to orient people in extraordinary ways. Like a refrain, the words acquire density, rhythm, and meaning through associations—those of contiguity and similarity understood, respectively, in the language of poetry as metonymy and metaphor (Jakobson 1960, 1987).[4] These tropes engage the intellect and the body to produce different ways of being in the world. In one respect, the rosary symbolizes biblical mysteries—the joyful, luminous, sorrowful, and glorious—about Mary and her son Jesus.[5] Participants conceived the contiguity of the past and present and the people who reside in them, constituting a world of epic proportions—timeless expression, cohesion, ideological closure, and wholeness (Bakhtin 1981).[6] While participants might have recognized distinctions that accompanied particular instances, for example, of suffering and death, they also realized life as a whole through the ritual's performance, creating an aesthetic that connotes, in addition to the empirical present, what the world ought to be (Langer 1957; V. Turner 1962; Kapferer and Hobart 2005).

In another respect, the rosary characterizes the participants' travel beyond rational boundaries, where each one experiences similarity by adjusting his or her behavior to the sacred and to other people's behavior. Gracie emphasized this suppression of reason by indicating that her journey constituted a sensual and emotional involvement with the biblical mysteries as they related to contemporary life. This experience drew on other people's rhythms and sentiments, orienting the body as a sensorial aperture to other people's dispositions (Rappaport 1999).[7] The body believes, Pierre Bourdieu observes, "in what it plays at" (1990, 73). The body produces tears for grief and for joy. This experience hinges on particular circumstances, broaches unknown conditions and open-ended outcomes, and emphasizes the participants' agency in the encounter of others.[8] This way of being resonates in words and images gleaned from emotion, gaps in logic, and pauses in the flow of conversation. Gracie's words and images implied something much more visceral and contentious, as if drawn from experiences forgotten or repressed or from a "vestige of linguistic identity" that she had lost (Ricoeur 1987, 75). These two ways of being-in-the-world represent a dialectical relationship between symbolism and practice. They locate where a subjective orientation to the sacred transforms an objective orientation to others and the inverse—a mutual permutation.[9]

Whether explored through the rosary or other rituals that sustain storytelling, this mutual permutation is uneven, evocative, tumultuous, and, often, hardly tolerable. Gracie asked me on occasion to turn off my tape recorder, suggesting that there were some things that shouldn't be recorded but needed to be remembered. This kind of contradiction surfaced in stories about, for example, a dream of California life—of working, of attaining prosperity, of making something of oneself—the individual pursuit and collective adventure defining notions of democracy as inscribed in America's literary tradition and marked by racial ideologies. The ideologies entailed an evaluative index—of hygiene, thrift, integrity, intelligence, and criminality, for example—that disqualified Latino people (and other people of color) from participating in the dream and justified relegation to a wage-labor force. This contradiction shouldn't be remembered because it involved acknowledgment that self-awareness was contingent upon one's own alterity, often emerging through crises and causing disillusionment and pain. The contradiction needed to be remembered because it epitomized others—empathy and estrangement, family cohesion and dissolution, safety and danger, prosperity and poverty—that defined life in Fresno and the region.

The contradictions form the content of data drawn from a few questions. Can you tell me about the rosary? Can you tell me about the Mass, the service, the procession, the pilgrimage, the journey? They were the right questions because they provided insight into identity formation, gender, citizenship, migration, capitalism, modernity, and people's interests and agendas—topoi for anthropological inquiry. These few questions, in other words, evoked a wide range of issues. They were the right questions, more importantly, because they gave insight into people's self- and collective awareness. Conceptual lenses, including those of psychology, history, tradition, and spirituality, helped give insight additional depth. The questions turned attention, mine and the participants', toward origins, often forgotten, repressed into primordial drives, sensate and inarticulate but referenced in language and experiences.

OPEN YOUR HEART REPRESENTS A TRADITION OF POETICS in the U.S. Southwest, or "Greater Mexico," that provides an emancipatory epistemology as an alternative to other, oppressive ones correlating with colonial, capitalist, and/or modern social conditions (Paredes 1958, 11). Américo Paredes helped define this tradition in scholarship of border balladry, most often sung in a décima or corrido and also related in story or evoked by playing a guitar melody. Paredes's *With His Pistol in His Hand* (1958) is particularly noteworthy in its study of the ballad of Gregorio Cortez, a south Texas folk hero known for having defended his brother against false arrest for horse theft and then eluded Texas Rangers, county sheriffs, and would-be lawmen on horseback. The study includes details that define a moral compass for the tradition and this project.

Paredes addresses Gregorio Cortez's appeal to people. The study incorporates an account of the region's history, the legend, archival documentation, and testimony. The study also entails a comparative analysis of the corrido, including treatment of a Spanish precedent, a Mexico City broadside, and ten other variants—nine collected from regional performers, and one made up of quatrains from the others and in accord with oral tradition to create an original "more detailed and factual than . . . later [ones]" (Paredes 1958, 180).[10] "By staying within the ballad traditions of his people," Paredes explains, the maker of the border corrido "succeeds in composing in a natural and often forceful style," to blend historical, literary, and social elements into a story recognizable and memorable for people to take as their own (183).

The legend represents the heroic figure of Gregorio Cortez as no less "natural and forceful." Cortez was born between Matamoros and Reynosa, Mexico, and buried somewhere on the border, perhaps on the Mexican or American side; no one knows for sure. And during his life, he accompanied his brother as far north as the Austin area to raise a family and make money with hard work. He was most adept at ranching, farming, shooting, and, of course, riding. Always polite, honest, and slow of temper, Cortez was a "good-looking man" with a "frank and engaging personality" (Paredes 1958, 95). On the fateful day in 1901, he escaped pursuers on a mare, outriding them, negotiating brush and watershed, and leaving no trail, as if, people thought, "he [were] riding through the air" (43). People gave him food, water, and advice to ensure his safety. On learning that his family members had been put into jail, that anybody who'd helped him had been beaten, thrown into jail, or hanged from a tree, Cortez ended the suffering by turning himself in. From the beginning to the end, Cortez's actions came naturally because he was native to this region, was familiar with the landscape, and embodied the characteristics of native inhabitants. The legend casts him as everyman whose heroism and forceful demeanor drew foremost from his morality; he sacrificed himself to the hands of adversaries so that his people could be free.

Performance of the corrido orients the individual into collective experiences fashioned over time and in places that define the region. "They still sing of him," Paredes declares in his rendition of the legend, "in the cantinas and the country stores, in the ranches when men gather at night to talk in the cool dark, sitting in a circle, smoking and listening to the old songs and tales of other days" (1958, 33). A guitar melody becomes a corrido that becomes a tale, carrying a rhythm, pitch, and tenor of speech to places that map an ever-expansive landscape.

Paredes contributed to this landscape by performing a song that became his scholarship and his story. With his guitar in his hand, Paredes performed corridos as much as he talked about them (Paredes and Herrera-Sobek 2012). In view of his years of instruction at the University of Texas, his story includes people who stay within a tradition of storytelling, illuminating historical, literary, and anthropological treatments.[11] Paredes's story also includes people whose lives parallel his own. The people offer in the spirit of Cortez something of themselves in different lines of flight. The lines of flight do not provide an escape from social injustice any more than does Cortez's flight on the mare. They draw out characteristics of native inhabitants, including work ethic, family, integrity, reciprocity, manners, and morality, to assemble an ever-expanding ground, channeling people into a collective, alternative way of being in contrast to a society that persists in social injustice. Paredes represents this ground as "Greater Mexico," inclusive of all who might call themselves Mexican not for national distinction but for a cultural one that "describes Cortez and his kind of people" (183).

The people have been subject to marginal social assignments and the abuse of power over the course of five hundred years. Timothy Matovina (2005) tells a part of their story by drawing on sixteenth-century pastoral debates about leadership of colonized subjects. The tenor of these debates carried over to those of regimes—Spanish, Mexican, and American—that define the course of time and lend understanding of contemporary parishioners at the San Fernando Cathedral, San Antonio, of their devotion to Our Lady of Guadalupe, and of their resistance to the powerful. Roberto R. Treviño (2006) picks up a similar story that draws on twentieth-century social, political, and religious history, providing a rich orientation to Mexican American Catholics in Houston. Kristy Nabhan-Warren (2005) focuses on the culmination of the past in a South Phoenix, Arizona, case study featuring Estela Ruiz, her family, and devotion to the Virgin and her healing powers. Nabhan-Warren documents ritual prayer, conversation, gatherings, and activities for their contribution to a story about replacing prejudice, hostility, individual aspirations, and social isolation with a sense of calm and unity. Luis D. León (1999, 2004) writes about religious devotees who undertake unorthodox practices, especially in times of negligible official, institutional support, to redirect beliefs and cope with hardships of barrio life, allaying fears, mitigating pain, and providing hope in the future. Anthony M. Stevens-Arroyo, Ana María Díaz-Stevens, and Gilbert R. Cadena (1994, 1995) have helped define unity and hope in editorial work on articles that feature popular religiosity, ethnic identity, community, and nationalism. Stevens-Arroyo (2002) has also presided over national studies of Latino faith communities, accounting for Protestant-based congregations and people who self-identify with different origins—Puerto Rican, Central American, and Mexican—and yet, in the spirit of Cortez, share experiences of oppression.

Other scholars have taken a different direction by focusing on religious devotees and events that shed light on the past. Yolanda Broyles-González (2002) tells a story about her grandmother's preparation for a good death, which involves fulfillment of a *manda* (promise) to a folk saint known for resistance to Porfirio Díaz's regime in life and service to the poor in death.[12] Her grandmother's story reveals Yaqui Catholicism as a spiritual orientation and a survival tactic that shows how people have incorporated Catholic religious symbols into indigenous ritual to disguise their beliefs from would-be oppressors. Patricia Baquedano-López (1997) addresses *la doctrina*, or children's religion class in Spanish at Saint Paul's Church, Los Angeles. Children learn to identify with a narrative about Juan Diego and Our Lady of Guadalupe's 1531 appearance at Tepeyac, Mexico. They also learn a means to recognize and resist discrimination. Stephen R. Lloyd-Moffett (2008) discusses how César Chávez drew inspiration from readings about Gandhi, Saint Francis, and Christ and clarity of mind from ritual prayer and fasting for leadership of the United Farm Workers. These examples give breadth to Cortez's kind of people. They show how actual life incorporates resources— social circumstances, dialogue, writings, legends, religious symbols, instruction, and ritual—for critique of and resistance to colonial conditions and advancement of ethical objectives, including ethnic identification, equality between genders, and unity across populations. The examples account for the substance of people's lives, which transcends to popular acknowledgment in story, décima, and corrido among other art forms, contributing to a tradition of poetics devoted to, José E. Limón explains, the interpretation of "aesthetically salient, culturally embedded textualities and enactments" (1994, 14).[13]

Cortez rode a mare with his pistol in his hand. Paredes performed with his guitar, and storytellers, with their voices. The pistol, guitar, and voices characterize performance, each with a "natural and forceful" style. These characteristics, Aristotle observed of art, support a truthful imitation of "one thing," "one action," a "complete whole," with several incidents so closely connected that none can be withdrawn without dislocating the whole (*Poetics* 1451a30–34). Aristotle gives an example in Homer's *Odyssey*, noting a journey as a plot that creates unity in a story about disparate events long ago.[14] In scholarship on Los Pastores, or the Mexican Shepherd's Play, Richard R. Flores helps define the one thing, action, or whole that comes out of performance, noting commemorative and constitutive elements. Performance entails ritual practices that draw on the past to remind people of who they are. Performance also combines structure and social and convivial disposition to produce a "shared sense of identity" (1994, 186; see Flores 1995). José E. Limón makes a similar observation of the corrido. Rhyme scheme, "narrated segments," "iconic account of events," "energy," and "dialogue" produce drama. The drama surpasses the moment by evoking an "'emotional kernel'"—a consolidation of performance, a performer, and an audience—that references an original, ineffable substratum of social life (Limón 1992, 13; McDowell 1981, 47).

Open Your Heart explores this substratum in silences—the pauses, emotions, gaps in logic, or spaces that participants dwell in, however provisionally, to mute the external world and make sense of its contradictions and of themselves. This space represents a radical position, a vehicle for being in one's own place and in the place of others with all of the heterogeneity that separates people and with the connections that join them. The people who open their hearts take up this position through rituals, moving themselves toward autonomy whereby the subject and other constitute a collective body, weighty in feeling and "virtual meaning" (Castoriadis 1998, 106).

Open Your Heart attempts to draw out this virtual meaning by following participants through their ritual life in different settings. The book follows Matachines dancers on a pilgrimage from Saint Anthony's Church, in Fresno, California, to Our Lady of Guadalupe, in Tepeyac, Mexico. The book follows participants assisting a daily Mass, in their performance of the rosary, and on a journey toward the sacred center of their lives. The virtual meaning expresses itself through utterances but ultimately remains embedded in symbolic action.

Symbolic action privileges neither a "semiotic concept of culture" nor materiality drawn into relief through struggles over social inequity (Geertz 1973, 14; Comaroff and Comaroff 1992; Jackson 1989; Wade 1999). Symbolic action evokes classical poetics and Marx's understanding of labor—people acting in and on nature—and locates people's fundamental humanity and sociality (Roseberry 1995).[15] This humanity and sociality lie at a juncture where people mediate sign systems and their embodied experiences of others to extract self-understanding. This movement toward self-understanding posits as an ideal a collective self—an inversion of Freud's maxim of psychoanalysis: "Where id was, there ego shall be" becomes "Where ego is, id shall come to be" (1961, 22:80; quoted in Castoriadis 1998, 383). For the people who open their hearts, symbolic action makes sense in relation to individual desires while signifying a prevailing cultural logic, which, at least initially, is dialectical, orienting people socially and advancing claims to humanity amid oppressive social conditions. I suggest "at least initially" because the dialectics do not equal an essential cognitive schema or cultural whole; rather, they are a point of entry to a social space that is sensuous, desirous, allusive, but nevertheless there.

Why do these people, Gracie and all the others who shared experiences, practice religion? What is the role of the rituals that define the religion? When I ask these questions, I am also asking about the purpose of this book and positing a thesis: the people practice religion because it enables them to approach origins or, as Sister Mary Tiziana suggested, the "sacred center" of all of the stories about power, strife, and abjection that define their lives and indicate the social body's pathology. The people tap the various streams that shape their experiences, including tradition, language, and symbols, and submit them to ritual treatment aimed at working out the tensions that separate one person from another and cultivating harmonies that bring them together (V. Turner 1967). Their movement toward origins, the sacred center, is as much spiritual as it is historical, psychological, and moral. The movement is their journey about following the heart.

THEIR JOURNEY IS ALSO MINE ABOUT SOCIAL RECONCILIATION. My journey began in May 1999 when I went to Fresno to initiate research about Latino people of faith. This trip led to an extended period of research between July 2000 and November 2001. For me, this time in Fresno was a return to the city where I had grown up and which I had left for travel and higher education. I returned, in part, to search for the place I had once called home and fulfill a longing that had become most acute upon the passing of my parents about a decade before. I returned, however, to the edges of my childhood experiences—the neighborhoods in the city's west and southeast sides. These neighborhoods had traced the difference between spaces that were familiar and comfortable and those that were not. This sense of comfort and discomfort, I soon learned, had shaped other social processes, including ways of speaking, people's comings and goings, the city's growth, and allocations of material resources. There was no better way to find the past, I thought, than through the social spaces that marked its parameters. I frequented a handful of Latino congregations in Fresno's west and southeast neighborhoods. Many of them were Protestant congregations—Assembly of God, Pentecostal, Nazarene, Methodist, or simply Christian and nondenominational. And the neighborhoods had seen better days; they were artifacts of past development projects left by the wayside as capital investment flowed toward neighborhoods and commercial centers in the North. I eventually arrived at Saint Anthony's Church, where, I surmised, I might find Cortez's kind of people.

I met Gracie in Saint Anthony's administrative office on a Friday afternoon in mid-May 1999. The office lights were low, and the curtains, drawn shut, offered relief from the glare and heat of the late spring that forebode the San Joaquin Valley's hot summer days. I explained that I wanted to undertake a study of the parishioners' lives, to participate in their faith. Gracie invited me to come and "get involved." She asked me to assist the Mass that afternoon. Shortly before 5:30 p.m. we entered the church sanctuary, where some parishioners, five or six women and a few men, kneeled in the first pew facing the altar. They were praying the rosary. I learned that the rosary was how things began around Saint Anthony's, in anticipation of the Mass, prayer groups, ministry meetings, and other gatherings. I also learned how the rosary and other rituals initiated stories, Gracie's stories and the parishioners' stories about their lives with others that became a part of my own.

I tell the story about ritual-in-stories in the capacity of a translator, adhering in particular to Gracie's way of telling because of her position as the most formidable teacher and storyteller in parish life. I undertake her poetic activity: the rhythms, transitions, associations, and the ways the form becomes content to combine one voice with other voices. This approach does not pretend to capture the parishioners' lives. Rather, the approach sustains, as Walter Benjamin observes, the parishioners' "afterlife" in the same way that they sustained the afterlife of people in stories. This afterlife does not lie in events or in what people may have said or done. One locates this afterlife in the stories' effect upon the storyteller and audience, marking the difference between the communication of information and verbal performance (1968b, 71; Behar 1995).

The performance mediates the effect by coordinating different elements of the effect's production, respectively a frame and framework. The framework, William Hanks comments, is the "immediate social field of time and space" that influences people's perceptions, orientations, and production of local knowledge (1993, 127; Cicourel 1985). The framework influences language's meaning as the latter occurs neither in the system of language nor in reality but in language's actual application (Bakhtin 1986, 86–87). Parishioners engage the framework of different places—which include the church's chapel, sanctuary, grounds, a convent, and a home—as emotive and constitutive forces through storytelling, integrating paralinguistic and linguistic features that add to the language's materiality.

The frame provides a prototypical and schematic structure for perceiving and interpreting objects, events, and experiences (Hanks 1993, 128; Bauman 1977). In this book, each chapter focuses on the formal features of a different ritual: dance movements, the Mass, rosary, pilgrimage, and procession. The movements of the Matachines dance, which I introduce in the next chapter, are the most noteworthy because they provide an overarching frame for each chapter, effectively drawing seemingly disparate matters—my return to Fresno, search for "home," meetings with Gracie and other parishioners, acts of "getting involved"—into a structure for taking them figuratively. The dance movements guide, in other words, a way of proceeding, reading, and gleaning different matters, enabling one to apprehend them according to their interrelationships. Each matter contributes to a matrix of experiences, forming, similar to Western Apache place names, "a web of shared understandings, which serve as an expanding context for interpreting meanings" (Basso 1996, 81).

This book retains the frames and the frameworks of different enactments as reflexive components that trace the transposition of past, verbal performances into a textual performance (Bauman and Briggs 1990; Briggs 1993a). The movements of a dance, a procession, or a journey toward the sacred center, for example, constitute patterns for ways of speaking. The patterns choreograph utterances, impose relative stability on the meaning of signs, and support discursive cohesion. They provide people, including storytellers, audiences, research participants, and the researcher, with common footing for subjective unity and mutual understanding. The patterns also help retain resonance with original environs as they guide a reproduction of conversation styles, inclusive of syntax, lexical choices, themes, and modes of interaction, in text (Bakhtin 1986).

The text centers on dyadic narrative (Briggs 1993a). Each chapter features at least two primary narrators who talk about the same things in different ways, marking distinct native and nonnative positions, perspectives, and forms of communicative competence.

A part of the competence includes a language repertoire of English and Spanish. Gracie and Eva Gonzales, who play roles, respectively, in chapters 3 and 4, spoke to their addressees in their maternal languages, pronouncing the proper names of saints accordingly. They switched codes, say, from Spanish to English, in the event of reported speech for modulations. They often provided translations. As a general consideration, they opted for one or the other language as necessary to best serve people and show a way of getting involved.

Despite these differences of position and perspective, the narrators come together in the time and place of a dominant frame that predisposes them to dialogue, their voices to similar tones, their words to common referents, and their perceptions to similar interpretations. The narrators deploy dialogue to create shared space and form bridges between social worlds without losing sight of the differences in power and resources that divide them (Bakhtin 1981; Tedlock and Mannheim 1995; Schieffelin 1985).

The bridges, however, fall short of completion. The narrators articulate on either side politics that shape social behavior—choices about where to live, eat, socialize, send children to school, and bury the dead, for example. The narrators show prohibitions that cause tension and conflict between people. They also create a structure of feeling for a fuller, more meaningful life gleaned through the absence of prohibitions. They show the need to belong somewhere else, encouraging people to leave their egos behind, cross over to another side, and engage in an unprejudiced inquiry about otherness.

One's progress toward the other side depends upon the stories told along the way and an ability to understand them as allegories. The Greek root of the word "allegory," *allos*, or "other," and *agoreuein*, "to speak"— generally, to speak in public or open space—denotes a practice in which a story "continuously refers to another pattern of ideas or events, . . . a representation that interprets itself."[16] Paul de Man (1979) shows that a story has the propensity to produce other stories in the mind of the reader or listener (Clifford 1986, 99). A story supplements a prior story in two ways in particular: (1) enrichment by adding new content and greater depth of meaning, a plenitude augmenting another plenitude, and (2) replacement altogether, signaling a new application of an old theme with a different epistemological orientation germane to new circumstances (Derrida 1974). Chapter 6, for example, addresses both of these ways through a discussion of the United Farm Workers' effort to unionize labor on California's Central Coast, accounting for why people who might have been amenable to the union in the 1970s rejected it in the 1990s. This story draws upon two well-known stories—the Passion play and Jesus's Way of the Cross—and the narrators rely upon stock characters and scenes to form a schematic structure for associations between different people, including César Chávez, union organizers, and farmworkers, providing insight into the nature of their roles and directing courses of action.

The allegorical strategy is inherently open ended; it outlines sufficient associations to ensure narrative cohesion yet broaches others through allusions. The explicit associations account for the narrators' use of cultural resources to heighten the audience's experience to the point of an emotive and intellectual engagement with a text. The narrators deploy figurative language that channels the audience toward what C.S. Peirce called "firstness"—qualities of feeling, unique, unadulterated, and without abstraction such as, in this book, the smell of ashes and dust, the hue of a rose, and the warmth of a mother's womb (1998, 150). These qualities exist as mere possibilities as if they were a part of an underlying psychic condition whose presence escapes logical assessment. Yet they dwell in the arousal of moods that range, Paul Friedrich (1991) suggests, from assertion to passivity, to distaste, to pleasure, and to irony, signaling deep organizing principles of speaking and acting in different settings. The settings appear as narrative spaces for the audience's imagination to paint scenes, animate the text's structure, and give the text greater significance than it might have appeared to have on its own (Iser 1980, 52).

This creative engagement is neither uniquely conscious nor embodied but rather experienced as a "psycho-physical unity" with a textual world (Husserl 1960; quoted in Hammond et al. 1991, 213). One experiences through the text the self according to its embodied nature understood as the existence of others. When an audience member perceives another person, he or she creates an "'analogical perception'—an experience of that other body, not merely as object, but as an 'other' subject" (Husserl 1960, 111; quoted in Berger and Del Negro 2002, 69). One recognizes, Harris Berger and Giovanna Del Negro elaborate further, the difference between one's individual subjectivity and another person's, between one's body and another's body, but the realization of both subjectivity and the body is contingent upon a shared experience (2002, 70).

When Gracie asked me to "get involved" in ritual in stories, she introduced the formal conditions of a journey. In one respect, I'd say, ritual in stories incorporates formal strictures that circumscribe a space for emotive, intersubjective, and intrapsychic play dedicated to restructuring the relationship between signs and referents, subject and object, and actor and acted upon (Benjamin 1968a; Jackson 2002). One apprehends this change through language's materiality. Immediacy, thickness, and weight connote something more than what is empirically present; it is in this circumscribed space that the present meets the past and the self encounters otherness, both sacred and cultural. In another respect, Gracie would say, you have to get involved with others in their joy, sorrow, suffering, and even death, cultivating along the way "the need to belong some place."

Open Your Heart supports this need by highlighting the formal features of a poetic tradition, accounting for a continuum of "enactments" within "aesthetically salient, culturally embedded textualities" (Limón 1994, 14). These features—respectively, the frame of ritual and the framework of place—orient cognition to associations between past enactments, including linguistic and paralinguistic signs, managing the effect of information.

The formal features also circumscribe spaces for an audience's entry into the text for interpretive engagement (Hanks 1989). The audience experiences these formal features for their immediacy and weight—the strictures of a different, textual reality. This change in disposition hinges on reflexivity, an account of an audience's position in a familiar world composed of people who speak a common (often scholastic) language that fortifies communicative competence, intertextual relations, and, unfortunately, verbal dominion over the people they talk about (Briggs 1993b). The change also depends on making this familiar world strange by placing pretensions in the foreground and then enabling the reader to acquiesce to narrative tenor, supplying unwritten parts to create links to others—storytellers, who were once the audience of other storytellers. This process entails a journey back to different times and places to explore alternative, subjective experiences and embodied dispositions that form "one object," "one action," or a "complete whole" of ritual in stories and writings about them (*Poetics* 1451a30–34).

THE DANCE

Open your heart. At least, that's what my seminarian friend Antonio Estrada suggested, when he gave me advice early in my research at Saint Anthony Mary Claret Church in Fresno, California. Antonio said, "If you want to understand the people, open your heart."[1] Back then I had no idea of what Antonio meant. My aim had been to see the things that the people saw, to understand the differences and similarities of perspective. After all, I, too, was from Fresno. And despite having left many years before to live elsewhere for higher education, I identified with the region and imagined that we, the people who lived there, belonged to the same culture. Antonio suggested a different way of imagining and getting to know the people. This idea of opening the heart seemed impossibly abstract and, at the same time, remarkably grounded, as if it entailed some kind of visceral experience.

To understand what "open your heart" means, imagine a group of dancers, about sixteen of them, ranging in age from thirteen to eighteen years. It was a Saturday morning in early June. School was out, and the dancers—called Matachines—were gathering with their parents in Saint Anthony's parking lot. The dancers piled out of their cars, their parents close behind carrying suitcases and packages filled with Mexican pastries, warm tamales, potato chips, bottles of Coca-Cola, and other snacks. The *compadre* (godfather) of Gracie Romana Adame, the group's leader, had made a manda, or promise, that if the dancers danced well

17

for Our Lady of Guadalupe, he would take them to see her in Tepeyac. They would join the thousands of pilgrims who make the trip annually.[2] And the dancers danced well.

The origin of the Matachines dance is ambiguous. If you ask Pueblo dancers in New Mexico, as Edward Dozier did, you might hear about how the dance was introduced by a "mythological figure from the south . . . an Indian god who wore European clothes, foretold of the coming of whites and suggested cooperation with them, but also advised the Pueblos to retain their customs and ceremonies" (1958, 444–45). Adrian Treviño and Barbara Gilles (1994) consulted their fellow folklorist Cleofas Jaramillo (1941). He had grown up in northern New Mexico in the early 1900s, and his answer increased the number of possible origins even more: "This aboriginal dance was brought from Mexico. Some say that it is an Aztec dance; others believe it to be of Spanish and Moorish origin. My mother told me it was the dance danced by the Aztecs when they went to meet Montezuma on his visits to the different pueblos" (Jaramillo 1941, 50; quoted in Treviño and Gilles 1994, 106).

Jaramillo and his successors—Champe (1983), Kurath (1949), Treviño and Gilles (1994), and S. Rodriguez (1991, 1996)—infer that the etymology of *Matachine* might reveal a more definitive origin. Gertrude Kurath found in a Spanish dictionary that "in the Middle Ages the *Matachini* were masked buffoons in motley and bells" who "cut capers and struck each other with swords or airfilled bladders." Her Arabic dictionary suggests that the term is derived from *mudawajjihen*, meaning either "those who put on a face" or "those who face each other" (1949, 97).[3] Sylvia Rodriguez adds to the Arabic definition by suggesting that *Matachine* "is of Italian origin, referring in the diminutive to *matto*, 'madman' or 'fool.'. . . In any case," Rodriguez continues, "it became associated with the Moorish-Christian conflict, a type of dance known in Spain as a *Morisca*" (1991, 236; see also Forrest 1984). The Spanish introduced the dance to the New World because "the drama portrays the advent of Christianity among Indians by referring to the expulsion/ conversion of the Moors" (S. Rodriguez 1991, 236). The search for a definitive origin of the Matachines dance involves a bit of buffoonery; any effort to pin it down adds to the number of possibilities and, moreover, to the explanations about what happens when people with different points of view and interests face each other.

The cast of characters contributes to this paradox about origin: it includes twelve Matachines; a masked clown called El Abuelo, or the Grandfather; El Toro, or the Bull; and two principal figures, El Monarca and La Malinche.[4] *El Monarca* means "the king," and observers and dancers accept him as the representation of Moctezuma, the last Aztec ruler, or a messiah figure (Champe 1983, 7; Parsons 1929, 219). La Malinche recalls Hernando Cortés's interpreter and mistress, who, as portrayed by Octavio Paz, represents "the violated Mother, . . . a figure representing the Indian women who were fascinated, violated or seduced by the Spaniards." She gave birth to Cortés's child and has become a symbol of Mexico indicating the Spanish conquest and the legacy of "foreign influences" (Paz 1985, 85–86; quoted in Harris 1996, 150).[5]

While this interpretation is common in scholarship, Max Harris (1996) argues that Malinche is Moctezuma's wife or daughter.[6] Following Susan Gillespie's 1989 account of indigenous mythology, Harris notes that Malinche legitimizes the cycle of the Tenochtitlán dynasty, whereby three nonconsecutive rulers—Acamapichtli, Moctezuma the Elder, and Moctezuma the Younger—are boundary figures marking the transition from one temporal and political cycle to another. In one cycle, if Malinche is the daughter of one ruler, or Moctezuma, then she is the wife of the next, and so on. She shares semidivine powers with her consort. And Malinche is instrumental in the restoration of power to the Mexica, the indigenous people of the valley of Mexico known for their rule over the Aztec empire. A mythological narrative tells of this restoration and calls for the return of a "king perhaps named Motecuhzoma," or a "messiah-like figure," who would "defeat the Spanish and initiate a new Indian hegemony" (Gillespie 1989, 166, 201; quoted in Harris 1996, 153). Gillespie and Lafaye identify this king, or messiah-like figure, as Quetzalcóatl. His feminine consort is Cihuacóatl, also known as Tonantzin, meaning "our mother," whom the Aztecs worshiped in Tepeyac. Tonantzin is known later as Our Lady of Guadalupe (Gillespie 1989, 166; Lafaye 1976, 211, 214).

Twelve Matachines, separated evenly into two lines, carry rattles and tridents or fans and move forward and backward. One line mirrors the other. And a bow marks the prologue to three acts.[7] The dancers' moves are sometimes fast, sometimes slow, rotating in opposite directions and integrating crossovers and exchanges; each move is choreographed variously to the melody and three-quarter tempo played on a violin and guitar, or to a drum, or to tambourines and bells hung from the dancers' ankles.[8] El Monarca and La Malinche weave among the Matachines and dance between their lines. In one dance sequence, El Monarca's footwork involves jumps and squats. La Malinche turns to the left and the right with a quick, bobbing curtsy. In another dance sequence, La Malinche's right hand rotates counterclockwise; El Monarca's, clockwise. Sometimes El Abuelo accompanies them, imitating their steps, and singing in falsetto; he also mingles with the audience, entertaining with his antics. El Toro marches alongside the dancers, sometimes on a leash attached to El Abuelo, waving his cumbersome skull until the end, when El Abuelo leads him to the center to be castrated or killed. The dancers move sometimes forward, sometimes backward, and always in procession, as if they were on a journey.

I saw Saint Anthony's Matachines on Saturday, 8 December 2000. They were in line with groups of Matachines and Aztec dancers from other Catholic churches near Saint John's Cathedral in downtown Fresno. They were preparing to begin a mile-long procession to the convention center, where Bishop John Steinbock was to give a speech celebrating the Catholic Church's Jubilee 2000.[9] Saint Anthony's Matachines wore blue-and-white costumes sewn by their mothers and grandmothers. The young women wore white stockings and blue satin sleeveless dresses trimmed in white, slit up the sides, and covered above the waist by white turtlenecks or sweaters. The young men wore black pants, white shirts, and blue capes trimmed in white and boasting the image of Our Lady of Guadalupe on the back. The dancers wore headdresses similar to those worn by the Aztec lords as described by the sixteenth-century ethnographer Fray Bernardino de Sahagún—"a basic crown, consisting of a headband, which ties in back, with a flat, oval-shaped front piece standing upright from the forehead" (Champe 1983, 5).[10] On the front piece, there was a small image of Our Lady of Guadalupe.

The tie at the back of the headband supported two pheasant feathers that rose high above the dancers' heads. The feathers recall Quetzalcóatl,

whose name, a compound of *quetzal* and *cóatl*, means "feathered serpent" in Nahuatl. *Cóatl* also means "twin" and implies the multiple bi-
nary relationships that Quetzalcóatl weaves through the fabric of Aztec
mythology (Gillespie 1989, 143). Various sixteenth-century documents
written by Spanish missionaries and Aztec elites portray Quetzalcóatl as
a mediator separating, as implied metaphorically by his name, the cosmos into earth (serpent) and sky (feathers), marking the time of creation
and of peopling the earth.[11] He is associated with Venus, the morning
and evening star, and indicates the junction of night and day (Gillespie
1989, 176). Quetzalcóatl is a historical figure, the last Toltec who resided
in Tollan, known for its attributes of civilization—religion, science,
crafts, architecture, and calendrics—a "fitting seat of Quetzalcóatl, the
creator of wisdom" (Gillespie 1989, 179; Sahagún [1590] 1975, 10:165–
69). And Quetzalcóatl is also a deity who, having been sent into exile
upon the fall of the Toltecs to Aztec rule, promised to return from the
east, following the path of the morning star, to save his people from oppression and restore a civilized society.

In the procession, Saint Anthony's queen, chosen by the church's
Guadalupana ministry, represented Our Lady in the place that La Malinche might have occupied.[12] A small boy dressed as Juan Diego, who
witnessed the Virgin's apparition in Tepeyac in 1531, replaced the role of
El Monarca. An assistant followed; she held a banner boasting the image
of Our Lady of Guadalupe.

I saw the same group dance the following Tuesday, 12 December,
Our Lady of Guadalupe's day. The dancers led a procession of approximately two hundred of Saint Anthony's parishioners: many elderly,
walking slowly or being pushed along in wheelchairs, and others quite
young, infants in strollers and children, playing games along the way.
The procession started in the evening around 7:00, about a mile north of
the church, and ended in the church's sanctuary, where a visiting priest
from Juarez, Mexico, celebrated the Mass. The air was cold with a bite
that comes after nightfall with the onset of fog. People found warmth by
huddling close together, singing hymns, imitating the Matachines' footwork, falling behind to accompany the slower members of the procession, or moving ahead to converse with the Mexican priest, who carried
the banner with the image of Our Lady of Guadalupe.

The Matachines dance, whether performed in Fresno, California, or in parts of the old and New Mexico, involves facing origins.[13] For participants and observers alike, these origins are ambiguous because they lie in no one place or time; rather, place and time emerge through a doubling and referral that takes place in the characters. El Monarca, for example, recalls Moctezuma, the last Aztec ruler; or a Christian messiah introduced to the New World by Spaniards in the early sixteenth century; or Quetzalcóatl, who, according to Aztec myth, promised to return and overthrow oppression; or, as suggested in Fresno, Juan Diego, whose relationship with Our Lady of Guadalupe has been a sign of God's grace in the midst of conquest and the model for the thousands of pilgrims who visit Tepeyac annually. La Malinche recalls Cortés's mistress and translator, who in 1519 was instrumental in the fall of a civilization; or Moctezuma's wife or daughter, who will be instrumental in the rise of another; or Our Lady of Guadalupe, the patroness of Mexico, who, Eric Wolf has written, "links together family, politics and religion; colonial past and independent present, Indian and Mexican" (1958, 38). Indeed, her role in the family shows through mothers and grandmothers who sew Matachines costumes for their children, and through the compadre who promises to send the younger generations to Tepeyac. Each action involves doubling and referral of identification that draws myth, legend, and history into the present, when one faces another, mirrorlike, the two seemingly different but the same, in step, one forward, another back, and always in procession.

Like the Matachines dance, rituals—the Mass, processions, pilgrimages, prayer—that define the Catholic faith direct practitioners toward a disposition, a primordial way of being. This way emerges through a key component: choreographed footwork that becomes embodied rotations in opposite directions, integrating crossovers and exchanges to be in the world of others—divine, human, powerful, and oppressed. In this region, the one I identify with, such steps mean meeting and facing people for how they acquire self-awareness, whether through ethnic identification or experience of, for example, prejudice, discrimination, and impoverishment. The steps also mean an expression of faith with moral commitment to how the world might be—just, fair, and ideal. This world begins with a reformulation of social relationships, a step in rotation, forward and backward, toward origins, or, as Antonio Estrada suggested, an open heart.

THE MORNING AIR WAS WARM, THE SUMMER HEAT ALREADY setting in and foreboding long days under the sun. With a deep breath, one could draw the faint smell of sulfur and dust from the surrounding vineyards, a smell that gave way to the fragrance of ripening fruit as one traveled south. Many of the young dancers had never before left the San Joaquin Valley, knowing at best the surrounding impoverished farm towns that had been home at one time or another when their parents were on a migratory labor circuit.[14] They knew the itinerary that would take them down through Bakersfield, Los Angeles, and San Bernardino to Mexicali, where they would cross the border, just as some of their parents, friends, and acquaintances had done while heading north from Sonora, Sinaloa, Guanajuato, and Michoacán. They, too, would pass through these Mexican states that sent an estimated 1.2 million migrants who headed annually to the United States, many of them to fill jobs picking grapes and stone fruit in Fresno County.[15]

The dancers' trip south into Mexico entailed as much apprehension as a migrant's heading north for the first time.[16] Gracie, who had spent her early childhood in El Paso and had lived in Fresno for most of her life, recalled how local lore influenced her first trip to Mexico.

"I never wanted to go to Mexico," Gracie explained. "My uncle, parents, and grandparents were always asking me to go with them. They told me how beautiful it was. But I didn't want to go."

"Why not?" I asked.

"Because the teachers always told us about how bad it was. They said that we would get sick. They said that we would get robbed. . . . They told us about kidnapping and the sale of children. They made it seem like a horrible place. I didn't want to go. I was scared."[17]

The words of Gracie's teachers weighed heavily, virtually transforming domestic space into a venue of popular talk. Their intentions were good, it appeared, because they taught Gracie about hygiene, safety, and order—something that to them was uniquely American and distinguished the United States from Mexico.

Gracie's fear of Mexico was a part of American nativism. Whether you inquire about the Mexican labor force in California's modern development at the turn of the century; the California state legislative deliberations over citizenship and constitutional rights for Mexicans (and indigenous residents) during the 1850s; the rationale justifying the U.S.-Mexican War (1846–48); or back further to President James K. Polk's desire for Mexico's northern territories in the 1840s, you'll find the influence of American nativism every step of the way.[18] George Sánchez (1993) reminds us in particular of the Americanization programs spanning three decades—well into the 1930s—that left an impression on people like Gracie's teachers.

Academics in the sociology departments at the Universities of Chicago and Southern California, for example, trained generations of social workers, public-school administrators, and teachers. In coordination with government, nonprofit, religious, and business institutions, these people went about assimilating migrants, mostly Mexican, into the labor force, teaching them English and the Protestant values of temperance, diet, hygiene, discipline, efficiency—roads to prosperity—and, above all, cultural loyalty. Social workers went into homes, and teachers, into schools, where they could reach immigrant women and their children, hoping that instruction in these venues would extend over time to the larger society (G. Sánchez 1993, 99).[19] For Gracie, facing Mexico was an awesome undertaking because it meant defining the contour of self-awareness, testing its tenacity. Going south, as her relatives had asked her to do on numerous occasions, was perilous because the journey meant forgoing a part of self-awareness and becoming something else.

Facing the United States, as many Mexican migrants have done in increasing numbers since the modernization of Mexico under Porfirio Díaz, has been no less difficult.[20] American nativism, as suggested in the language of public policy, the juridical system, and various acts and programs during the twentieth and into the twenty-first centuries, has tirelessly defined these people as a source of social contagion to be "assimilated," "naturalized," "repatriated," "deported," or simply sent back (after finishing their work).[21] Sociologists, anthropologists, and various kinds of "social scientists" working in academic, nonprofit, and public institutions have added layers of commentaries to public opinion about the migrants. They have created migrants' biographic profiles and characterized their social networks, the economic stress of their "push" communities, the relief offered by "pull" communities, and their place within the "world system," effectively formulating a theoretical framework for trade agreements between the United States and Mexico, for immigration policy, and for border control aimed at sustaining a low-wage labor force while allaying the anxieties and frustrations of those who feel threatened (Durand and Massey 1992; Mines and Massey 1985; Massey 1999; Wilson 1993).[22] One must ask: what have these activities created for Mexican migrants as they face the United States and make their way north? They face dry, merciless landscapes, dehydration, robbery, forced prostitution, and civil rights abuses by self-appointed border vigilantes and official border patrols. They also face death.[23] Facing the United States, and to a much greater degree, going there, are perilous beyond a Mexican migrant's wildest dreams because doing these things entails vulnerability that accompanies a journey in the persona of a Mexican from a dangerous and horrible place.

In Saint Anthony's parking lot, the Matachines prepared for their trip. No Toro was visible, but his presence was surely felt among many signs around the church. On the rectory's north wall, there was a mural featuring a procession led by Juan Diego; the first secular bishop of Mexico, Juan de Zumárraga; the Indian convert and interpreter, Juan González; and a handful of priests and Indians.[24] They made their way through the desert environs of Tepeyac to see the Virgin. In the parking lot near the sanctuary's side door, where many of the dancers gathered, there was a fountain with a tile mural. The mural portrayed Juan Diego kneeling before the apparition, his mantle full of red roses, a fine image of Our Lady impregnating its course fibers. And in the sanctuary, right of the altar, there was a replica of Juan Diego's mantle framed and hung at eye level behind a waist-high table. Parishioners had left fresh flowers. In each place, Our Lady of Guadalupe appeared in a ring of fire, like the woman described by John in Revelation 12:1–2 (RSV): "And a great portent appeared in heaven, a woman clothed with the sun, with the moon under her feet, and on her head a crown of twelve stars; she was with child."

In her study of the image, Jody Brant Smith observes that Our Lady's "head is tilted to the right. Her greenish eyes are cast downward in an expression of gentle concern. The mantle that covers her head and shoulders is of a deep turquoise, studded with gold stars and bordered in gold. Her hair is black, her complexion olive. She stands alone, her hands clasped in prayer, an angel at her feet" (1984, 3; quoted in J. Rodriguez 1994, 19).

According to the ancient Nahuatl manuscript *Annals of Cuauhtit-lán*, the mantle indicates a divinity sought by the messiah figure Quetzalcóatl: "And it was said that Quetzalcóatl would invoke, deifying something in the innermost heaven: she of the starry skirt, he whose radiance envelops things" (León-Portilla 1963, 29). This divinity, Miguel León-Portilla explains, refers to the "double role of Ometéotl, the god of duality who inhabits *Omeycan*, 'the place of duality.'" One role, Citlalinicue, is designated as "'she of the starry skirt,'" and the other, Citlallatónac, as "'celestial body which illumines things.'" The vestment is woven of myth, wraps truth, and is the product of wisdom (29, 30).

The Matachines knew how they should act on arrival in Tepeyac, having experienced processions to Our Lady of Guadalupe numerous times in Saint Anthony's sanctuary. On one occasion in August 2001, a family of four, the children approximately four and six years old, entered the sanctuary through its primary double doors in the rear, allowing clear light to penetrate the somber space. Dust and sweat clung to the father's T-shirt and sandals, which had soaked up a day's work in the fields as he brought in the annual harvest. The mother wore blue sweatpants and a patterned blouse, her hair still damp from bathing. They stood for a moment in the back, in the aisle between two rows of pews leading to the altar. After making the sign of the cross, they lowered to their knees and shuffled forward slowly, heads bowed. On arriving at the altar, they stopped for a moment, turned to the right, and shuffled farther toward Our Lady, where they stopped and said prayers. To face the Virgin, to look upon her face, hair, prayers, and "gentle concern," engenders, James Fernandez explains, "the perfection of being . . . in the inclination to consider the perfect or near perfect beings of our existence as mirrors themselves." The Virgin is one such mirror, the "*Specula sine macula,*" providing an image for reflection and for an act of homage (1986, 165).

The act of homage is usually made amid great commotion. In the sixteenth century, it was of no great significance to many Spanish missionaries that roses appeared in Juan Diego's mantle, blanketing Our Lady's fresh impression, during a season that produced no flowers. Instead, they fought among themselves. Divided by secular, Franciscan, Dominican, and Augustinian affiliations and by power in the New World, they made the people who paid homage the object of debate, evaluating their humanity, arguing for and against their worthiness of God's grace and their capacity to be Christian (Ricard 1966). Much of the debate focused on the nature of the apparition to verify its occurrence and validate Our Lady's dedication to the people who paid homage.

In 1648 Father Miguel Sánchez, a priest of the Oratory of Saint Philip of Neri, provided the first written documentation of Juan Diego's vision. He posited in New Spain a providential order of epic proportions. The time and place of the primitive church became the setting for a story about a mother who comes in the midst of conquest and colonial oppression to protect her children from foreign influences (Brading 2001). The following year, the vicar of Guadalupe, Luis Laso de la Vega, published in Nahautl the *Nican mopuhua*, presumably documenting an oral tradition in the indigenous language. Writers see the strength of this devotion in native identification of an indigenous god with Our Lady of Guadalupe (Burkhart 1993; Campbell 1982; Jiménez Moreno, Miranda, and Fernández 1963; Lafaye 1976).[25]

The historian Stafford Poole (1995, 2006), however, raises concern over the absence of documentation for more than a hundred years after the apparition. He argues that *criollos*, people of European background born in Mexico, were responsible for the spread of popular devotion. Criollos, who experienced subjugation by peninsular Spaniards, seized upon Sanchez's 1648 publication as evidence of divine favor for their role in New Spain. Other scholars direct attention to the nature of devotion, citing indigenous precedents to a Christian future within an oppressive, colonial setting—conditions ripe for acts of devotion that create breath for oral accounts and, over time, create a story for written documentation (Elizondo 1983, 2001; J. Rodriguez 1994).

The claims of past and contemporary writers reflect a tradition from the Iberian Peninsula involving a formal *relectio*, a lecture; *relectios* were enacted whenever the Castilian crown faced uncertain moral circumstances (Pagden 1987). It was simply not enough that Spain had papal endorsement of its activities in the New World, or that advisors assured the Spanish kings that they were the guardians of God's expansion of Christendom. The Castilian crown needed pronouncements, drawn from classical—specifically, Aristotelian and Thomist—interpretations of law and nature and crafted by advisors at the University of Salamanca. Francisco de Vitoria, his students, and the students of his students crafted a moral philosophy that provided a theoretical framework for the crown's policies regarding the Indians, their tutelage, and the *encomienda* system of labor.[26]

This moral philosophy articulated an understanding of property or, in the language of natural jurisprudence, *dominium*, and more precisely in this case, *dominium rerum*. *Dominium rerum* referred to the dominion of private property, goods (*bona*), and also of people's actions and liberties, including actions by and the liberty of their own bodies. According to advisors, *dominium* was contingent upon specific qualifications—a social contract whereby "men had [to] renounce their primitive freedom in exchange for the security and the possibility of moral understanding which only civil society could provide; but they retained certain natural and hence inalienable rights of which *dominium* is the most fundamental" (Pagden 1987, 80).

Dominium was the basis of a civil society, a concept that had significant ramifications in the New World. The Spanish conquistadors reasoned that if members of a society possessed no dominium—and therefore no civility—then they could not claim dominium rerum when confronted by invaders intent on taking their land. In addition, dominium, albeit an inalienable right, was ultimately contingent upon moral or Christian understanding, thereby raising the question of whether or not the Indians were capable of attaining it. And even if they were, their dominium could not be realized until their tutelage was complete. The Indians had their advocates and detractors, represented, respectively, by

Bartolomé de Las Casas and Juan Ginés de Sepúlveda, who went head to head at a famous debate in Valladolid in 1550.[27] But regardless of what either side said, the Indians' claims to humanity and the manner of their oppression were always at stake.[28]

By 1556, the hermitage in Tepeyac was too small to accommodate the pilgrims, and Alonso de Montúfar, a Dominican and Mexico's second archbishop (1551–72), began construction of a church. Through the seventeenth and eighteenth centuries, Montúfar's successors built even larger churches on the same site for pilgrims who arrived in increasing numbers from throughout the Americas.[29] Additions made in 1893, and again in the 1930s, constituted the Basilica of Our Lady of Guadalupe, large enough for thousands (Chauvet 1978).[30]

Eva Gonzales, who attends Saint Anthony's, recalled her first trip to Tepeyac; it was in fulfillment of a manda made by her mother at her birth. "That was the one," Eva explained about the manda, "where I couldn't cut my hair until we went to Mexico to visit the Virgin."

"How did you get there?" I asked.

"By bus. It took three or four days. . . . It was the middle of June, and there was a storm. And the weather was bad. We went in the middle of a hurricane. But it was fun. I was twelve. I cut my braids and left them there."[31]

Eva left her braids with Our Lady of Guadalupe like her predecessors who had left parts of themselves. In the basilica, Eva must have approached the altar, shuffling on her knees with her mother by her side. As they approached Our Lady, the exchange must have been relatively brief, marked by her mother pulling a pair of scissors from her pocket and handing them to Eva, who clipped her braids and left them. The exchange must have felt impulsive, occurring as quickly as it disappeared. Whatever intention Eva and her mother might have had waned with the onset of a prevailing logic, a cultural grammar that predicated the act as it had done for those who had come before.

At least for Eva's mother, this exchange between Eva and Our Lady had been part of a twelve-year plan. Eva was born, and her hair started to grow. During this time, Eva's mother, an Arizonan, and her father, from Michoacán, were on the migratory labor circuit, following seasonal work in the San Joaquin Valley's vineyards and in the Central

Coast's canneries.[32] They spent days in the valley's heat and nights outdoors, traveling when their work had finished, living for the dreams that brought many migrants to the Golden State.

Alfonso Suárez, who attended Saint Anthony's, had heard about the dreams when he was a young man in Guadalajara. "I heard others say," he recalled, "'Oh, the United States, you can earn a good living there, what a great adventure.' I didn't have to come, not because I was rich, but because my parents supported me. But I came for the experience, and nobody was going to stop me. I didn't have papers [documentation]. I entered and left however I could. And in 1988 I had the opportunity to arrange my papers under the amnesty. That's how I came to stay, for the experience, to know."[33]

Ana Rodríguez shared Alfonso's desire to know life in the United States. "I was not able to make it in Mexico," Ana explained about her decision to leave in the late 1990s. "I am able to do something here, so I am going to do what I can, to do the best that I can, to improve my way of life, my learning. Everything is a matter of changing. Everything is a matter of improving, of education, of doing the best that you can. Since Benjamin Franklin, all of those people, geniuses, that invented things—they didn't do it by [staying where they were]. They kept on moving. And they kept on moving. So for me, not being able to move, staying in the same place, that's a total failure."[34]

These migrants followed dreams and played a role in a cultural grammar that prescribes an American past. William Bradford's Puritan pilgrims, after escaping religious persecution in England and dispiriting hardship in Holland, looked upon the Plymouth Colony as an opportunity to spread the gospel, transform their lives, "a place wher they might have libertie and live comfortably, . . . though they should be even as stepping-stones unto others for ye performing of so great a work" (1898, 30, 32). The transcendental implication of these words became the prevailing ethos of Ralph Waldo Emerson's "Self-Reliance." "Insist on yourself," Emerson urges us, recalling the examples of Franklin, Washington, Bacon, and Shakespeare; "never imitate. Your own gift you can present every moment with the cumulative force of a whole life's cultivation; but of the adopted talent of another, you have only an extemporaneous, half possession" ([1841] 1945, 60–61). Wonderfully individual, yet universal, these words resonate in the formation of an American self with which Walt Whitman began his *Leaves of Grass* ([1867] 1921):"One's-self I sing, a simple separate person, / Yet utter the word Democratic, the word En-Masse." And at the turn of the century, Frederick Jackson Turner, who feared that the American frontier was coming to an end, and with it, a unique American identity, recalled nostalgically the immigrant's encounter and mastery of the wilderness; that "out of his wilderness experience, out of the freedom of his opportunities, [the immigrant] fashioned a formula for regeneration—the freedom of the individual to seek his own" (1920, 213).[35] "Liberty" and "opportunity" to deploy one's "gifts," to "regenerate" and to reinvent one's self, account for a brand of democracy and a way of thinking conducive to enterprise, production—to progress. The value of progress depends upon differences—from a repressive England, dispiriting Holland, the wilderness (and its native inhabitants), and, as suggested by Ana, Mexico—that follow in progress's shadow.

To face the United States—the adventures, opportunities, and promise of making something of one's self—is another act of homage that, similar to sixteenth-century devotion to Our Lady of Guadalupe, people made amid great commotion. The century-old debate about predominantly Mexican migration to the United States came to fruition in the 1986 passage of the Immigration Reform and Control Act (IRCA). Co-authored by Senator Alan K. Simpson (R-Wyoming) and Representative Roman L. Mazzoli (D-Kentucky), the IRCA represented the first major reform since the Immigration Act of 1965, aimed at controlling undocumented immigration.[36] The bill's life in congressional hearings began in 1972 and showed, it appears, the best of a democratic process devoted to honoring the immigrants, their hard work, and their right to self-determination, and at the same time to protecting American workers and industry. From all parts of society—academic institutions, labor unions, government services and bureaus, agriculture boards, special-interest groups—experts spoke with earnest formality, upholding the government's decorum and supporting its authority to look after the people's interests. This extraordinary effort, which endured for years and filled volumes, might be reduced, arguably, to reconciling a contradiction in the popular perception of the immigrant: illegal and by implication criminal on the one hand, and required labor on the other.

Such a contradiction, the inherent tension that guided the tenor of debate, ultimately revealed the underlying objective of power. In response to Senator Pete Wilson's (R-California) ambient flourishes about "illegal immigration" run amock and the needs of California growers, Senator Simpson cleared the air: "When God's bounty is ready to harvest, they have got to have the horses to harvest, and when the figs get hammered to the ground, you got to have it done; when the peaches are ready, it's got to be done."[37]

"Horses" is an apt metaphor for labor, characterizing precisely the implications of illegality or criminality: it refers to a subhuman, beast-like agency to be harnessed and controlled, ensuring economic and social well-being for those in power.

Senator Simpson's insight into the status of California's labor was secondhand news to many of the migrants who worked in the fields. In one of many conversations, I asked my friend Alfredo Reyes about social justice. Alfredo, who arrived from Guanajuato in the late 1980s, worked on the migratory labor circuit, and was never able to "arrange his papers," drew from his experiences.

He asked rhetorically, "Why don't many people in this country, when they speak of migrants, the undocumented, why don't they stand up for them? Why don't the people stand up for [the migrants] when they benefit from them, if [the migrants] are a living presence that help the country? Each time that we go to eat in a restaurant, we benefit from them. Each time that we drive on a highway, we benefit from them. And [the migrants] are paid wages much lower than what people from here make. Nobody gives them the benefits that people here have."[38]

Like Alfonso and Ana, Alfredo stayed in California. He worked for low wages harvesting God's bounty for the benefit of others and for the country's promises of "liberty" and of the "opportunity" to "keep moving," to make something of himself—the adventure that hinged upon his own alterity and, once again, the denial of dominium.

PEOPLE ASSERT, NEVERTHELESS, SUCH A LIBERTY OVER time. Eva's hair grew, and by age twelve, she had woven it into braids. She climbed into a bus with her family, and they traveled south through a hurricane to see Our Lady. She approached the altar, clipped the braids, and left something of herself among the many things left by those who had come before.

When the Matachines arrived in Tepeyac, they were dressed in their Aztec costumes, preparing to see Our Lady. El Toro appeared. "[He] told us," Gracie recalled, "that we couldn't go inside in costume to pray. It was one of those rules, I guess. . . . We couldn't go inside with costumes because we would disturb the people who were praying and all that. . . . My compadre said, 'Well, we'll see.' We got there, dressed up like that. . . . [My compadre] told us that we were going to see our Holy Mother. . . . We went in. We kneeled down in the front where they have rails. And we all kneeled down, some stood up, and we all looked at her. And you just look at her; it's so emotional to see her up there. It's like she comes out of the picture to hug us. So we went inside with our costumes, with our feathers. . . . It was beautiful."[39]

I might have asked about the feathers, about whether or not Gracie knew their significance as related by Susan Gillespie (1989), Miguel León-Portilla (1963), Jacques Lafaye (1976), and numerous others writing about the feathered serpent. But the question would have trumped a much more important revelation that had come in her recollection of that unique moment of crisis, when El Toro told Gracie, her compadre, and the Matachines that they couldn't enter the basilica to see their Holy Mother. Her utterance of "feathers" displaced a historical narrative about this feature and whatever authority the narrative entails, and replaced that narrative with the driving force of history itself, neither visible nor conscious, but an intuitive, sensuous expression of the social existence that determines consciousness and shows claims to humanity.

THE PEOPLE IN THE CHAPTERS THAT FOLLOW MOVE LIKE Matachines. They move forward, sometimes backward, and always in procession as if they were on a journey. Each turn, crossover, or exchange through a ritual, whether the Mass, prayer, or pilgrimage, is a compulsive action with provisional intention, occurring as quickly as it disappears, and at the same time, a symbolic action that orients one toward origins. This orientation resonates at seemingly inconsequential moments—when two people who perceive each other as different face one another, when a Mexican migrant faces north, or when a pilgrim faces south. Each step entails facing oneself in the face of another, moving forward and sometimes backward toward a collective history, a place of conception, the Holy Mother, inside the Basilica of Our Lady.

Each chapter addresses at least one ritual—the daily Mass, rosary, and pilgrimage, for example—and imitates the form to help give meaning to content. I learned this technique from Gracie Romana Adame, Eva Gonzales, Alfredo Reyes, Alfonso Suárez, Ana Rodríguez, and Antonio Estrada, among others. They told me in their own ways to come and get involved. They told me how to say prayers such as the Our Father and Hail Mary. They taught me how to say "amen" even as they took me by the arm, inviting me to sit in church, attend meetings, retreats, and festivals, and visit them in labor camps and homes; even as they told stories about migration, work, family, fear, love, and dreams, sometimes personal, often collective. I followed their footsteps through parallel experiences, each building upon the others by incorporating ritual form that shapes a way of moving about and doing things with words. Gracie and the others would argue, I believe, that the rituals create a way of opening the heart.

Toward this end, I play the role of El Abuelo, dressed as a clown and wearing a mask. In fact, this Abuelo wears many masks, fashioned by an investment in human behavior, sympathizing with beliefs, imitating activities, and advocating morals. El Abuelo also wears the mask of a writer whose voice provides critique within a narrative aimed at inducing an audience to understand the lives of people whom it might perceive as different. This strategy follows Max Weber's (1958) discussion of the politician's ethic of responsibility (Rosaldo 1989). The ethic, Weber suggests, entails "passion and a cool sense of proportion . . . forged together in one and the same soul." This passion means "the sense of *matter-of-factness*, of passionate devotion to a 'cause,'" and the "cool sense of proportion" means "the ability to let realities work upon [one] with inner concentration and calmness" (1958, 115). El Abuelo mediates an affinity with and distance from people; he enables an audience to engage in subjective and objective experiences that broach diverse relationships with clarity and mystification, logic and sensuousness. Regardless of whatever degree of ambiguity, one thing is certain: El Abuelo will bring El Toro to the center for castration or death.

And who is this Toro, you might ask? We have already felt his presence in Saint Anthony's Church, on the border, in the Spanish university, in Vallodolid, in congressional hearings, and in Tepeyac. El Toro is pervasive, marching along, waving his skull at all who care to look at him, causing great commotion, and threatening to subvert every human action that is symbolic of humanity. El Toro's end is something to look forward to and celebrate.

In the meantime, remember the Matachines in Tepeyac. Gracie said, "So we went inside with our costumes, with our feathers. We went outside, and we danced."[40] Follow the dancers; imitate their steps, moving forward, sometimes backward, always in procession. And dance.

THE DAILY SERVICE

I'm late. I can hear the final verses of the entrance song, "*Unidos como hermanos.*" The priest has already arrived—"*Venimos a tu altar.*" Heading down the short, dark corridor toward the chapel's door, I approach the parishioners' call inside, "*Que llenes nuestras vidas de amor y de amistad.*"[1] The small room for about thirty is nearly filled with the people I always see here: Maria, Señora Paz, José and his wife Paloma, Juanita and the children. And Eva has saved a seat for me next to her. The daily Mass is about to begin with liturgical readings—stories from the Bible. The liturgy involves a kind of service suggested by the term's Greek origin, *leitourgia*, which combines *leitos* and *ergo* to translate into "person who performs a public duty." The term's verb form, *leitourgeō*, emphasizes the performance of such a duty (Lebbe 1949).[2] I wonder what the priest will say about the readings, what they might mean, and for whom they might lead us to pray.

The event subsumes any individual life; it encompasses a past that people engage by wheeling back, gleaning stories along the way. One story is about the time when Jesus drank wine and ate bread with the apostles shortly before the crucifixion, a sacrifice designed to free humankind from sin. This story commemorates another story about the Jewish emancipation from slavery. For centuries, people have celebrated these stories by breaking bread and drinking wine together, imagining being there, like the apostles, with Jesus, among the Jews, thanking God for love, and wondering what the stories mean now. The Mass, a primary ritual defining the practice of Catholicism, enables people to undertake a collective journey of love and friendship.

The daily Mass took place precisely at 5:30 p.m. and lasted for about twenty minutes; it was a part of my introduction to Saint Anthony Mary Claret Church, to its neighborhood in southeast Fresno, California, and to the people who shared their lives with me. The Mass's elements of time, love, and friendship were vague ideas but nevertheless characterized the role of the ritual and a way of life. People transcended their sense of self-awareness to inhabit the lives of others especially through an understanding of the past—the biblical period and the more immediate past contributing to a history of the region, the state, and parts of Mexico and Central America. This practice involved apprehension of barriers—regional, ethnic, ideological, and psychological—that separated people, and then involved efforts to overcome those barriers. Imagine, then, your own transcendence and realize what congregants mean by love and friendship that accompany the daily service.

THE SPACE OF A CHURCH

Imagine a Catholic church near the corner of Jensen and Chestnut Avenues, a crossroads marking the flow of people through rural and urban spaces. Chestnut leads south toward Malaga, a small community named after the Spanish city and its native grape (Salley 1977, 131). In the early 1880s, the "celebrated fruit producer" Charles G. Briggs saw opportunities for enterprise supported by irrigation, the Southern Pacific Railroad, a schoolhouse, a packing plant, and the "great advantages" of soil and climate in this region. He acquired large masses of land and sold them in twenty-acre lots to settlers from as near as San Francisco and as far as Scotland and the Scandinavian countries. These people were "excellent citizens," devoted to land improvements. They invested energy and capital in leveling land, building dikes, and digging ditches to turn sunscorched, weed-ridden soil into farmland, displacing sheepherders who had displaced cattlemen in the struggle over a free range (*History of Fresno County* 1882, 111, 115).[3] Farther south, Chestnut leads to the fruit of such labors: rows upon rows of vineyards, large corporate farms, the seasonal homes of largely Mexican migrant workers, and the center of the county's annual three-billion-dollar agribusiness (Mason, Alvarado, and Palacio 1996).

Imagine yourself in the church's parking lot after the 10:30 a.m. Sunday Mass. It's summer. Temperatures of 100°F or higher have already burned away the cool morning air. Join the flow of traffic that heads north on Chestnut. Pass by a water basin, an elementary school, and Church Avenue, honoring Moses J. Church, renowned for bringing irrigation to the region in the 1870s. Continue by empty lots and orchards of "stone fruit"—peaches and nectarines—that survived the last wave of urban development in the 1970s, creating a neighborhood of stucco, tract homes and high-density apartment complexes. This neighborhood fulfilled the dreams of people who had spent a part of the post–World War II era migrating from labor camp to labor camp according to an annual rotation of regional harvests. English-language and trade skills enabled them to settle in Fresno, where agriculture's satellite industries— fruit packing, food processing, shipping, light manufacturing—provided steady wages. This largely Latino population (48 percent of the total) has been joined by Southeast Asians, most of them refugees, who accounted for 6.3 percent of the total population in 1990 (Mason, Alvarado, and Palacio 1996).[4] These residents have reduced the monotony of stream-lined home production with personal touches of color, children's toys, cars, and landscaping. They have cultivated vegetable gardens. They have planted shade trees and lawns that take the edge off summer heat.

Head farther north on Chestnut, and the temperature rises. The road is lined with parking lots and strip malls. Drivers of old cars have their windows rolled down, and those of late-model cars have the windows rolled up, the air-conditioning going full blast. Supermarkets, discount clothing stores, and Mexican and Asian fast-food restaurants offer cool places to pass the time.

This time, turn right out of the church's parking lot. Take an immediate left, and travel east on Jensen. At quarter-mile increments, pass Willow and Peach Avenues and begin to understand the logic of this space. Chris P. Jensen was a resident of the Central California Colony in the 1880s. He was a civil engineer and grower of vineyards and orchards.[5] Chestnut, willow, and peach trees, providing shade and fruit, respectively, made up a refreshing, bountiful landscape cultivated by men of industry.

Continue east toward the town of Sanger and the Kings River, one of two Sierra Nevada watersheds that nourish the dreams of valley residents (the other is the San Joaquin River, north of Fresno). Pass by five- to twenty-acre lots that make up small farms with single-family dwellings, horses, goats, sheep, dogs, and other animals.

Juan Ramirez, who attended Saint Anthony's, lived out this way, just south of Jensen. He had a small house on about five acres. I visited him one day. He was unemployed and had been spending his time taking care of a cow, goats, hens, and cocks for fighting. They were "hobbies," he explained. He could never make enough money selling cocks or other animals to have a "real business." Nevertheless, he had wanted a little ranch like this one since he was a boy in Guadalajara, living on the streets and shining shoes. He was under pressure to sell to developers who wanted to expand a nearby industrial park.[6]

Head west on Jensen and pass Chestnut to Highway 99. Travel the same thoroughfare used by commuters from rural, impoverished farm towns and truckers who keep commerce flowing to other parts of the state and country. The speed limit is 50 miles per hour, and the signals are synchronized to keep traffic moving through the community of Calwa. Officials of the Santa Fe Railway coined the name Calwa from the first letters of the California Wine Association in 1913, when they moved the railroad company's yard, roundhouse, and freight offices south, just outside Fresno's city limits. In place of this installation, members of the association established a winery (Hanna 1946). The winery has produced sweet wines from grapes with high sugar content, the result of a hot climate, and is still open for tasting. The offices of the association closed in 1936 after twenty-two years of controlling the production and sale of 84 percent of California wines.[7] The defunct namesake and routing of traffic make Calwa today an easy place to miss.

Consider what might be missed. There is the United Methodist Church on Tenth Street. The church was founded in 1915 and has been maintained in its original form of a white, wood-sided sanctuary, steeple, and social hall. The church has had no pastor for years. Its members hold services on Sunday and organize an annual barbecue to raise funds to feed and clothe the poor. Half a dozen other churches in the area share similar responsibilities.

Have an early-morning breakfast of instant coffee and eggs at the coffee shop with the men who work in the train yards. A Mexican *telenovela* (soap opera) is usually on the television. See mothers walking their children to school, just as their mothers did for them. Meet extended families whose members will tell you, "I was born in Calwa. My entire family is here. This is where I belong."[8] Recognize the depth of memory and activity that keep this place alive amid overwhelming hardship—widespread unemployment, poverty, and a good dose of street violence.

Imagine yourself in Saint Anthony's parking lot again. It's early evening. The sun is setting. The San Joaquin Valley's hot air rises and creates a vacuum drawing cool air from the San Francisco Bay 180 miles north. The air collects along the way the faint, sulfuric odor of fermenting grapes, a hint of pesticides, and dust that creates spectacular sunsets. Migrant laborers convene in the parking lot among old vans with California, Oregon, and Washington license plates. Their workday, which began at 4:00 a.m., ended a few hours earlier. They have come to pick up clothing from the outdoor boxes, pray before the memorial of Juan Diego and Our Lady of Guadalupe. They draw holy water from a tank located outside the rectory door.

Begin to understand the people's religiosity according to the church's location at a crossroads marking travels through rural and urban spaces. In the early 1920s, Reverend Thomas Nealon of Saint Alphonsus's parish held services in Spanish on the Southern Pacific Railway station platform in Malaga, a few miles south of Jenson Avenue. Later, Ramon Vasquez allowed priests to use his farmhouse as a chapel. He wanted to help in "acquiring a church for the community" that had begun to form. In 1935, Mr. Vasquez gave the Cathedral parish, Fresno, land to build a chapel and named it El Cristo Rey (Christ the King) (*Central California Register*, 7 September 1935). In February 1952, Claretian Fathers took charge of the chapel and a new parish. The fathers first offered Mass in a room at the Calwa Hotel. Then ten months later, the fathers acquired a nineteen-acre site at the Jensen and Chestnut Avenue location. Volunteers converted old Air Force barracks that had become a school into a church (*Central California Register*, 29 August 1952, 10 July 1953). This history charts changes from transient to permanent places, from a railroad platform or hotel room to a chapel and church, acknowledging alternative usages and giving definition to the crossroads.

The character of this crossroads has hinged on prevailing geographical conditions of heat and availability of water. The heat posed a challenge to early settlers who faced the region's dry, weedy soil, suitable for herding cattle and sheep. They added water by tapping the Kings River with a vast network of canals, ditches, and dikes, and the heat became a resource for vineyards, orchards, and shade trees—fertile ground for industry and progress that made up dreams of a bountiful life. Entrepreneurs have pursued these dreams by transforming the landscape into subdivisions and corporate farms. Migrant workers and Asian refugees have also pursued the dreams as they took residency in tract homes and apartment complexes, forming communities like the one Mr. Vasquez wanted to help in Malaga. Juan Ramirez pursued them in his effort to transform his life as a shoeshine boy on Guadalajara streets into the life of a valley resident and small rancher. Fresno residents have harnessed the sun for gardens; farmers, for table grapes and raisins; and wine producers, for local port. Small-business owners have harnessed the sun to lure people into their air-conditioned places. The heat and water have helped orchestrate the relationships between people.

The relationships have acquired further definition through undertakings that account for different kinds of movement. Early settlers and developers established farms and subdivisions and left namesakes on streets, towns, and neighborhoods. They displaced sheepherders, who had displaced cattle herders. The railroad men who made space for a winery and named Calwa created a place that residents in outlying areas have learned to overlook with the development of thoroughfares and prominent industries. The seasonal harvests have depended on migrant workers who have found provisional homes in camps hidden among vineyards. The workers' movements have adhered to work sites and other "safe" places like the church parking lot with little threat of officials checking legal status. The workers have led lives of perpetual displacement from all other places.

The movement is analogous to the pouring of cool evening air into the San Joaquin Valley. The cool air replaces the hot daytime air, provides relief, carries the smells of industry, mixes rural dust with urban pollution, draws some people into yards, and draws others to the church parking lot, where they pray to the Virgin and nourish their bodies with holy water. The movement characterizes the crossroads, the flow of people, rural and urban spaces; each parallels a mind-set that comes to fruition in moments of prayer and other ritual acts of devotion.

The acts of devotion show a great concern for time. The sun begins to set. The temperature drops. The wind picks up. And in Saint Anthony's parking lot, the faint smell of pesticides fills the air. A migrant worker sits on the stone fence encircling Juan Diego and Our Lady of Guadalupe. He holds his face in his hands. Another drinks holy water. These moments entail a social quality derived from the past, inclusive of legend, physical exertion, odors, and talk among experiences that give people a sense of where they are and where they might go.

At Saint Anthony's, people talked about religion, migration, work, and other topics that showed ways they thought about the past. Juan Ramirez talked, for example, about enterprise embedded in a childhood dream of living in California, having a small ranch, and making a "real business" out of raising and selling animals. Yet this dream emerged from adverse effects of enterprise, the industrialization of a Mexican city that left children on the streets. Mr. Ramirez recalled times and places from a perspective that showed a marginal place in history. He was a protagonist, a proponent of enterprise and claims to progress—a better life. He was also an antagonist by virtue of having been denied the benefits.

This odd position of protagonist and antagonist fashioned a way of thinking characterized by contradictions. The contradictions led people like Mr. Ramirez to examine the past with a desire to resolve inconsistencies or, at least, better understand themselves. In this respect, people became historians; they talked about the past through a variety of stories that gave substance for reflection, reason for pause, and direction for courses of action.

The stories always came with rituals—the adoration, rosary, communion, sign of the cross, a drink of holy water, manda, and many others of small and large proportion. The rituals gave structure for address-ing all kinds of things—events, people, the things they have done and things done to them—with remorse, laughter, fear, affection, and other emotions.

This combination of ritual structure and narrative reflection en-abled parishioners to realize religion in a way similar to how their clas-sical and Christian predecessors did. Cicero related the Latin term *religio*, a supernatural feeling of constraint, with *relegere*, to read over again. Early Christian writers saw a connection to *religare*, meaning that which ties believers to God.[9] The parishioners undertook a reading of the past characterized by repetition. They read the past over and over again to acquire a comprehensive understanding, grasping diverse ele-ments into a form that made sense. They created stories in ritual. On performing the ritual, they achieved an embodiment of history and of ties to God.

IT'S NEARLY COMMUNION TIME. MEN, WOMEN, AND CHILDREN anticipate filing out of their seats into the aisles. Children will nudge one another while adults negotiate the pace of other communicants, con-verging toward the altar to receive the Host and sip of wine from a chalice.

Assistants of the Mass took the eucharistic food to commemorate the time Jesus ate with the apostles. Jesus taught the apostles that the bread and wine were, respectively, his body and blood, to be sacrificed so that humankind could live. He also taught them that this life de-pended on the memory of him in stories. The apostle John recalls, for example, when the Jews were wandering in the desert, and God gave them manna, a kind of bread, so that they could live (John 6:48–58). And when they were thirsty God gave them water from a rock (Num. 20:10–13). The water was also a sign of baptism and indicated the nour-ishment of the body and soul (Hamman 1967).

The Old Testament is full of these stories. They make up typologies leading to the time of Jesus; each one shows in one way or another how God gave people something to live by when faced with life-threatening circumstances. The apostle Paul mentions that remembering Jesus's death assures believers that Jesus will come again, thereby showing how memory is also about anticipating the future (1 Cor. 11:23–26). The eucharistic food provides so much, including a lesson about how remembering the past is critical to surviving the present.

REMEMBERING CALIFORNIA

To remember the California of the Mexican Period (1821–48), before its annexation to the United States, means seizing upon a romantic opposition to the region's future modern development. This California comes from Californios who in the 1870s, after having lost their domination of politics and land tenure in the coastal regions, gave their accounts of the past to the agents of Hubert Howe Bancroft, the founder of California's historiography. They recalled a better California, where the temperate climate, rich soil, and green pastures provided an ideal setting for the cultivation of a society. The society was neither Spanish, Mexican, nor Franciscan but drew the best parts—liberalism, secularization, Catholicism—from these people to create a regional identity and, as Rosaura Sánchez (1995) argues, an ethnic identity.[10] The Californios defined their land and ethnicity, respectively, according to a pastoral landscape where people of different social classes shared language, reciprocity, equanimity, faith, and history, a place of great hope for the future.

Never mind that this place overshadowed the political, economic, and aristocratic pretensions that helped create oppressive conditions, particularly to Indians.[11] Never mind because these Californios faced formidable adversaries who, according to Mexican policy, could settle only below the forty-second parallel in the Sacramento and San Joaquin Valleys, away from coastal settlements. These adversaries were Anglo American immigrants, different from the earlier Anglo immigrants who had arrived by ship and assimilated to Californio life. The later immigrants followed the footsteps of the infamous trappers Jedediah Smith, Sylvester and James Ohio Pattie (father and son), Ewing Young, and Joseph R. Walker, who, beginning in 1826, had founded overland trails to California. Like these trailblazers, the immigrants were uncouth and eschewed legal documentation, naturalization through Spanish-language acquisition, and religious conversion.[12] They valued self-reliance devoted to the transformation of the wilderness into development and to material accumulation—industrious individuals who exercised their talents often at the expense of amicable social relationships.[13] The immigrants represented a threat to Californian sovereignty as defined by Mexican federalist and centralist political commentaries, which became increasingly prevalent after Texas's independence (1836).[14] To Californios, these immigrants were barbarians, living outside civil society, and therefore relegated to the interior regions known for hostile Indians, runaway neophytes, and questionable survival.

In the 1870s the Californios, who gave interviews to Bancroft's agents, had good reason for harsh judgment. The rhetoric advocating the U.S.-Mexican War continued in its aftermath, but this time directed at local populations and specific people rather than just a nation. From 1855 to 1859, the editor of *El Clamor Publico*, Francisco Ramirez, espoused values of Jefferson and Jackson—values of popular government, economic progress, civil rights, and religious tolerance—that shaped the U.S. Constitution and the Treaty of Guadalupe Hidalgo (which ended the U.S.-Mexican War), and buttressed a foundation for a healthy democracy. At the same time, Ramirez documented aspersions cast on the Mexican population —ascribing to it a proclivity to religious superstition, violence, robbery, intoxication, idleness, and debauchery (Pitt 1971). The people who promoted these stereotypes, Ramirez reasoned, threatened to undermine democratic values and a prosperous future.

The hostility coincided with Senator William Gwin's Land Law of 1851, which established the Board of Land Commissioners, an agency empowered to review all land titles and rule on their authenticity. Claimants faced several complications that damaged their cases. Their surveys were vague according to the commissioners' standards, marking property lines with geographical descriptions—a hill, tree, or fork in a creek—that reflected the Californios' transformation of the wilderness into a range. Their titles were often inaccessible, stowed away or lost in Mexico City's government archives. Their documentation was in Spanish and written with archaic legal language untranslatable in American courts (Pitt 1971).

The Californios' most formidable adversary was far more insidious: the social and political climate of the period. The Land Law of 1851 made claims vulnerable by implying fraud and creating a legal environment fecund for lawyers and squatters. Of the fifty lawyers who specialized in claim law in the 1850s, most were "shysters"; only a few were qualified (Pitt 1971, 91). Californios paid lawyers often in land for services rendered over the course of years. The process filled lawyers' coffers while raising doubts about the authenticity of claims, which for squatters became signs of opportunity.

The squatters, who saw so much land—millions of acres in the hands of a few hundred families—wanted a piece of paradise and hope for the future. Many, tired of digging for gold, moved onto what appeared to be vacant land and made improvements by turning the soil, planting crops, and building fences and places to live. They were "hardy immigrants" and "industrious settlers," in contrast to the beneficiaries of "special privilege."[15] Squatters ingratiated themselves with juries, judges, and legislators (Pitt 1971, 87). The legislators accommodated squatters by passing laws that enabled them to make improvements and secure claims to unsurveyed land. These laws fully satisfied no one and provoked violence and litigation that made the Californios' ordeals insufferable (Pitt 1971).

The Californios' problems were compounded by other factors: property taxes (based on assessments as opposed to revenues), high freight rates, low cattle prices, and droughts and floods in the early 1860s that wiped out one-quarter of the state's wealth, including 40 percent of its livestock (Pitt 1971). Land rich and cash poor, many Californios sold percentages of their land and grazing rights to Anglo cattlemen, who later petitioned under state law for partitions.

The cattle barons Henry Miller and his partner Charles Lux were, arguably, the savviest negotiators of land claims. They acquired, Leonard Pitt says, "all of the most substantial parts of the fifteen northern Spanish-Mexican ranchos (1971, 99). Their holdings eventually consisted of a mosaic of fertile lands that extended from Mexico to Oregon (Pitt 1971; Acuña 1972; Treadwell 1931).

The natural, legislative, legal, and social conditions of the 1850s and '60s had a cumulative effect of making Californios in debt and vulnerable to lawyers, legislators, squatters, and other people who felt justified in predatory interests. Between 1848 and 1870, the Californios' claims to land worth $10,000 or more declined by 75 percent. Many became small landholders; most became members of a landless class, stripped of whatever political and social credibility they had enjoyed in prosperous times (Acuña 1972; Pitt 1971).

To understand predatory interests, consider Bancroft's *California Pastoral* (1888). In this tribute to an allusive paradise, the author highlighted the region's inhabitants during the Franciscan and Mexican periods (1769–1848). These inhabitants, Bancroft says, enjoyed the bountiful gifts of "soil and climate" and wasted them through social decline (180). The missionaries, Bancroft suggests, appeared to reflect serene, beneficent shepherds of the classical period. They appeared to have the "kindest motives," devoted to the amelioration of the "most abject races" (268). But in reality, the missionaries were "wolves," manipulators, and commercial agents whose "humble guise" of religion obscured their despotism of Indians (182).

Likewise, Bancroft explains, the Californios did not represent the "best of people" (269). They had sufficient "energy," but it was "a spasmatic kind which aroused by passion subsides before beneficial results are secured" (269). Compared to Indian counterparts, the Californios were "alike in natural indolence, love of luxury, fondness of amusement, and hatred of menial occupations" (269). They "passed away their time without care, . . . and never gave any thought to their future" (275). Bancroft drew a caricature of Californios similar to the one that had justified Manifest Destiny, the U.S.-Mexican War (1846–48), and the United States' annexation of northern Mexico.[16] He made the Anglo Americans' displacement of native and Californio populations appear as a natural process facilitated by the Anglos' "patient and self-denying industry, [laying] the foundations of superior political institutions" (269). Bancroft's pastoral raises the specter of paradise lost under the stewardship of one population and his anticipation of a better, modern society under another.

This reasoning, which posits an ideal place and time for the creation of a pragmatic alternative, has helped define regional conceptions of progress ranging from large industry, particularly in agriculture, to neighborhood projects. Pastor Marc Rosales of the Malaga Pentecostal Church, for example, envisioned a future ministry on a ranch with many acres for children, "where kids can come and live," where "they'll have a father figure who'll love them unconditionally." Meanwhile, he carried out his work with the "throwaways"—kids without parents and the incarcerated—people who, Pastor Rosales explained, have been denied love because the "separatists" judge them as different "by how they appear" and by the things that they have or don't have.[17]

Pastor Aurelio Lopez of the Rapto Divino Church in Calwa envisioned his future while alone in the mountains, where the Lord had sent him to fast for thirty days. "I got a revelation," he recalled, "from God for my life, for my whole family, for the church. And since then, my spiritual life has been so strong." Pastor Lopez devoted his time to cultivating the spiritual life of neighbors who were like he had been before his revelation: people who "control the neighborhood," "sell drugs on the corner," have "nice cars, lots of girls, . . . trouble with the law," who beat their wives and just "go day by day." He envisioned opening churches in the nearby farm towns—Kerman, Sanger, Selma, Tranquility, Los Baños— "daughter churches" to his "mother church" showing the growth of a community.[18]

The Californios, Bancroft, and Pastors Rosales and Lopez suggested that community occupied a space born out of nostalgic, imaginary, and actual places. The green pastures, social harmonies, despotic missionaries, uncouth immigrants, loving fathers, "throwaways," "separatists," and a mother church, among other perceptions, produced affection that enabled a person to conceive an idea of position, sometimes predatory and other times not, and create future plans. The plans gained rhetorical traction and impetus by holding out for the mind's eye an object of repulsion on the one hand and, on the other, a sense of urgency and order and a course of action for social well-being.

Wheel back to the 1930s, 1920s, and before, when Bancroft's vision of modern development had made considerable progress; economic and technological investment marked a path toward the future. The federal government had endorsed a geographical transformation by passing the Land Reclamation Act of 1902, which, Carey McWilliams explains, "outlined a development policy for the arid West and made possible the

use of federal funds in the construction of large-scale irrigation and reclamation projects." Irrigation turned arid land into productive farmland, enabling the development of "intensive farming," producing high
yields per acre (1990, 162). Small family farms gave way to large, high-
technology farms that produced products for national markets. The
construction of railroads in Mexico under Porfirio Díaz's administration (1876–1910) and in the United States (largely by Mexican and Chi-
nese labor) assured the Southwest of a steady supply of labor by enabling
workers to travel easily.[19] The railroads also provided California farmers
of citrus, stone fruit, and grapes with access to national markets. This
development confirmed Bancroft's assessments of racial character and
natural outcomes. The Californio and Mexican residents were reduced
to an impoverished working class. They were unable, it appeared, to
compete with Anglos, whose American ethos, composed of individual-
ism, work, industry, production, and material accumulation, justified
their domination of politics and resources.

This mind-set guided labor unions, public officials, and social
groups in efforts to set policy and pursue economic goals. The American
Federation of Labor excluded Mexicans, African Americans, and other
people of color in the early 1900s. To the AFL's members, work, productivity, and masculinity constructed notions of not only patriotism but
also whiteness.[20] Similarly, the League of United Latin American Citizens (LULAC), committed to fostering the "best and purist form of
Americanism," opposed Mexican immigration when it increased due
to the Bracero Program (LULAC as quoted in Gutiérrez 1995, 81).[21]
Mexican immigrants threatened Mexican American labor's collective
bargaining power and, on account of "cultural differences," Mexican
Americans' ability to be recognized as "American" by the dominant society. The League's reasoning reflected Americanization efforts among
academics, social reformers, and government policy makers during the
interwar period aimed at making Mexican Americans "civil," "clean,"
"healthy," and "productive," adopting the "customs of the [American]
community" (G. Sánchez 1993, 119).[22] We may also consider Daniel
Patrick Moynihan's idea of "black pathology," which, like critiques of
Californios and Mexicans, accounts for the people who fail to assimilate

to an American mainstream. Moynihan's handiwork shaped thirty years of domestic social policy (Glazer and Moynihan 1970).[23]

Pastors in Fresno's southeast neighborhoods expressed similar reasoning, pitting health and progress against social contagion and decline. Pastor Jorge Alvarez identified a line between La Gracia Church in Calwa and the corner bar "not more than five hundred feet away." "By law," Pastor Alvarez explained, "the bar should be closed, but somebody gave it permission to open." At night, "cars peal out, their wheels screeching. . . . And if a Hispanic gets drunk and kills a family of Americans, in reality all of us Hispanics look bad, not just the one who killed somebody. . . . The scriptures tell us," Pastor Alvarez continued, "to fight against what is morally incorrect." So Pastor Alvarez organized a block party and invited dignitaries from the local and state governments— Mayor Alan Autry, city council members, the chief of police, the sheriff, and INS officials. They came, and Pastor Alvarez drew attention to the neighborhood and his church, showing its dedication to teaching values and "lifting the morals of the society." Pastor Alvarez explained, "many Hispanics think, 'Well, the Anglos have all of the good things because they're Anglos and it's the good part of their country.' And this is right, but we can also benefit if only we do something right for the society in which we live."[24]

Other pastors also saw the well-being of their congregations coinciding with economic development. Pastor Dan White of the English-speaking Assembly of God congregation remarked that the growth of his congregation came with second- and third-generation Hispanic families moving into new subdivisions. "They're different from their parents and grandparents," Pastor White explained. "They're not Spanish-speaking only. For most of them, Spanish is their second language. For some of them, they don't speak Spanish at all. They are that far removed from that culture."[25] Pastor White's observations concurred with regional studies showing that the children and grandchildren of immigrants from Mexico and other parts of Central America escaped the hardships of farm labor through acquisition of English-language skills, education, and jobs in urban areas (Allensworth and Rochín 1995). His observations also indicated a line between his ministry and "that culture."

What is "that culture" that Pastor White referred to? I asked Pastor César Pérez of the nearby Nazarene congregation. He explained that

> most of the people who are here come from *pueblos*, small towns in Mexico. What they do here is work in the fields. So they don't have the opportunity to do something different. . . . It's a different culture. . . . They like to drink a lot because . . . their duties are too hard in the fields. When they finish their task, they feel tired, hot, miserable, alone. And they drink. After they drink beer, they take drugs. They fight with their families. Something that surprised me a lot, is a lot of police cars here, a lot of criminality. At least 70 percent of my church members have problems with the law.[26]

Pastor Pérez explained the culture of wage labor born out of the California pastoral. The culture consists of people who come from the most impoverished sectors of society and who by necessity undertake a livelihood defined by tasks, fatigue, misery, and feelings of loneliness. It's a culture of limited experiences—detachment from home, family, and friendships across generations. The culture offers no luxury of reflection or hope even within the scope of California dreams—only the frustration of these things denied. It's a culture that deprives people of their history and provides means sufficient only for small, immediate gratifications. Ironically, Bancroft perceived these characteristics among the Californios, justifying their social decline and incorporation into a labor force, epitomizing a part of modern progress.

The southeast Fresno pastors saw lines like those addressed above as a social problem facing their ministries and not facing the people situated, presumably, on either side. Pastor Rosales clarified this point by asking rhetorically, "What's wrong with the United States? . . . The people in prison, if you study the people in prison, you are studying the people in the United States."[27] The people in prison and presumably other "throwaways" reflect the larger society and, more precisely, the "separatists" who define themselves by caricaturing and repelling others. These people channel resources to different sectors of the economy, producing affluent farmers, shopping centers, well-paved streets, and other forms of opulence in one part of the city and impoverished, ethnic neighbor-hoods in other parts.[28]

Who are the separatists, one might ask—the city mayor, politicians, farmers, and other well-to-do people? Not exactly—the separatists reflect a part of a cultural psyche. The latter is also represented allegorically by the California pastoral and literally by the prisons that mark the landscape.[29]

To put this issue another way, Pastor White and his wife, Cory, recalled a fence that once enclosed their church. "There was a fence," Pastor White said, "and yet inside, the property was real run down. The grass was brown. Everything looked bad; it looked seedy. . . . And when I was behind it, I felt like the people who walked past, I felt separated. I felt like, 'O.K. I'm *out* here and you're *in* there.' We had an attitude of, 'Well, you stay *out* there and we'll stay *in* here. We'll have church and we'll be happy'" (emphasis added).

Pastor White found documentation in the church files revealing the fence's history. A former pastor had gone to city hall to fight a code prohibiting the construction of fences taller than forty-eight inches on corner lots. He had won an exemption from the code and built a six-foot chain link fence. "There was a pride," Pastor White continued, "that they had won their battle and were able to put up the fence. . . . They put up the fence and, like Samson, didn't know that the Holy Ghost had left them."

"They were afraid of the community," Cory interjected.

"They were trying to protect themselves," Pastor White added. "And there was a hold-the-fort mentality."

So Pastor White gathered the members of his congregation to decide what to do about the fence. "We prayed," Cory explained. And they prayed for about six months until "the Lord spoke" to them, "saying that the fence wasn't just around the property but around the hearts." They decided to take the fence down, "open their hearts to the neighborhood," and show their "love for the community."[30]

Similarly, Pastor Rosales showed his love for the community of people that resided behind bars in California prisons. Pastor Lopez showed his love for the neighbors who were like he had been, inviting them to his mother church.

And at Saint Anthony's, the priest announces that it's time to turn to your neighbor, reach out your hand or open your arms, and profess your love with the words, *"Paz de Cristo."*

UNDERSTANDING THE PRESENT

My friend Devon Sanders and I were on our way to lunch. We went periodically during the time I was in Fresno. We had known each other since childhood, attended the same schools in north Fresno, traveled together, and even lived together. We had competed in the sport of alpine ski racing, which drew our lives together for summer training in European resorts and winter competition in California. I thought of him as a brother and mentor: he always achieved more than I did—NCAA and professional athlete, and an Ivy League education. He went to law school, returned to Fresno, married, had a family, and worked in his father's firm, representing real estate developers, ranchers, and dairy farmers.

I sat in the passenger seat of his late-model sports car, with German technology that combined luxury and power. We headed south on Highway 41, which cut through Fresno, connecting the north side of the city with the south. We moved along at about seventy miles per hour, talking about our children. We exited right on McKinley Avenue and traveled west through one of Fresno's older neighborhoods, where my family and I lived during the time of research.

We passed by Fresno City College, the city's oldest institution of higher education, providing vocational training and general education, shoring up a foundation for students who planned on attending a four-year university. We passed by the Old Administration Building, a 100,000-square-foot "eyesore," a writer for the *Fresno Bee* had commented. The building had been condemned and closed for twenty-seven years (20 June 2002). A chain link fence lined with barbed wire surrounded the 86-year-old brick building with boarded-up windows. The city council, State Center Community College District, or other public entities could not muster up enough public support for a $25 million bond measure to fund a renovation, priorities being elsewhere.[31]

We approached Fresno High School, the city's first secondary school, founded in 1889. The school had produced, Principal Bob Reyes declared, "many of Fresno's finest business, civic, and political leaders," and continued to promote "leadership and group skills."[32] The school grounds were full of students involved in physical education activities. All of them, it appeared, represented the Latino families that lived in the area. Devon, who lived farther north but within Fresno High's geographical parameters, looked out and across the school grounds, saw all of the dark hair and brown faces, and said, "I would never send my kids there."

"Why not?" I asked.

"They'd get picked on or hurt. They just don't think the same way we do. They're not motivated. Their parents don't provide good role models."[33]

A few minutes later we arrived at a restaurant that served our favorite Mexican food.

DURING THE TIME OF MY RESEARCH, ALMOST EVERY SCENE and display of customary behavior depended on discriminatory gazes. The people perceived variance in hue, gender, idiom, and style, posing a question, "What might that be?," followed by an answer that formed another part of a social imagination.

In California, talk about an ethnic other has focused predominantly on a "Mexican" subject, demarcating a cultural process anchored in a psychological condition. The talk articulates the Mexican subject as complex symbols of labor, piety, family, cuisine, and a glorious missionary past, or of indolence, vanity, violence, crime, and decadence. The talk predicates legislation, public policy, labor rights, Cinco de Mayo celebrations, mission tourism, and a proliferation of Mexican restaurants, prisons, and police forces among other things that define the life of the state. In the language of psychoanalysis, the talk is a rebus that represents a depository of desire, abjection, investment, and expenditure—Freud's unconscious and basis of cultural heteronomy.

The relationship between culture and psychology gives insight into subjectivity. In *Écrits*, Jacques Lacan identifies symbols in relation to incest taboo, which he calls a "subjective pivot" that orients people in language and predicates—Lacan following Lévi-Strauss (1951) here—social patterns: gift-giving, marriage ties, kinship relations, and so forth (Lacan 1977, 66). The symbols are not "icons" or "stylized figurations," Alan Sheridan explains. They are "signifiers, in the sense developed by Saussure and Jakobson, extended into a generalized definition: differential elements, in themselves without meaning, which acquire value only in their mutual relations" (1977, ix). This distinction characterizes the way that symbols function in discourse or talk. Meaning comes from correlations among symbols that chart different domains defined by topical foci and, as shown above, positive and negative valuations. The domains orient the mind's eye to a feedback loop between what the mind perceives of social relations and one's experience of them, a hermeneutic circle that combines social laws with, in Lacan's terms, "the law of language" (1977, 73).

The law of language always represents something else that resides outside of one's purview or direct apprehension. Similar to a drama, language's symbols are so compelling because they say something about us that we cannot see or wholly understand; they refer to an a priori, unconscious condition that guides ways that we socialize with others and the values assigned to them. Devon Sanders's look out of the car window and across the schoolyard, for example, entailed a plethora of impressions—danger, hurt, lack of motivation, social decline. The impressions supported his self-awareness by drawing a line of defense against youth and their families. He fortified this line with accouterments: the car, luxury, and power. What Devon produced in talk—a line of defense with himself on the one side and, in actuality, unknown others on the other side—refers as much to his perception of what's in the world as to the perception's origin in the mind.

Devon Sanders's look contributed to a drama with other actors in the San Joaquin Valley, including developers, ranchers, and dairy farmers. The drama draws intrigue and compulsion through contrast between racial assignments and, accordingly, between insiders and outsiders, the powerful and subordinated, supporting, as self-evident, outcomes of a labor force and poverty.

The media, police, government officials, and other institutional authorities also played a role in this drama. They said things and created images for popular consumption, only to reinforce common perceptions and interpretations of people. Television news, for example, covered the trial of Josefina Sonia Saldana, featuring Ms. Saldana for having kidnapped and killed Margarita Flores for her unborn fetus and then scattered body parts throughout Southern California and Mexico. Coverage lasted for months until Ms. Saldana committed suicide. Salvador Estrada Jr., a fourteen-year-old Sunnyside High School freshman, was "fatally stabbed." He was a "fun-loving, churchgoing youth who respected others and had no place in his life for violence" (*Fresno Bee*, 5 May 2001). Juan Manuel Gonzalez, aged 50, veered off Whites Bridge Road near Kerman at "70 mph" and crashed into a cement-mixing truck. "He never knew what hit him" (*Fresno Bee*, 2 February 2001).[34] The police held Jesus Gutierrez, aged 20, and Antonio Gutierrez, aged 19, in connection with the fatal shooting of Andrés Castro, aged 26, near J's Mart and Gas. Castro "was born in Tijuana . . . moved to the United States when he was a boy and graduated from Kingsburg High School. . . . [He] was a good mechanic and always kept his car clean. He liked to garden" (*Fresno Bee*, 28 May 2001). Day after day, the media displayed images of people whom one knew at school, saw in front yards, or passed on the road. The familiar, including names, places, and activities—Jesus, Josefina, Andrés, a country road, good mechanic, churchgoing youth, courtroom, corner market—became known through shocking impressions—body parts strewn about the countryside, fatal stabbing, shooting, or accident. Order and comfort accompanied horror, showing a mysterious reflection to the things that people related to.

This odd combination circulated through different means of communication with various degrees of intensity. Newspaper articles featured contorted faces, mug shots, handcuffed prisoners, and school photographs of victims, prompting wild stories and drastic security measures. "Saldana doctor: holes in brain," the headlines read, recalling a psychiatrist's testimony that explained the defendant's "stress," "confusion," and "irrational behavior" (*Fresno Bee*, 2 February 2001). County Assembly Member Dean Florez lobbied the state Board of Corrections for funds to build a new juvenile hall. He argued that the hall was necessary to relieve overcrowded conditions and threats to "public safety, inmate safety and staff safety" (*Fresno Bee*, 31 March 2001). The mayor, Alan Autry, "push[ed] hard" for a daytime curfew in public schools. The curfew, he argued, would "reduce crime," presumably by keeping potential criminals in "safe, clean" schools. The schools helped students become "satisfied, informed, self-sufficient citizens" who make "positive life choices" and develop a "sense of commonality and brotherhood" (*Fresno Bee*, 26 March 2001). Police officers routinely took extra precaution with potential criminals like Alberto Sepulveda, aged eleven. He "was shot in the back as he obeyed . . . commands to lie down" during a SWAT team's narcotics sweep (*Fresno Bee*, 1 January 2001). The media, dignitaries, and other officials imposed order through references to walls, fences, curfews, and force among other lines of defense that contained irrationality, criminality, violence, and death, as if to say, "We've got a handle on it; the public is safe." If he had lived, Alberto Sepulveda might have said, "It's got a handle on you," asserting a turn of logic whereby what people perceive defines what people become.

Alberto Sepulveda, of course, didn't have a chance to say anything. Others had said enough for him to ensure his placement on one side of a line, the side that came with presumptions of criminality and demanded swift action.

I did not know Alberto, and the newspaper didn't say anything about who he was. But I assume that he might have been like other boys of his age, attending neighborhood schools, even learning to make "positive life choices" and become a "satisfied, self-sufficient citizen." These objectives defined the terms of moving forward, "improving," and "doing the best that you can." They defined the terms of "education." For Alberto as for many others in his position, the terms of education also meant taking a step back, and looking into the eyes of another. The terms meant seeing, if only for a brief moment, a perspective of the past with race and prejudice that brought about the event of his death. Who knows? Perhaps it was such a double take, a step back, another forward, and a glance, that triggered the bullet that pierced his back.

This kind of movement involves changing from one side to another, double takes, and new impressions. Gracie Romana Adame learned the moves as a little girl when she migrated with her parents from Arizona to California in the 1940s. She traveled with her parents on California's migratory labor circuit, moving from camp to camp as different regional crops came into season. Letters followed them, forwarded until they caught up. She slept often outdoors, struggled to maintain hygiene, and had limited formal educational opportunities. But this moving about is what her parents had to do to change their lives, so that one day they could "settle down," "sink roots," and "have a real home" with kids going to school. And they did; her parents found long-term employment "in the city," and Gracie went to school, became a schoolteacher, and lived in Fresno, a few blocks from Saint Anthony's.

At this juncture where everything seemed right, somebody showed up to give different meaning to the word "movement." A priest asked her, "Why don't you leave? You have been here for a few years." Gracie also recalled when she first moved to the neighborhood in southeast Fresno. "Anglos expected us to move on," she said, "but we stayed."[35] Movement for Gracie meant making something of herself. For the priest and Anglos in the neighborhood, movement meant getting out.

This predicament of mixed messages produces ambiguity and angst about what to do. Alfredo Reyes felt this way one day at Saint Anthony's. He'd come to the United States from Guanajuato, Mexico, in the late 1980s and spent a few years on the labor circuit picking peaches in California and apples in Washington State before going to Fresno to be near family members. He worked at Saint Anthony's as a caretaker, youth leader, and coordinator of church ministries, wearing many hats and being involved in the lives of most parishioners. Father Alba, the pastor of Saint Anthony's, once told me, "I've seen Alfredo in the church sanctuary alone, kneeling before the cross in deep prayer." Alfredo was a part of the place in body and spirit.

It was no matter that Alfredo had never been able to "arrange his papers" and become a legal resident. Everybody knew; Pastor Alba, the staff, parishioners, his housemates, and I knew. We knew the Alfredo with whom we'd shared meals, retreats, and the Mass. That is, until one day when an office manager was reviewing personnel files. She ran a tight ship and, drawing from her experience in the military, wanted to make sure that "everything was in order." She called the diocese's office for advice. Someone recommended that the parish "let Alfredo go."

"Why did she do that? Why did Father Alba let you go?" I asked Alfredo.

"You know, David, it's politics."

Politics indeed, but whose—the office manager's, Father Alba's, mine, or somebody else's? Politics pervaded the language we spoke. We kept them at bay for the most part, until a momentary lapse in judgment made us forget who someone was and imagine what someone might be. Years of anti-immigration rhetoric, legislative initiatives, and fear of fines must have pressed upon the office manager. Her phone call to the diocese transformed Alfredo into something else—illegal and a threat to parish life. The irony, of course, lies in the fact that the office manager herself became a threat when she had Alfredo, a person central to parish life, removed.

These moments came to pass. Alfredo stayed away for a while, holed up in his apartment, "thinking things over." Father Alba called Alfredo to see if he'd gone to a local nonprofit for advice about his papers. Then Alfredo came back. He started assisting in the Mass again and resumed his work with the youth group. About his termination, Alfredo was philosophical, saying, "This is God's way of urging me to move on and make something more of my life."[36] For the time being, Alfredo stayed at the parish, and the possibility of his moving on was more imminent than ever.

VICTIMIZATION BRINGS ABOUT CIRCUMSPECTION; IT GIVES insight into the meanings of words and their relationship to actions, enabling one to empathize with the people who take those actions. Alberto Sepulveda was a victim, one that gave insight into the police officer who took his life. One might empathize with the fear the officer must have felt, a visceral hardening that provided sufficient stamina to take aim. Similarly, one can empathize with the office manager, how she made the call and let Alfredo go. One can also empathize with Devon Sanders, with how he looked out and across the schoolyard. And, of course, one should also empathize with the victims of these situations. This kind of empathy means acknowledging something of oneself and also leaving oneself behind, a crossing, exchange, and exploration of alternative possibilities.

The Mass takes people on a similar journey in commemoration of Jesus's sacrifice. Christ was a Jew with all of the markings of an ethnic identity who became a symbol of a collective destiny.

The people file out of their seats and into the aisles and head toward the altar. Their approach entails a preoccupation with others—the others with whom one negotiates steps and stories about heat, water, and movement, among other themes that help configure all of the possibilities of heritage.

The altar is near, and the anticipation builds. The priest asks if you accept the body and blood of Christ. If you say, "Yes," then you too take on a body and a movement forward, sometimes backward, and always in procession.

The Mass has ended. The priest tells everybody to go in peace. And we begin to sing, "*Caminando unidos para hacernos uno.*" Again, we file out of our seats and head toward the door—"*Caminando unidos con nuestro Señor.*" Waiting patiently, one by one, we funnel into the dark, narrow corridor. "*Caminando unidos para hacernos uno,*" we make our way into the parking lot and the world. "*Caminando unidos con el Redentor.*"[37]

THE JOURNEY HOME

THREE

I was driving to Gracie Romana Adame's home. It was a chilly weekday morning in early October. The days were becoming short, and the nights, cool. The dust, so prevalent from the summer work in the fields, had cleared. I turned onto Church Avenue and headed east through a warehouse district. Truck traffic carrying fruits and vegetables had died down; the harvest was nearly over. Many field workers had gone north to Oregon and Washington to pick apples. Others had gone to Mexico. And many had stayed, often unemployed, to enable their children to attend school.

Fall in the San Joaquin Valley is a time of transition. It is relatively short compared to fall in other regions. Long, hot summer days give way to a few weeks of cool temperatures and crisp blue skies, with Sierra vistas to the east often boasting the first snowfall in the high country. It's a time of anticipation—of short gray days damp with morning and evening fog, of holiday festivities and indoor decorations. It's a time to think about the procession for the Virgin of Guadalupe, the *novenas* and *posadas* for the Christ child, the celebrations of past years, and what's to come.[1] It's a time of meditation.

Gracie lives a few blocks from Saint Anthony's in a white stucco home, not very different from others along Church Avenue. Her old white Oldsmobile was my landmark indicating the right place. I approached Gracie's security door—black sheet metal perforated with fine holes that allowed one to see out but not in—and thought about the rosary. Gracie and I were going to talk about the rosary, as we had on previous occasions.

You may have seen a set of rosary beads. They are often wooden with five decades of small beads, each separated from the next by a distinct one. Each small bead designates a prayer to Mary, and each distinct one, to the Father. The beads also represent biblical mysteries—the joyful, luminous, sorrowful, and glorious—about Mary and her son Jesus. These mysteries are bound in the biblical stories about birth, God's kingdom, crucifixion, and ascension into heaven.

You may even have heard a recitation of the rosary. Catholics, at least those whom I know, manipulate the beads, say the prayers, and meditate on the mysteries in churches, homes, or wherever they go. At Saint Anthony's, prayer groups begin their meetings by saying the rosary. One person initiates the ritual by announcing a meditation upon a particular mystery. For example, during Lent, forty days of preparation for Christ's crucifixion, Catholics focus on the sorrowful mysteries. These include the events expressing Christ's suffering and passion for the sake of humankind. The group says an Our Father. Then, one person leads the others by saying the first half of a Hail Mary, in honor of the Lord's mother. The entire group follows with the second half, repeating this pattern ten times, completing a decade. A session is usually devoted to meditations upon five biblical mysteries, accounting for five Our Fathers and fifty Hail Marys. A complete rosary consists of meditations upon twenty biblical mysteries, twenty Our Fathers, and two hundred Hail Marys. This ritual provides a formal frame for participants to evoke biblical mysteries and apply their meaning to contemporary life while cultivating solidarity with others.

The solidarity goes centuries back in time. Two fifteenth-century Carthusian monks, Adolf of Essen in 1439 and Dominic of Prussia in 1460, claimed to have received the rosary by divine inspiration from Saint Dominic (1170–1221). According to legend, Saint Dominic had used it in the early thirteenth century as the "invincible sword to destroy the nefarious heresy" of the Albigensians, who "threatened the peace and tranquility of Christendom" (Pius IX 1980, 37). The rosary's life in the crusades entails another mystery. Despite confirmation by Dominican observants and papal instruction long afterward, there is no historical record of Saint Dominic's use of the rosary.[2]

I've suggested that the rosary "is a journey," as Gracie informed me.[3] It takes us back, for example, to the biblical and medieval periods. It enables us to imagine the joy of a child's birth, the horror of a crucifixion, and even the militant march of Catholicism in Southern France a long time ago. Gracie insisted that the rosary is a journey. "[It] tells," she said, "how Mary followed her heart. Mary lived. Mary obeyed. Mary got involved. So a journey of her life, today, brings me to this journey that I am so involved with."[4]

I stood waiting on Gracie's porch, thinking about how sensational the rosary is, recalling Gracie's instruction. "Yes, you have to see the suffering," the death, the joy, the "need to belong some place. The rosary tells me all that."[5] The rosary takes us to other places and times, shows us how to imagine and feel. It tells us what to see. The rosary lets us into Mary's life and, as Gracie suggested, into Gracie's life as well, enabling us to relive the experiences with the emotion of having been there. But wherever the rosary takes us and whatever it enables us to experience, it also involves mysteries.

This chapter begins with meditation upon the rosary and provides an account of its performance. The meditation coincides with a visit to Gracie's home, where my return to Fresno, California, intersected with Gracie's stories about her journey.[6] The ritual in stories, I argue, elicits memory for insight into the afflictions of contemporary life—wage labor, migration, violence, isolation, and social decay. The combination also enables one to "see the need to belong someplace," a better place understood through "get[ting] involved" with otherness. Otherness entails slippage between the known and the unknown, the tangible and intangible, or between the mysteries that refer to the sacred, and other people represented through maternal images, inducing a sense of flow, harmony, or connection between one human and another.

But what does Gracie mean by a need to belong someplace? "Where could this place be?" I wondered.

The door cracked, and I heard Gracie's soft voice, "*Hola, mi hijo* [Hello, my son]. Just a minute." She placed a key into the security door's lock. The deadbolt slid back. And Gracie opened the door and stepped back, allowing me into the entryway. Gracie had a small frame, standing about five feet high. I noticed it when we embraced and greeted each other.

Gracie's living room was a place for visiting. A twenty-four-inch television dominated one corner, the low volume creating background noise. On this October morning, Judge Judy sat behind her bench and prescribed candid, commonsense advice to disputing neighbors. There were three worn sofas along three walls, enough space to accommodate the entire family. Gracie had four children and lived with her daughter, son-in-law, and two grandchildren. Her grandson knew "a lot about computers" and had one situated at the end of the room that opened to the kitchen. Pictures of her granddaughter in a soccer uniform stood on a table full of trophies. A pencil drawing of Jesus's face hung framed in glass on the wall at eye level. And a figurine of Our Lady of Guadalupe sat on a table among old photographs of Gracie's grandparents and parents. The light was dim because Gracie had drawn the curtains over a large window to the street, allowing warmth to penetrate the room while cutting off the morning glare from the east. The room boasted an intimate, cozy feeling accentuated by the busy murmur of the outside world through the computer, television, and occasional street traffic.

This morning, Gracie was animated. The evening before, she had gone to a youth group meeting at Saint Anthony's.[7] And the day before that, she had attended the first support group meeting for mothers of incarcerated children. These activities indicated more involvement in church functions than she had had for several months.

This news recalled for me a moment two and a half years before (May 1999) when I had called the church secretary with hopes of finding a home for my research. I remember inquiring about a church leader who could tell me about the ministries, hearing, "That would be Gracie." I remember asking if the church had a youth group. The secretary responded, "You need to talk to Gracie." I met Gracie a week later and learned that in one way or another—through her roles as catechism teacher, youth group leader, office volunteer, eucharistic minister—she was involved in most parishioners' lives. Her activities were the culmination of many years that she characterized as a blessing she had never expected.

Gracie's involvement at Saint Anthony's began many years before in Cheyenne, Wyoming. She had gone to visit relatives there and found, she explained, "a community that [had] something to offer."[8] At church, she saw people helping the priest with the Eucharist. "I wondered," Gracie recalled, "if they were priests, deacons, or people studying to be priests. But they were just people who wanted to help the priest. They were married—that was one of the requirements." When she returned to Saint Anthony's, she told the priest about it.

"No, that's wrong," he said, implying that only priests, deacons, and acolytes should administer the Eucharist.

"But a few years later," Gracie continued, "we had another priest. I told him about the people who helped with the Eucharist."

And the priest said, "That's a good idea," and asked Gracie to make a list of people who might help him. Gracie made a list of all the married people who might help and gave it to him. A short time later, he asked Gracie if she herself wanted to help.

"Of course, I was divorced," Gracie recalled, "and he knew it.[9] But, he asked me anyway. I felt so happy that I went home and cried. You see, you never know what you're going to learn when you go to places and how it's going to affect the place you live."

Gracie's trip to Cheyenne had provided insight into her own parish. The first priest had sustained his authority by preventing parishioners from administering the Eucharist. This prohibition struck at the heart of Catholicism, creating a rift between priest and people, when this most sacred Catholic ritual is designed to facilitate quite the opposite, unity through an encounter with God. In the journey to Cheyenne and subsequent events in Fresno, however, Gracie's patience exemplified her faith. When the time was right at Saint Anthony's, when a new priest with a different perspective and openness arrived, Gracie allowed the significance of her Cheyenne trip to resurface, bringing about a fundamental change in parish life. The event also changed Gracie herself by enabling her to realize her worth. Instead of a stigmatized divorced woman, she was a viable parish member. The Cheyenne trip initiated a logical sequence of events, as if this sequence were a natural process in the development of a community, while its essential vitality remained a mystery. As Gracie reminds us, "You see, you never know . . ."

What Gracie did not know was how future priests would influence parish life. Shortly before Christmas of 2000, about a year before my early October visit, Gracie announced that she was planning to retire; she was "just too tired." So she resigned from her positions as office volunteer, catechism teacher, and (after finding a replacement) youth group director. I no longer saw her white Oldsmobile in the church parking lot when I came around. As time passed, I no longer saw many people— the church's caretaker, the secretary, and other parishioners; somehow the community was losing its cohesion through the separation of its members.

This separation was not part of a natural process. Father Rick Alba had been the pastor of Saint Anthony's for about two years before my arrival. During his tenure, he initiated many changes to help people experience what it means to be a Christian. As he explained, "To really be a Christian means you have to get involved in some way. But not everybody can get involved in the same way. We are all parts of a whole."[10] While his primary duties were "caught up in the administration, saying the Mass," and other "details," he was particularly pleased with the parishioners' initiatives—the *communidades de base*, or base communities, the migrant labor ministry, and the support group for mothers of incarcerated children. He was surprised with the last-mentioned group upon his return from vacation. "The people," he explained, "are very responsive . . . they see a need and they do it." Father Rick also attributed this quality to his own staff, which had recently "changed over." This one was a "much more responsive staff" to the congregation's needs and "not being busybodies in the parish and everywhere else."

Father Rick used the word "responsive" often. His meaning is derived from his order's founder, Saint Anthony Mary Claret, an early nineteenth-century Catalonian who was a master of marshaling people according to their charismata and addressing the diverse needs of the church. He served primarily the poor and is noteworthy for establishing a library in Barcelona and schools and hospitals in Cuba. At Saint Anthony's, "responsive" also means efficient, timely, and ordered—in contrast, as Father Rick implied, to the chaos brought by people pursuing their personal agendas.

Gracie had retired from her activities at Saint Anthony's until one day her friend Helen came to her door. Helen must have knocked and entered Gracie's home just as I had. Helen was upset because her son was in prison. She worried constantly that something would happen to him—injury, rape, or worse.[11]

"Mothers know their sons, their good and bad character," Gracie explained, relating to the way that Mary knew her son. "It's a part of the journey to think that this young lady cooked for him, fed him, washed him, . . . taught him to pray. This young lady took care of this beautiful baby who grew up to be the savior. And so you think about this boy, he ate tamales probably, or bread [laughing], things that she cooked special like we cook for our families today. And, as she was walking, she was experiencing life too. It wasn't easy for her. It wasn't easy for him. So they had to persevere with the love they had for each other. . . . Mothers know that prison makes their sons into people they don't recognize."[12]

Helen and Gracie's insight into prison life resembles Christian Parenti's (1999). He articulates the role of institutionally sanctioned violence—rape, beatings, murder, sexual slavery, the cries of trauma and agony echoing throughout cell blocks—that reinforce a social structure among inmates and order for prison officials. The structure and order are expressed in a prison nomenclature. Names are assigned to inmates by word of mouth. The identities are spread in a flurry, heard but not seen because inmates reside within earshot and not sight of each other. Everybody knows his place: "man," "daddy," "husband," "booty bandit," and "punk," the most abject position.[13] These terms refer to an essential status reinforced through coercion, physical domination, and threat of death.

The threat of death to an inmate can be literal. However, the threat is more often to an inmate's subjective existence, a threat executed in part by a prison management that resembles Foucault's panopticon. The illusion of continual surveillance, Lorna Rhodes observes of contemporary prisons, causes inmates to disassociate the "seeing / being seen dyad. . . . He who is subjected to a field of visibility, and who knows it, assumes responsibility for the constraints of power; he makes them play spontaneously upon himself. . . . He becomes the principle of his own subjection" (Foucault 1977, 202–3; quoted in Rhodes 1998, 286). This self-vigilance and subjection show the realization of the subject according to delimited behavior named by the inmates, assigning an exchange value in a social economy.

The chaos and order of this world haunt the world outside, with a dangerous proximity that escapes perception. This sense of closeness and distance, Angela Davis observes, dwells in the public imagination, where "fantastical notions of 'the criminal' translate into fears of a stranger (of color) who lurks in dark corners," while cultivating feelings of safety because that "stranger" is "somewhere far away," locked up, and poses "no threat to society" (1999, x, xiii).

In Gracie's living room, Judge Judy struck her gavel, passing judgment on her world and restoring it to order. And Gracie recalled how she reacted sometimes when the telephone rang: "Please, don't let it be him"—referring to her son. "And it's never him. He calls me, and all that. But there is always that fear that something is going to happen to my son. And I am sure that Mary felt that because she knew. She knew that this was going to come."[14]

So Gracie and Helen decided to say a rosary and "see what happens." They contemplated, I suspect, the sorrowful mysteries, enabling them to experience the passion Christ felt for humankind in the garden before his crucifixion. They realized that others in a similar situation might also like to say the rosary and share their experiences. Gracie and Helen organized a meeting, and many mothers came. Gracie and Helen didn't know how the group would "grow," "evolve," or "become something."[15] They did know, however, that the group started with the rosary, which was all the confirmation they needed about whether or not it was the right thing to do.

On that early October morning, Gracie was animated. The rosary had taken her to another place where she was able to see the suffering and joy as she had seen them on her journey to Cheyenne, Wyoming. Recall Gracie's reflection, "You see, you never know what you're going to learn when you go to places and how it's going to affect the place you live." On this occasion, the rosary took Gracie to Helen's place, the place of Helen's heart and suffering. It also took them to other mothers who were undergoing similar experiences. The rosary enabled them to con-

ceive bonds of affection and anticipate their growth, "becoming something." They didn't know what. But, of course, that's a part of the mystery.
On that morning, Gracie was animated, and, I assume, Helen and the
other friends were animated as well.

Gracie showed me to my usual place on the sofa, next to a robust
arm where I placed my tape recorder. She sat next to me, both of us
across from the drawing of Jesus on the wall. "That was a gift," Gracie
explained, "by a youth many years ago."[16] When he first came to the
youth group, "he was a smarty," Gracie continued, laughing at the memory. "Very like . . . 'Yaaa!' you know kids. Very much 'Show me and I'll
believe.'" This young man started praying, got involved, and received his
confirmation. "Then one day," Gracie recalled, "he came and said that he
was going back to school."

"Did he drop out?" I asked.

"No, he was asked to leave," Gracie said, laughing again at the memory. "He went back to school. And where he went after that, we don't
know," Gracie said before pausing. "Maybe he became a big painter."
Gracie's recollection of the gift expressed the hope that a mother invests
in a child, confident that things will work out.

Likewise, Gracie's experiences at the support group for the mothers
of incarcerated children raised hopes about her own son. He had hung
out with the wrong friends and gotten into trouble, and was in prison.
As much as I could surmise, he had been there for a long time. I knew
that the loss of her son was difficult for Gracie. She mentioned him from
time to time, sometimes on the edge of tears, but never provided too
many details. She said, "Mary saw her son. I see my son. And everything
that happened, happened. Mary's a woman that teaches every woman;
look, love, cheer, persevere, and so much more." The meaning of these
allusions to the biblical period lies between the stories about Mary's life
and those about Gracie's. It's a nebulous space identifiable by tracing
where the edges of the stories meet emotions, moods, and visceral experiences. These edges mark charged liaisons between Gracie's and many
others' lives, providing solace from loneliness and understanding and
optimism about the future.

This space between stories provides refuge when the experiences of
daily life become overwhelming. Gracie recalled, "What we experience

is something the disciples experienced, Mary experienced, Jesus experienced [pausing]. Jesus saw all of the hardships, the beatings of people, coming to take men away, the pushing of people at that time. Like when today, we fear it. Then they had Roman soldiers. Today, the police are dressed in a different way. But when you hear that knock, when you hear that siren, when you hear somebody coming, it was the same way."[17] Gracie's son had been taken away and had become a child of the state, raised in the order and chaos of prison amid the abuse, the suffering—a constant reminder to the average citizen on the outside that all is right in the world.

Gracie's dwelling on Jesus and his perception of human fodder initiated a journey through an imaginary landscape of the past. It raised the image of her grandfather, captured and to be shot with other Mexican villagers until Pancho Villa's soldiers intervened and escorted them to safety. "That was very frightening for my grandmother and my grandfather," Gracie explained. "So they decided to go to El Paso. And then the kids came. They were married. And grandkids came. And I remember [my grandmother] taking me to the church and praying with me: 'Wow, this is something!' But then at home, there were terrible things, violence and abuse," Gracie recalled and then paused. "[My father] spent a lot of time out in the streets, learning from the streets. So, I think that made him feel hard. He had to be a 'man,' a man in the home. 'This is my kingdom; I am the king,' and that sort of thing. It was very hard and painful [pausing]. My grandmother was like my protector. She would tell me that somebody loved me."

Fear and love fill the spaces between the production of one image and of the next as images accumulate to create a historical montage, replacing a logical understanding of linear time and geography. "That time" of Jesus is that time of the Mexican revolution, her father's education, and Gracie's childhood. The images signify persecution, abuse, protection, and refuge that characterize biblical society, revolutionary Mexico, a modern American city, and a child's home.

Gracie's recollection of her childhood remained obscure to me, as if it were too close to home to talk about comfortably. Yet she talked about the youth at Saint Anthony's, their homes, their fathers, their pain and love, with the clarity and vision that come from hindsight.

"I tell the kids," Gracie explained, referring to the children in the youth group, "we are going to pray this mystery. Think also of the kids who are suffering, who are into drugs that are waiting for the police to come and knock on their door, to come and get them. Think about your own families. How maybe there's drugs, there's no love there. What we experience is something the disciples experienced, Mary experienced, Jesus experienced. He wanted to see what he could do . . . and, he said, 'You know there's a way we can get out of all this.'"

These images reveal human suffering under the influence of power. In a modern setting, this suffering is epitomized by street life, which kids turn to, Gracie explained, because they feel "loneliness" brought about by the hardships of wage labor, long hours spent for little in terms of food, shelter, family time, and self-worth. So kids go to the streets, where other kids offer some other kind of family, but no less painful.

"I remember going to see my brother one time in Stockton," Gracie explained. "And, we were going to the church. And on a corner in an empty lot, there were young men hitting this one young man. It was like five or six of them around this one person, boys and girls. And, they were hitting him, beating him up. And my brother blew the horn, and they just looked at us. My brother came to the stop sign; they were there right on the corner. . . . My brother said, 'Stop beating that kid.' And they said, 'Get out of our way man, it's none of your business.' And then one of the guys yelled out, 'He's gonna be in our gang.' . . . If this young man could stand the pain, he belonged there. Now, what made that young man get out of his home to go to that place in order to get beat up and to belong to a group?"

Gracie's memories of her childhood surfaced in fragments amid stories about other people. When she was twelve or thirteen years old—"somewhere around there," Gracie recalled—her grandmother died. She didn't know for sure because she'd moved to California with her parents. "We became migrant people," she said. "And you could see a lot of the things that were happening on the farms. Camp to camp, we went from camp to camp. . . . And she died during that time."

The family had been able to "settle down and make Madera home," but departures for farm work disrupted any true stability. "So when the letter came," Gracie continued, "it followed us to different places where we were going. But, we moved so many times that we never got it. Finally, we went back to Madera, and the letter came saying that my grandmother had passed away sometime back. So it was very hard for my mom. She cried a lot. And we never saw her again."

"Did your mother become the grandmother to your children that your grandmother was to you?" I asked.

"In some ways," Gracie responded, "not in everything. Very little. I think that it was my father being so abusive with her and with us. She was afraid to get close."

"Kids tell you straight out," Gracie explained further, referring to the youth group. "They don't hide very much. 'Nobody loves me.' 'My mom treats me this way; my dad treats me that way,'" Gracie said, imitating the youths' voices.

"How do you know if your father loves you or if your mother loves you?" Gracie asked them.

One child persisted, "I know my father *doesn't* love me."

"Why not?" Gracie asked.

"Because he never calls me 'son.' He always calls me by my name."

"Don't you think that means he loves you?" Gracie asked.

"No."

Gracie told the youths that she was going to try to help them, and she called a meeting with all of the parents. She was talking about loving the children, how they feel, and how they say nobody loves them, "when a man raised his hand and said, 'You know that my son tells me that I don't love him because I call him by his name. He says that I should call him 'son, mi hijo.' And then another man raised his hand and said, 'My son doesn't get too close to me because he tells me that I don't love him.'"

"What do you mean by that?" Gracie asked.

"The same thing that [the other man] just said."

"Why don't you start calling him 'my son' or 'mi hijo'?" Gracie suggested.

And the man said, "Well, . . . I am going to try because everywhere I go I call him by his name. That's his name."

"Everywhere" the father goes, he calls his son by his name, a seemingly harmless gesture, a formality at worst. This practice becomes significant in view of the term of endearment that the name replaces.

Names make a son feel "hard," socially accountable—a public figure in such-and-such a place, in such-and-such a time, and worthy of such-and-such a "treatment," similar to circulation of labor that Gracie experienced among migrant people on the farms of her childhood. Such formalities deny authorship or the relation between fathers and sons, between mothers and daughters, and grandmothers and grandchildren. These formalities, accounting for systemic conditions that pervade domestic spaces, abnegate compassion and drive intimate sensibilities deep into a remote, private place.

No wonder sons say their fathers don't love them or fathers say their sons "don't get too close." This repulsion of intimacy is a part of commodity logic. Names represent the social value of autonomy, a value that shapes egos, individual attitudes, and provisional associations and identifications that are exchanged according to time, place, or setting. This exchange value is defined by the ritual expulsion of that which pollutes and defiles—those intimate feelings, for example—an expulsion that cultivates accentuated expressions of ego and, paradoxically, non-ego.[18] This paradox is represented by the father who was "going to try" to call his son "son," only succeeding in calling him by his name because "that's his name." This paradox has real effects on homes, as Gracie had recalled about the home where she grew up—hard fathers, abuse, and suffering. Boys respond by getting out. They go where they get beat up and allow isolation and fear to define their membership in a group that is no less painful.

Gracie's images of her childhood home also signify an allusive place of refuge that called attention to itself through the exclamation "Wow!," a comforting prayer, and a grandmother who told her granddaughter that "somebody loved [her]." These images, which include a "component of emotion and perceptual response," are similar to Charles S. Peirce's "category of 'Secondness'" (1940, 76, 87; quoted in Friedrich 1991, 76). "'Secondness' involves an awareness of difference, of a second reality, with its action and reaction, effect and resistance, ego and non-ego, 'the element of struggle . . . mutual action between two things'" (Peirce 1940, 89; quoted in Friedrich 1991, 32). This awareness emerges from the play between opposing things that shows a combination of fear and love—a nervous tension and an impetus of Gracie's journey.

"How did you first learn about fear?" I asked.[19]

"When I was in the orphanage," Gracie began to explain. "My parents were separated. My brother and I were put in an orphanage. We were driving up this long, long drive. I don't know if you are familiar. You start going up like that; you see the trees. And there's just one straight road, and you turn around and come out again. Well, my mother left us there. No goodbyes or anything; she said, 'Be good. *Portate bien.*' She gets out, and the door [of the orphanage] closes next to me really loud [slapping her hands together]. When I close the door sometimes loud [claps her hands], I say, 'Oh my God, that's scary.' The sister came and got us. That was horrible. What am I doing here? Did I do something wrong? Why was my mother leaving us there?' And then I heard the car take off. It was a nightmare there with the sisters. It was horrible, horrible. You'd think that because they were nuns, they'd be nice. It was then that my mother left us, the first time that I experienced fear."

Strangely, Gracie's arrival at the orphanage and the slam of the door separating her from her mother and her home are all too familiar. This separation marked her entry into a world of an entirely different order, largely symbolic and in contrast with previous experience.[20] The Depression hit people like Gracie's parents hard, reducing their value as wage laborers to nothing and creating fathers who could not support their families and mothers who could not keep their children. Ironically, this systemic failure became to Gracie the responsibility of her parents, who, after all, were "able-bodied" and could do something. Gracie's and her brother's status as "Mexican" only added to their jeopardy; they were required by the "Americanization efforts" of academics, social reformers, and government officials either to become "clean," "healthy," "productive," and worthy of the "[American] community" or to be repatriated to Mexico (G. Sánchez 1993, 119).[21] Indeed, the mother's final words, "Be good," or, "Portate bien," meant, "Follow the rules so that you can be worthy of this community." Gracie's entry into the orphanage meant receiving the new names with pejorative connotations—"undeserving poor" and "Mexican"—that symbolized human waste and substantiated the nuns' mean treatment.[22] The human waste, this little girl in an orphanage, betrays the horror of this symbolic order: its positive signification of value, hygiene, productivity, and "community" is contingent upon the negative signification of worthlessness, squalor, indolence, and social deterioration. Gracie's entry into the symbolic order meant adopting a dialectic that shaped her subjectivity and longing to escape by returning to her mother.

"How did you first learn about love?" I asked.

"I think it was in the orphanage," Gracie said with a cracked voice and tears. "It's so funny, [pausing] in the orphanage [pausing]. There was a picture there of Mary, holding a baby. Every day, I prayed the rosary. There was this picture of Mary [pausing]. And there used to be a little girl. She stayed close to me [pausing]. She was blond, an Anglo girl. Very beautiful. So she would come and sit, and smile. I only spoke Spanish then. But I managed to find some words to talk to her, you know, in English [laughing]. And she would take me [with her]. She's beautiful [pausing]. And she would sit with me. And I started to like her. I didn't speak the language. I only spoke Spanish. But, with her there, we would like, [pausing] she was looking for love, and I was looking for something. So when they'd take us to chapel, she'd always run to get in the line near me, a straight line. We didn't speak to anybody. We didn't look anywhere. And the sisters were real mean to her because she used to wet her bed. And it was my turn to take her to get a shower one night. And [the sister] said, 'You give her *agua fria, no le dejes agua caliente.*' And I thought 'Ooh, *agua fria.*' And when the sister left, I turned on hot water. And she started smiling."[23]

Tears and laughter trace Gracie's passage down that "one straight road" where "you turn around and come out again," the same place, strangely familiar. This place is also symbolic but in a different way. Pictures of "Mary," "Mary holding a baby," the symbol of all mothers, broach feelings of intimacy and warmth in lieu of language's abstract and often essential signification. Words feel out of place, leading Gracie to laugh at her attempts to use them. The rules of orderly conduct—getting in a "straight line," and not "speaking to anybody" or looking "anywhere"—define a place of immediacy, rhythm, and presence that rejects the logical identification of others according to differences in time and place. Gracie's friend is "beautiful." And this experience of love also shapes Gracie's subjectivity, enabling her to identify the relation between people and the scandal of its oppression.[24]

"So, then your journey starts," Gracie continued.[25] "You have meetings. You talk to families. Hopefully they say, 'Hey, that's neat. Maybe I should do that.' And then one day this guy comes and says, 'Gracie, Gracie, guess what?'

"'What?'

"'My dad said to me, "*Mi hijito* [my little son], I love you."'

"'Oh, my God.' My tears came, and I hugged him. It was very special, not always cussing him out or saying things to him [pausing]. Can you imagine, 'mi hijito, mi hijito'? Kids feel unwanted. If you don't touch them and you don't go with them and stop feeling about yourself for a while, 'me as a father, me as a mother, me as a grandmother.' But just accept them."

"What about your son, when is he coming home?" I asked.

"His sentence is coming to an end," Gracie said. "So when he tells me, 'Mom, I am beginning to see things different,' something's different, something's working—the prayers, the Mass, or whatever we do in his name. And then he says, 'I am playing guitar again.' O.K. That's a good thing."

Gracie expressed a home characterized by the harmony produced by whatever "we do in his name" or the music of a guitar. Home entails a change of perspective that is devoid of conflict. It indicates the realization of another place that throughout Gracie's journey has served, albeit implicitly, as the underlying basis of her orientation in the world and participation in civic affairs.

Gracie's remembrance of the past entails forgetting her names of mother, grandmother, catechism teacher, and youth group leader and moving decisively toward a radical subject position, the place of other people, that enables her to heal social wounds.[26] The children who "feel unwanted" issue from the social body's pathology. And the children won't feel better, as Victor Turner explains in another context, "until all of the tensions and aggressions of the [society's] interrelations have been brought to light and exposed to ritual treatment." Gracie "taps the various streams of affect," including tradition, language, and symbols, often entailing the logic of commodity structures that reinforce alienation from feelings, warmth, and the relations between fathers and sons and between mothers and daughters (1967, 392; quoted in Taussig 1992,

109). Alienation, however, is defined by the implication of a mystery—in the idiom of psychoanalysis, the mother and her storehouse of psychic impulses that trace a connection to the past, both biological and cultural. Gracie taps this stream too, creating a watershed that fills language and human relationships with rhythm, empathy, understanding, and the substance of new, positive human relations.

Gracie's position represents social scars that show the contiguity between the symbolic order and another place, abstraction and intimacy, ego and non-ego. The scars enable her to traverse from having critical insight into the workings of power on the subjugated to being as the subjugated—as a youth, father, son, and mother.[27] The scars show healed wounds and the path of a journey toward home recognizable through strangely familiar gestures—a father's call to his son, "mi hijito," a grandmother who tells her granddaughter that somebody loves her, a guitar's rhythm, a splash of warm water, and a smile.[28]

Gracie's meditation on the mystery is characterized by the flow of her love and fear into a social landscape defined by stories about the past and the realization of hope in the future, or, in metaphorical terms, the cultivation of a rose garden and vision of salvation.

Gracie brings to mind the rosary's fifth sorrowful mystery, when Jesus is crucified and sees his mother and the disciple. The apostle John tells us that Jesus said to his mother, "Woman, behold your son!," and to the disciple, "Behold, your mother!," and "from that hour the disciple took her to his home" (John 19:26–27 RSV). Jesus identified a place where people like Mary and the disciples transcend their individual lives and share the lives of others. Gracie shows us that arriving at this place involves the difference between being alone and "just too tired" on the one hand and feeling animated on the other. Gracie also shows us that arriving at this place requires a change of attitude and ethics. The arrival entails an involvement with others in their joy, sorrow, suffering, and even death, cultivating along the way "the need to belong some place."

An integration of Gracie's storytelling with my own supports this need. This strategy relies on tropes entailing formal features—respectively, the frame of the rosary and the framework of the home—that indicate different operations. Gracie's enactment of the rosary in her home realizes the ritual's designation as a metaphor that draws parallels with enactments in other past settings, including their paralinguistic and linguistic signs; the enactment guides transitions from one topic to another, managing the flow of information. The home's characterization as a maternal space highlights the ritual's designation as a metonym indicating the origin of the whole of associations and a place, a better place called home.

That October morning, my place was in Gracie's home, on her sofa, both of us admiring the pencil drawing of Jesus on the wall. Gracie stood up, walked over to the drawing, leaned on a sofa, and lifted it off the hook. She said, "Let me show it to you."

Gracie sat down next to me again and said, "See, after getting to know [the young man] and talking to him, one day he did this. Look at this," pointing to each line of the face, lips, nose, beard, strands of hair, crown of thorns, tears—every part of Jesus. "It says 'love.'" And indeed, every line of lead that formed the image was not a line at all but tiny inscriptions of the word "love." "And see there," Gracie said, "happiness, sadness, suffering, your body gets all out of shape at times. You speak, you hear, and you see. And why do you do it, because he loves so much."

"Yes," Gracie continued, "he took time to sit down. And the tears of course, when we talked about Jesus, he had his moments, and we have our moments and tears come to our eyes. . . . I still take it to catechism and to the people I work with. I tell them, this is by a young man who came, he learned, and he left. Maybe he kept going with love, love, love."

Gracie showed me to the door and inserted the key into the deadbolt, which slid back. We embraced and said our goodbyes in anticipation of our next meeting.

I headed west on Church Avenue, and the day was warm.

THE SACRED CIRCLE

FOUR

We sat on folding chairs in a circle, Eva Gonzales, Sister Mary, and I, and about ten others whom I didn't know: a pregnant woman, a retired couple, a mother and her teenage daughter, and several elderly women. Sister Mary had instructed us to read Luke 24 while we waited. It's about how, after the resurrection, Mary Magdalene, among others, visited Jesus's tomb and found it empty. They were bewildered. Two men approached and asked, "Why do you seek the living among the dead? He is not here, but has risen" (Luke 24:5 RSVCE).

We had gathered for a morning of contemplative prayer, one of a few annual retreats organized by Sister Mary of the Sister Disciples of the Divine Master. This religious order was founded by Father James Alberione on 10 February 1924 in Alba, Italy. Father Alberione followed Saint Paul's instruction "It is Christ . . . who lives in me" (Gal. 2:20 RSV) by cultivating a life characterized as "contemplative and apostolic, in loving and active silence"—a "life . . . hid with Christ" (Col. 3:3 RSV). Father Alberione's first rule for the order was silence, a medium for attaining an interior life receptive to an enlightenment that he once described as an obligation "to prepare himself to do something for God and for the people of the new century with whom he would live."[1] The sisters have followed this direction in years of service marked by their order's growth. They have established convents throughout the world, including Stanton, New York, in 1947 and Fresno, California, in the early 1950s. In Fresno, the sisters were originally at Saint Anne's Church, the Diocese's Pastoral Center, and later, at their own location on Cornelia Avenue in northwest Fresno. Despite the encroachment of nearby subdivisions, the convent retains a country atmosphere, covering a few acres of manicured gardens among vineyards and small farms. This atmosphere complements the order's focus on Christ, particularly his manifestation through the Eucharist, priesthood, and liturgy.[2] It's quiet.

Sister Mary spoke in a low, soft voice, loud enough to reach our ears but not fill the room. She said, "Leave your obligations and schedules outside. Don't let them control you." The room was not large enough for everybody's agenda. At times, it doubled as a dining room. But just then, it had no tables, just a circle of chairs, approximately twenty feet in diameter, situated adjacent to another circle of similar size; it was a quilt laid on the floor. The room's simplicity was characterized by beige walls, a few portraits—one of Christ and another of Mary—and stained-glass windows looking out and on the garden. The glass cast a rosy hue throughout the room as the spring sun rose in the east.

Sister Mary instructed us to take off our shoes and leave them by the entry (if we hadn't done so already) because we were about to begin our "journey" through the labyrinth. The quilt was a replica of the labyrinth in Chartres Cathedral, labyrinths being a standard feature of the Gothic architecture in this region of France. The labyrinth in our room followed a unicursal design, consisting of one entrance and one circuitous path that initially drew near the center, then to the perimeter, then turned back to the center, which was marked by a six-petal rose. This unique ornament was of classical origin: Virgil and Ovid credit the architect Daedalus with having built a labyrinth to imprison Minos's Minotaur, the offspring of his spouse Pasiphaë and a fierce bull. Minos sacrificed Athenians by feeding them to the Minotaur, venting his shame of his wife's betrayal.[3] The sacrifices continued until the hero Theseus ventured into the labyrinth and slew the Minotaur.

At Chartres, the labyrinth signifies pilgrims' journeys. Chartres has been the destination of pilgrims since the ninth century, about 876, when Charles the Bald from Aachen donated the Virgin's tunic. It had been a gift to Charlemagne by the empress and emperor of Byzantium, Irene and Constantine Porphyrogenitus (mother and son). The Virgin had worn it at the Annunciation and at Christ's birth and had left it behind upon her Assumption. The tunic lies in a reliquary casket located in a crypt where there is a deep well, its waters known for their miraculous healing powers.[4]

In her instructions, Sister Mary recalled the pilgrims' experiences and prepared us for our journey. She said, "The journey is personal. One may acknowledge another, but don't be mindful of others. We travel our journey alone. At times, it might be frustrating. It might feel as if you are wasting time. But, you are never far from the center. The center is everywhere. The circumference is nowhere. A pilgrimage is a journey to a sacred place. The sacred place is our heart, a journey to the heart."

Sister Mary instructed us to contemplate a paradox that compounded with each turn of phrase. We were in the midst of a circle for which there was no one center and no circumference, embarking on a solitary journey accompanied by several others, searching for a sacred place called the heart, which was as much a part of our interior being as our exterior world. As frustrating as this paradox might have been, one thing was clear: the journey was marked by signs—the tomb, heart, and rose—that became the objects of our contemplation, guided our progress, and linked the stories that we learned about along the way and their relationship with the ineffable—the life of silence.

This chapter begins at a retreat that entailed three days of contemplative prayer characterized by walking a labyrinth of medieval design. Eva had invited me to this retreat just as she had invited me to other places—church, restaurants, and parish social events—where she told me about her life, bit by bit. The invitations enabled me to follow her footsteps; we walked along the circuitous path of her past that brought us together in the present—a medium of a spatial and temporal journey.

Our movement entailed much pushing back and forth. A part of this effort had to do with loss in our lives. Eva and I had suffered the loss of a parent, and our respective efforts to figure out the meaning of this event brought us to Saint Anthony's Church. The effort also entailed inquires into each other's identities. Eva looked upon me in a way that reflected how I looked upon her. She speculated that I might have been

a student, seminarian or, worse, a northerner, referring to Fresno's affluent north side—exterior labels shot through with explanations about
differences in gender, social position, and power. These labels entail objectification that places human life in a conceptual framework similar to
that which contains death. In the idioms of the social sciences and of
psychoanalysis, respectively, the other person and death are understood
as the "other." Eva and I were drawn to the other (referring to each other
and the deaths in our lives) but also repulsed by our limitations. The
other entailed an interiority that we could not enter—not even to whatever degree such might be possible without losing ourselves entirely.

Our experiences of these oppositions—exterior/interior and
attraction/repulsion—centered on a tension that directed our inquiries
of the self and other, of what we were, then, and of what we might become toward larger circumstances impinging on daily life. We probed
social, mythological, and historical forces, often implicit but nevertheless influential, in an effort to find the place where tensions subside,
allowing for psychological, social, and spiritual equilibrium. We walked
the path where our lives converged and headed toward the place one
might call home.

I argue that this walk is a prayer whose objects of contemplation—a
tomb, a heart, and a rose—lead to stories, some tragic, about a mother's
death, devastating fires, unfulfilled desires, trails of blood, and quiet moments of solace that define a social landscape. The objects also mark the
way along a path where the social meets the personal, where the exterior
world meets an interior one, and where the verbal meets the ineffable,
representing an ethical and spiritual intersection. This position enables
one to recognize the logic of the social system shaping life in California's
San Joaquin Valley and yielding by-products of racism, crime, and
human suffering, particularly among wage laborers.

The chapter acquires substance and rhetorical force through tropes
that mediate the intersection of human agency and stories, precisely the
implication of "the walk is a prayer." The tropes channel an audience's
mind and body into the narrative for an imaginative, emotive investment that animates characters, dialogues, thoughts, and objects in an
organic play that engenders human qualities: pity, fear, suffering, and

love. This poetic approach aims at cultivating a sense of weight, thickness, or the real that comes through labor. The approach also aims at cultivating immediacy to people who otherwise remain obscure amid general perceptions of poverty, social isolation, and other modern social conditions.

WE FORMED A LINE TO ENTER THE LABYRINTH, EACH OF US edging forward with small steps. I walked behind Eva, allowing her to set the pace, just as she did with the person in front of her. While everyone remained silent, heads turned toward the floor, I could sense the anticipation. What would we encounter in the labyrinth—the sacred, or perhaps the Minotaur? One by one, we entered the labyrinth: Our journey had begun.

THE TOMB

Eva had been looking forward to this journey. About a month before, in late February, Eva had asked me if I wanted to go on a retreat of contemplative prayer for three consecutive Thursdays. She said that it would mean a lot to her and be a good thing for Lent. *Lent* is a Teutonic word denoting "forty-day fast"; its Latinate equivalent is *quadragesima*, meaning "forty days" in preparation of Christ's Passion and the feast of the Ascension. The actual duration of the fast has varied according to regional customs. And while the significance of the forty days and the fast has always been a topic of debate, theologians from the classical period to the present have conceded that the number forty "possibly" comes from the forty hours that Christ lay in the tomb, and that the fast is a sacrifice facilitating a communion with him.[5] In our own times, Lent usually involves sacrificial or modified behavior, giving up something for something else, like three consecutive mornings for contemplative prayer.

Eva's sacrifice was already well underway as we proceeded into the labyrinth; she had walked a similar path about two weeks before, on Ash Wednesday, at Saint Anthony's. If the significance of a religious event were measured solely by popularity, then Ash Wednesday would be the most important at Saint Anthony's. Thousands of people convened in the church sanctuary for services and Masses on the half hour from 7:00 a.m. to 8:00 p.m. and received an ashen cross on their foreheads.

This custom takes place on the first day of Lent and dates back at least to the eighth century, when the Anglo-Saxon homilist Aelfric wrote, "We read . . . in the books both in the Old Law and the New that men who repented of their sins bestrewed themselves with ashes and clothed their bodies with sackcloth. Now let us do this little at the beginning of our Lent that we strew ashes upon our heads." Aelfric reinforced his recommendation with a sobering story about a man who had refused to receive his ashes on Ash Wednesday; a few days later, he was killed in a boar hunt when a boar turned and made the hunter the hunted (Skeat 1881, 262–66).[6]

The ashes signify this proximity to death. According to *The Catholic Encyclopedia*, a number of Old Testament passages connect ashes, *efer*, with mourning: "A mourner . . . rolled himself in . . . [or] sprinkled his head with ashes." In the same passages, however, the Latin word *afar*, "dust," appears. Likewise, a mourner may have undertaken these activities with dust, presumably from a grave, showing empathy with the dead.[7] These accounts also involve a form of humility. A mourner repents of sins, dons new clothes, or provisionally forgoes self to identify with an other—an ironic affirmation of one's own life apparently overlooked by the man who went boar hunting.

At Saint Anthony's, parishioners approached the altar, each following in the other's footsteps in a slow, steady pace, as if walking in a funeral procession. An assistant dipped a thumb into a brass bowl of ashes that came from palm leaves blessed on Palm Sunday the previous year and raised the thumb to each person's forehead while uttering, "Remember that thou art dust and unto dust thou shalt return." Eva was among the parishioners who received ashes and heard those arresting words, commanding her to think simultaneously about beginnings, endings, and, presumably, much of what falls in between.

A bit overwhelmed by the masses of people who continued to file out of the sanctuary, I met Eva and her sister, Juanita, in the parking lot. "Why is Ash Wednesday so popular?" I asked.

"To them," Juanita explained, "it's a chance to change.... They think that perhaps now they might be able to start a new life with Christ. Over at Saint Helen's, the priest said that some people think that if they don't receive the ashes ... they will die that year. I have never heard of this. I think that people believe they have one chance to change, and this is it."

"People see this as an opportunity," Eva continued, "to begin living with Christ. They don't realize that they can do this anytime. But, now is especially important, as if there is one opportunity and it's now."

"What will you do for Lent?" I asked.

"I don't know," Eva said before pausing, "Well, I have thought of giving up work."

"Work?" I said, surprised.

"Yes, I want my life back," Eva said, and then explained, "Eighteen months ago, [when my mother died] my entire life turned around. Since then, I haven't had time to take care of my house, see my children or see Tom [my husband]. Everything is a mess; the house is a mess. I can't stand it anymore. At least if I quit, I can get my house in order."[8]

Eva worked at the public library for the blind. For thirty hours a week and about eight dollars an hour, Eva was in charge of filling orders for books on tape by retrieving, packaging, and sending them to Fresno residents with visual impairments. The first time I visited Eva at work, she took me on a tour and introduced me to her co-workers. Each greeted me, took a break, and explained his or her contribution to the library's operation. The job was a godsend. Through audio books, Eva and her co-workers were able to open worlds to people for whom those worlds would otherwise remain obscure. The work's significance shaped values of the workplace. Eva and her co-workers enjoyed the goodwill and companionship that they extended to others.

The job was for Eva also a source of frustration, another turn in a path that didn't appear to go anywhere, a form of entrapment resembling the predicament of the young men and women of Athens sent to the Minotaur for sacrifice. Her frustration stemmed from a history of wage labor that the job recalled, taking Eva back to her mother's childhood, her father's migration from Michoacán to California, and her dreams in life.

ASHES

I first revisited this history with Eva in her late-1980s blue Ford minivan. We had attended the noon Mass at Saint John's Cathedral in downtown Fresno and were on our way to lunch. We approached the van. Eva inserted a key into the lock of the passenger door and pulled the handle. The door creaked as it opened to a whiff of meals consumed on the road and revealed a thin layer of dust, worn seats, old receipts, parish bulletins, pamphlets, a Bible, a rosary, and a small figurine of the Christ child mounted on the center of the dashboard. Eva apologized for the "mess."

"What is that?" I asked, pointing at the figurine with its unique Bohemian markings.

"That's El Niño de Prague. He's the one that goes in our *nacimiento*.[9] It was passed down in our family. I don't know," Eva said, pausing. "Oh, I know why. Because when she," Eva began, referring to her mother and stopping in midsentence. "Their house burned down, completely. Everything was no good. And my mom went through it, and she was a little girl. And she found this [figurine]. She felt attached to him, because he had allowed her to find him."

Thus Eva began the story about her mother, among the ashes of her mother's former home in Mesa, Arizona. The parents packed the things they could salvage; Eva's mother, the figurine, and they went to California to find work. Eva's grandfather got a job as a labor contractor. And when Eva's mother was old enough, she took care of her father's finances. She met Eva's father in 1958, had two children, and traveled with her family from job to job on the labor circuit.

"My dad worked at different places," Eva began to explain. He worked first in the San Jose fruit canneries, and then in Bakersfield as an "ice man," packing ice on boxcars for the Southern Pacific Railroad. Her father took a similar position in Fresno. This position was better, Eva explained: "He got health benefits. He needed that because of his bad heart."

Eva and her sister, Juanita, attended school full time. Eva graduated from Roosevelt High School, and Juanita, from California State University in Fresno.[10]

Many scholars have written about migration, filling in the gaps in Eva's account with remarkable detail. They attempt to follow the path of strife and capture experiences through interviews.[11] Manuel Gamio (1930, 1931) recorded the dreams of people who, due to economic hardship, went to the United States. They took jobs on the railroads and in the packing sheds and fields "all over the state of California" (48). The migrants sought "fortunes" couched in their appreciation of American life—the variety of foods, music, movies, "good money," "good clothes," democracy, and equality (50). They talked about their wages: "There they paid me $2.50 for eight hours work" (23). "I worked very hard to earn my $4.00 a day. . . . I want to give a little schooling to my children so that they won't stay like I am" (44). The migrants packed so much hope into so little money, and their memories most often entailed disillusion, recalling excruciating work, hunger, abject living conditions, and racism. In his California research in the 1920s, Paul Taylor recalls migrants who traveled from other parts of the United States to California with hopes of "finding work, keeping off or getting off relief, of maintaining morale, of finding surcease of trouble; yes," Taylor emphasizes, "and the climate, which even the poorest can share" (1983, 176). Vicki Ruiz (1996) relies on the oral histories provided by thirteen women who recalled their adolescent dreams of going to California—freedoms, upward mobility, self-esteem, professional status, and material accumulation—often aspiring to the Hollywood glamour represented in Spanish-language media.[12]

One of these women whom Ruiz writes about could have been Eva's mother. "My mother had goals for us. She really did," Eva said emphatically. "And then things just got . . ." she paused for a few moments. "Things just didn't work out. She wanted each of us to have our own house, all of us to be okay. She wanted to have a family business."

Eva's parents did their best to ensure the family's assimilation into American life by providing what they could. "As kids," Eva recalled, "we had everything we wanted. Well, not everything: we still lived in poverty. But if we wanted something, we got it. That doll, that dress, we'd just say, 'I like that,' and there it would be the next day."[13]

Eva's recollection of her mother's hopes for the future entailed the double edge of an apology. In one respect, she defended her mother's dreams and the dreams of those who contributed to Gamio's, Taylor's, and Ruiz's ethnographies. The dreams accounted for a public anthem that legitimized life in the United States and the cultivation of a new self. They were substantiated by consumption—the doll, the dress, and other things that appeared to fill a void and confirm hope in the future.

In another respect, Eva expressed regret by recognizing that her mother's dream had played a restrictive role in her family's life. The "things" that "just got . . . just didn't work out" signaled Eva's own dreams and disillusion. In the early years of her marriage, Eva and her husband, Tom, took strolls on Huntington Boulevard, a few blocks southwest of her high school. The boulevard's namesake is Henry E. Huntington, the promoter of electric railroads and founder of Pacific Light and Power and the Huntington Land and Improvement Company in Southern California during the early 1900s (Gudde 1960, 140; Friedricks 1990, 377). Huntington Boulevard features a median with grass and mature fir trees, large lots of an acre or more, and spacious homes, both Spanish and Western styles, built by entrepreneurs between 1910 and 1930. The homes display their owners' prosperity and their nostalgia for a Spanish past and investment in the region's development. During the 1920s, novelists, politicians, journalists, and real estate developers cultivated California's heritage according to the myth of a Spanish Arcadia. This movement lent moral and civic authority to the Franciscan (and presumably Spaniard) colonizers and denigrated the Mexican period. Anglo residents drew from this ideal impression of a Spanish past to substantiate their hegemony and self-identification with the region's development as a counterdistinction to the Puritan East.[14] "We walked arm in arm," Eva recalled. "We dreamed about having our own home one day on Huntington Boulevard."

The couple was young and naïve. But their dream was nevertheless common among migrant families—Eva's own and also that of Tom, who was originally from Oklahoma, a place of origin well known among Californians because of John Steinbeck's *The Grapes of Wrath* (1939). Despite their grandeur, the dreams seemed tangible. Eva and Tom had high school educations and steady jobs. Eva worked at K-Mart, and Tom, in inventory at the Fresno State University bookstore. Their life had so much potential. "When we first got married," Eva recalled, "Tom and I used to drive around looking at houses. They were houses that we wanted to buy. Then, we had the money, with Tom's job. We found out that we could get an $85,000 house."

This financial potential, however, started going toward other purchases. "We just got so full of ourselves," Eva said. "I went out and got a credit card. And," Eva paused, "we just got full of ourselves. We never got the house. I had to get [another] job, and Tom, a second, just to pay off our debt."

"Do you own the house you live in now?" I asked.

"No, we rent it. When we first got it, it was so run down. I think they were going to condemn it. . . . We have the place over by the freeway. I've let it run down. So now, it's harder, but we realize that none of that matters. We just live and have what we need."

Like Eva's mother, her father wanted more for the children. Eva related her father's disappointment about her living conditions: "He always told us that we should have more. 'You were born here,' he'd say. 'You didn't have to start in Mexico with nothing. You should have more— better jobs, a better house.'"[15]

Hope lies at the center of the California dream fashioned by a history of testimony. From Gamio's and Taylor's ethnographies of the 1920s and early 1930s to Ruiz's, which recalls the World War II and postwar eras, one hears about beliefs in democracy, equality, and their role in enabling migrants to work and "have more." The migrants have defined "more" according to upward mobility, status, "good jobs," "good clothes," "a little schooling [for] children," a child's doll or dress, and a home, among other things—certainly not much to ask for from a land so bountiful that it even provides a mild climate for everybody to share. And "more" is there, in the images of Hollywood glamour permeating Spanish-language media and the spacious houses along Huntington Boulevard—so near to any young couple planning a future. Eva's father legitimized one's license to claim good things by virtue of being "born here," in California, not having to negotiate arrival, documentation, and citizenship, but rather being born into the dream that enables people to become something.

But the dream is always elusive, just over there, in Hollywood, in that neighborhood, in a "better job," in a few more years, a little farther down the path, constituting, as Habermas says, "a formal universality whose substance [lies] in something external to it" (1991, 118). People substantiate, it is important to recognize, that universality through consumption. The dress or doll for the child, new clothes, and a car, for example, are tangible milestones adding substance to people's lives and marking progress toward something much larger. And the credit card, as Eva indicated, appears also to be a link to that larger thing. The card enables one virtually to transcend the boundaries of an individual self and entertain a world of possibility for new identification through material consumption. This process, as Eva expressed, evokes the cruel irony and disillusion of being "so full" while so impoverished.

The "substance" that Habermas refers to is not so elusive. The migrant workers whom Gamio and Taylor interviewed referred to it constantly. The "$2.50 for eight hours' work" or "$4.00 a day" is the product of modern progress—a system whereby people assess labor's value according to a monetary exchange. While that exchange value can be a sign of great hope, as suggested above, it is also one of humiliation—a devaluation of life to what one produces and the little one can consume.

This system is also full of apology. In one respect, employers, government officials, politicians, and journalists, among other public figures, have defended a social hierarchy that situates people of color, and particularly Mexican and Mexican American migrants, in a labor class. This defense is of classical origin, entailing one group of people's identification with civilization over nature and with citizen over barbarian.[16] Tomás Almaguer recalls, for example, popular conceptions of Mexicans in Ventura County, California, that circulated through the media and exemplified the fabrication of race in the 1870s: "Yankee genius and enterprise has done more for this country than four hundred years under the reign of the lazy greaser, stunted in growth and benighted in the intellect, by the religious enslavement of both mind and body, the effect of which are still visible in the ancient adobe structures which disfigure the town, but which, thanks to the ravages of time and the intrusion of modern American civilization, are fastly crumbling away" (*Ventura Signal*, 4 October 1873; quoted in Almaguer 1994, 90).

SO MUCH—ANGLO INTELLECT, FITNESS, AND PROGRESSIVENESS in contrast to Mexican biological and cultural inferiority: the uncivilized, wild, barbaric—packed into so few words, constituting a version of Southwest history.[17] This history is thinly veiled in theory, Richard R. Flores reminds us, by "Anglo-Mexican relations that have been structured along an axis of classic capital-labor relations within a representative democracy" (2002, 9).

Over a century after the Ventura County media report, I interviewed two Fresno County farmers of grapes for raisins and nuts and learned how this specter of the past haunts the present with similar acrimony, justifying racial segregation and labor segmentation. Mike and Kyle Jameson represented in some respects the quintessential American family farm. The land belonged to Mike's father, and before that it had belonged to his father's father. Indeed, this heritage was my impetus to interview Mike. A representative of the local Farm Bureau told me that Mike "knows a lot about valley history."

I met Mike on a cold February morning, his office strewn with brochures, papers, bills, receipts, and old books, among them a copy of Vandor's 1919 *History of Fresno County*. The floors were dusty from mud having been tracked in from the yard. Mike and his nephew Kyle ran the farm, searching for innovative ways to compete with the large corporate farms that absorbed increasing costs of production and withstood volatile markets through their integrated industry, volume, and diversification. Mike and Kyle also fought, as most farmers in the San Joaquin Valley, over water, its adequate supply threatened by urbanization. Mike and Kyle were not rich people; they lived in "accommodations," as Mike suggested, "not much better than the workers." But labor was labor, and they were landowners. This distinction became clear when I asked about the migrant families from Central Mexico and South Texas that returned annually for the harvest.

"I live across the street from a labor camp," Kyle explained. "They have six bathrooms, three showers, running water. And yet, we still find shit in the rows."

"To them," Mike intervened, "it ain't natural to use a toilet."

"Some of our workers," Kyle continued, "complain because they set the box down on top of the row and put their knee right into it [feces]. They say, 'Look at this, I got shit all over. It smells.' And they ask if we can do something about it. So we go and disk and clean the mess up."

"These days," Mike concluded, "you've got to be careful about getting toilet paper in the raisins."[18]

The classic capital-labor relation is a euphemism for what Mike and Kyle perceived as a "natural" relation defined according to rancher/nature and civilized/uncivilized dichotomies that justified their dominion over the land and labor. Kyle provided unique insight into this relation through his proximity to the labor camp. He identified with the elements of hygiene most often inaccessible to the people who needed them: for laborers working in remote sections of vineyards and orchards and under time constraints, making a trip to the latrine is unfeasible. In addition, Mike represented what the Mexican and Mexican American laborers meant to him and, presumably, to a larger (Anglo) population: a source of contagion, a most unsettling revelation to the naïve consumer of raisins.

Employers, politicians, and the residents have also expressed regret about the wage labor system. They focus on laborers and the laborers' families. Mike Jameson, for example, regretted increases in the minimum wage because "everybody thinks that they need a cut"—the packagers, drivers, and so forth. The wage was $5.75 with a proposed increase to $6.25, or 8.7 percent. That 8.7 percent, compounded many times, "comes right out of our revenues, and we barely recover our costs some years."[19] In 1994, 59 percent of the California voters expressed their regret about the system's reliance on undocumented labor. Believing that the politicians were ignoring their concerns about illegal immigration to California, the voters passed Proposition 187, which cut off health and social services, including public education, to undocumented immigrants and their children. In 1998, 60.9 percent of the California voters expressed their regret about the public schools' accommodation of immigrant children by providing bilingual education. The voters, considering bilingual education an unjustified burden, passed Proposition 227, which provides an English-only education after a one-year intensive language immersion program.[20] Journalists have expressed their regret about Fresno County's high unemployment (ranging from 13 percent in the urban areas to 30 percent in rural towns), low tax base, and the bankruptcy rates of local businesses.[21] Fresno city council members have expressed their regret for having to work with a shrinking budget and develop innovative job training programs.[22] Fresno County even adopted a program aimed at "generating a savings for taxpayers" by "connect[ing] companies searching nationwide for workers with frustrated local job-seekers." The program provides assistance to workers and their families to move to other parts of the country, find a home, and start a new job.[23] Government officials have expressed regret about the by-products of such hardships: crime rates, "public drinking and urination," and "gunshots at night." Richard Mochado, former head of Fresno County's Economic Development Corporation, expressed what is arguably the regional regret about the San Joaquin Valley in view of the country's 1990s economic boom: "[We] missed the train."[24]

The apology for the wage labor system places workers in double jeopardy. In one respect, it ignores the system's reduction of these workers' labor to a low exchange value that California residents have justified through racial caricature. In another, the apology represents popular talk that defines the workers as the source of social problems rather than as victims of those problems. The talk suppresses what is truly at stake: an indictment of the system itself, the beast that has caused a history of suffering and censure largely recognizable through Eva's faltered speech, indicating what is felt and unspoken.

Eva expressed an acute awareness of this double jeopardy. She was one of its victims, as were her father, mother, and other members of her family for whom "things just got ... just didn't work out." While employers, politicians, journalists, and other members of the population who endorsed this system may have understood Eva's desire—her hopes "of more," of a better job, a better home, of making something of herself—that she had invested in wage labor, they didn't understand the desire's jeopardy. This desire is a love affair with the work itself and the system it supports, a form of bestiality represented by Pasiphaë, who made love with a bull and gave birth to the Minotaur. Eva was well aware of this beast that, when taken for granted, turns and makes humankind its fodder. Similarly, the beast preyed on the Athenians sent by Minos for sacrifice and on the man who refused to receive his ashes on Ash Wednesday.

STRING

So when Eva said, "[For Lent,] I have thought about giving up work. . . . I want my life back. . . . I want my house in order," she was recognizing a turn in the path, an ethical transition, analogous to that which Theseus recognized upon slaying the Minotaur. Virgil and Ovid credit Theseus's love of Minos's daughter, Ariadne, with his escape from the labyrinth's winding, confusing paths. Ariadne had provided Theseus with a ball of string that enabled him to trace his journey and form one circuitous path toward the labyrinth's center, where he slew the Minotaur, and then to return back to the labyrinth's entrance.[25] In his reflection upon the labyrinth, the architecture historian John James imitates a neoplatonic gloss of the myth, drawing together the contexts of the classical period and of twelfth-century and contemporary Chartres: "Was Theseus the Pilgrim and Ariadne the Virgin Herself whose string guided the seeker home after he slew the beast? Then what of the beast? If he was the devil within us then the message is a remarkably modern one—for without guidance we risk madness in any internal struggle with the beast. And in those Platonic times guidance was considered to lie in the knowledge whose patron was the Virgin, which may be why she held the string" (1979, 472).[26]

Eva represented her guidance, her escape from madness, through love, which, like the string that bound Theseus to Ariadne, bound her to other people—her husband, children, father, and mother, and members of her broadly defined extended family. This love involved the practice of "religion," according to the Latin word *religare*, meaning "to bind," which became particularly acute for Eva when her mother died.[27]

Eva's mother had died suddenly of a heart attack—an event that marked a transition in Eva's life. It is not that Eva had any less love or less religion before her mother's death. She had always been "the same with friends." She had always been *"sentido con Dios"* (close to God). "But," Eva explained, "I wasn't *sentida con Él,"* emphasizing *"Él"* (him) and implying additional meaning. "With my family, I had a lot of anger."[28]

Her mother's death changed everything, and others knew it. One day Eva was driving with her father and asked, "Do you think I look different?"

"Different from what?" he said.

"Different since Mom died," Eva responded.

"He said," Eva explained, "that I looked softer. I was so angry with him [God], I felt like he had cheated me. He didn't give me a chance to grow up for my mom."

"What do you mean by 'grow up'?" I asked.

"There are just so many things that I wanted to do for her. I got one week. After she had the heart attack, I was able to take care of her for one week, feed her and bathe her. Our roles had changed. I was the mother, and she was the daughter. Just like I am to my own children."

The mother's death brought into relief a paradox entailing a sense of loss, separation, hardness, anger, and the frustration of not having done "so many things," while also incurring a sense of closeness, softness, of Eva becoming a mother herself. Just as Juanita had explained about Lent, the death "was a chance to change," give up something for something else, a pivotal moment demarcating a new direction.

From that time on, Eva's life did change; she began to "heal" by spending time with her family—her children, father, sister, niece, and nephew. All of them were together, riding around in the blue Ford minivan to church events, including a Wednesday night prayer group, choir practice, and catechism, which Eva and Juanita taught. On weekends, Eva and Juanita attended at least two Masses, one on Saturday evening and another early Sunday morning. On weekdays, Eva and Juanita went to the noon daily Mass at Saint John's and then again at 5:30 p.m. at Saint Anthony's. Eva's father began to spend his evenings at Eva's house. Her niece and nephew began to spend time with her children. All of this activity was "working," Eva assured me. "The family was better," "wasn't worrying so much," "more relaxed," "getting just what they needed."

These words were cryptic, signifying a private life that was working miracles with her family. And frankly, nothing made sense to me until I encountered a pivotal moment and had to get involved.

THE HEART

My son, Alejandro, who was three years old, had an accident at school. He attended a Montessori preschool for three hours a day. In the afternoon, the teachers allowed the children to finish the day in the playground. My wife, Gabriela, and I often met at the school about that time, taking a moment to watch the children before they formed lines, walked back to their classrooms, and waited to be released to their parents. It was a Thursday in April, the weather was warm, and when I arrived, Alejandro was in Gabriela's arms, fast asleep.

"What happened?" I asked.

"I don't know," Gabriela said. "When I came, he was under the slide, face down. He wasn't moving. I went to him, and found him crying, one of those deep cries with no sound, only tears. He said that a stick went into his eye. I took him to the bathroom and tried to wash it out, but couldn't find anything."

Alejandro's body had undergone a shock, and he was sleeping it off. We took him to a pediatric ophthalmologist. She prescribed antibiotics and had us schedule another appointment for the following Monday. We learned that a "foreign object" had pierced his cornea directly over the pupil. Scar tissue had formed, precluding sufficient light for the eye to process images. The eye was healing, but not with the same sight. His vision was now 20/200, or, as he explained, "I see squiggly things."

"What happened?" I asked him.

"A stick went into my eye."

Gabriela and I felt that there couldn't be any greater pain than that of a parent whose child has been hurt; we wanted Alejandro to be as he had been. I went to Saint Anthony's one afternoon and stood before a statue of Jesus placed on a glass-topped table in the rear of the sanctuary. This image of Jesus showed his heart surrounded by a crown of thorns. He showed a wound on his torso. Drops of blood oozed from the heart and wound, appearing to drop onto the glass below. The feet were worn smooth from parishioners touching them. Parishioners had slid small scraps of paper and photographs under the glass. I had been there for a few minutes before Alfredo, the church caretaker, approached and stood by my side, also gazing at the image.

"Do you know who this is?" he asked.

"That's Jesus."

"But, do you know which Jesus?"

I said that I didn't.

And he explained, "This is the Sacred Heart of Jesus. His heart is exposed to show that he receives people with an open heart, not with the mind. He shows his compassion and sympathy for those who come."[29]

I looked down to where the blood would have formed a pool and found traces of all the people who had come before me: parents, children, relatives, and friends. On a piece of scratch paper, a parent had written [unedited], "Te bien to ruego que cuides a mis hijos siempre y que todo en mi casa marche bien en bendisiones todos." And on another piece of paper torn from a school notebook, a child had expressed suffering most exemplary of the other children who had visited the Sacred Heart of Jesus [unedited]: "Dear Jesus pesle help my family come closer and make me realse what I am doing. I feel like no one loves me. My dad and I fight a lot. I can't talk to my mom about my problems because right away she gets mad. I am only 11 years old and I am worried about the bills and my future because my parents."[30]

The blood led to many people who were in pain. They experienced anger, economic insecurity, loneliness, and feelings of separation from others and were longing for direction, another "*camino*." They were longing for love and exposed a private part of their lives that one can understand only through compassion.

EYES

In the parking lot I found Eva, who was on her way to the daily Mass. I told her about Alejandro's eye. She gave me a hug and said that she would pray for him. The following day, Eva, Juanita, and two other friends piled into the blue Ford minivan and drove to Saint Lucy's in Fowler, a farm town located about thirty miles southwest of Fresno. Saint Lucy (283?–303?) is the patron saint of blindness, her name derived from the Latin word *lucius*, meaning "light," "shining," "radiant," and "understandable." She is generally portrayed holding a dish with two eyes on it, referring to the eyes restored by God after her torturers gouged them out.

The dire events of Saint Lucy's life are legendary but often conveyed as history. She was born of a noble family in Syracuse, Sicily. She devoted her virginity to God and vowed to devote her services and wealth to the poor. She earned her parents' blessing after taking her mother, Eutychia, to Catania to pray at the shrine of the virgin martyr Agatha. Her mother, suffering from a hemorrhage, was cured. However, a young suitor thwarted Lucy's intentions by denouncing her to Paschasius, the Sicilian governor. Paschasius, acting in accordance with the Roman emperor Diocletian's persecution (AD 284–305), condemned Lucy to prostitution. When she resisted, Paschasius condemned her to death by burning. Lucy survived the burning, but lost her life by the sword.[31]

For Eva, Saint Lucy was a beacon of faith: human suffering— Eutychia's hemorrhage, poverty, prostitution, blindness, and burning— provided insight into the horrors of the world and illuminated a path toward God. On that day Eva, Juanita, and their two friends followed that path on Alejandro's behalf, going to Saint Lucy's. Shortly thereafter, Alejandro was fitted with a hard contact lens that drew light around the scar tissue and into the eye, restoring his sight to normal.

BLOOD

Eva's direction, enhanced by her companions and driven by her desire to do something for somebody else, also entailed hazardous turns, inducing confusion and feelings of alienation from her family and others to whom she felt attached. One turn began with the murder of her aunt and uncle, who lived in Malaga, a community three miles south of Fresno. Saint Anthony's has a mission there. "I was taking a break from my depressing job," Eva explained. "I had the radio on. I heard that 'an elderly couple . . .'" She paused. "We didn't even consider that he was elderly," Eva reflected upon her uncle. "I didn't even think that he was 'elderly,' that an 'elderly couple' had been killed in Malaga. Then I went back to work, came home, and started thinking, 'Oh my God, they live over there.' We were watching the news, and all of a sudden, they started showing pictures. It was just very . . ." Again she paused. "I was screaming, 'Oh my God, that's my dad's brother.'"

"They were elderly and small, but they put up a spectacular fight," said Fresno County sheriff's Lt. Greg Burton, who "identified the victims as Julia Avila and her husband, Delores González."

"Avila, who was born in New Mexico," the *Fresno Bee* reported, "lived on Calvin Street for more than 50 years. González was born in Mexico and worked as a handyman. . . . The tranquility of this close-knit Malaga community was shattered by the news of the slayings. Most people, including Burton, could not remember the last time there was a homicide in this neighborhood. . . . Across the street from the Avila home is the Catholic church where Avila was a fixture. 'She'd walk across the street all the time to go to church,' said her niece. 'Who could kill her?'" (1 February 2000).

The media's coverage of the violent deaths evoked a self-transformation for Eva. She initially failed to connect the media's representation of the dead couple with her aunt and uncle because they were indeed different people. She had known her aunt and uncle for most of her life, just as she knew their children and their children's children, accounting for stories about family gatherings, first communions, quinceañeras (fifteenth-birthday celebrations), and other events that filled time with meaning. Eva never really thought of her aunt and uncle as "elderly." The media, however, focused on the passage of time by identifying an "elderly couple," who had lived "on Calvin Street for more than 50 years." The media endowed time with a "tranquility" represented by a matriarch and patriarch whose work, faith, and presence in the Catholic church "across the street" made it seem ideal, permanent (or at least not subject to going down without a "spectacular fight"), formulating a legacy that was bigger than any individual life.

Eva's response to the news highlights its privileged status over her own oral history. The "we" that Eva used when she was speaking for her

sister, father, and other family members became "I," indicating a rhetorical compromise from a collective perspective to a less authoritative
individual one. In addition, Eva referred to her uncle as "my father's
brother," creating distance between herself and her uncle by abnegating
a term of endearment. Eva's handle on the story became increasingly
particular and incredulous. She gave way to the public account and an
invention, arrangement, style, and memory that define the personhood
of those who use it. The logic of this transformation is endorsed by an
assumption of utopian universality whereby people are able to transcend
the "given realities of their bodies and their status" (Warner 1993, 239).

The logic entails more than compelling rhetorical components; it
represents a dialectic whereby family members, neighbors, parishioners,
and officials representing institutional power (of the media and government) endorse a positive identity based upon an implicit other, the
mysterious killer. "There was no sign of forced entry, leading investigators to say the victims may have known their attacker," the *Fresno Bee*
continued. "Investigators said . . . they had several leads. . . . More than
35 drops of blood stretched from the victims' home out to the street, 50
feet to the street corner, and then another 100 feet down Grand Street"
(1 February 2000). These leads suggested that the killer was close, familiar, yet perilously elusive—an insidious irony characterizing also the
rosary people said for Eva's uncle at the church.

"It was creepy," Eva recalled. "Everybody's all looking at everybody,
like accusing people. Nobody said anything. They knew it was my dad's
brother," Eva continued before pausing. "And the women pulled away
from my dad," pausing again. "All those rosary women; they were like
afraid. They pulled away."

"From your dad?" I asked.

"You know, 'How could you?'" Eva paused. "My dad was the good
one. He was always at church. The brother was not good. They thought
he was not good. He had lots of money."

The rosary was a stage on which human actors portrayed a battle
between the transcendental forces of good and evil. The assignment of
these values was as furtive as the killer, linked interchangeably to the
victim, the victim's relative, and others, by reasons that seemed provisionally plausible—signs of piety on the one hand, and bloodline, gen-

der, material wealth, greed, envy, or the legacy of original sin on the other. Just as it was for Saint Dominic in the Albigensian crusades, the rosary served to root out evil at all costs.[32] The trail of blood led to everyone and no one; it nurtured a precarious environment characterized by the exchange of discriminatory gazes and values, creating winners and losers bound by a way of thinking that sustained itself through an economy of difference. The trail of blood led to a beast, a killer who wanted more and was willing to exchange others for it; the trail led to a system of exchanges nourished by human objectification.

These exchanges came to a halt, Eva said, "when this guy came in and he had like a bandaged hand. And people said, 'It's possibly him.' I did see *him* at the funeral," Eva continued, referring to her uncle's grandson, her cousin's son. "[My cousin] said that he had just got back from somewhere. He might have left the country and then come back."

This talk of return defined the killer. The *Fresno Bee* followed the trail of blood to where the killer presumably got into a vehicle and escaped into the night. Sheriff's detectives compiled a family tree and found a criminal who, nine years earlier, had killed one and wounded two others with a sawed-off shotgun in the nearby town of Sanger. He was convicted of voluntary manslaughter, and after serving six years of a ten-year prison sentence, was deported to Mexico, his country of citizenship. The detectives suspected that the criminal "had returned to the United States, violating his parole, and might be living in Fresno" (1 June 2000). The trail of blood led to a genealogy and a popular caricature of violence and criminality of Mexican origin that had always returned to California in one form or another—the "illegal" migrant laborers, their families and their children who spoke that other language, became a burden to the state, and threatened the "tranquility" of American life. The talk of return has produced two images defining California's past and present, one of the common good and the other of the common threat, born of the same mentality and cultivated as mirror images of each other.

Popular identification with the common good relies upon the escape of the common threat from law and order, ensuring the possibility of return. "I heard on the radio," Eva recalled. "They had arrested him. And by 4:30 that afternoon, he had committed suicide. They said that he had spoken to one person. Then we started imagining, 'Who could it be?'" In its report of the suicide, the *Fresno Bee* picked up the same trail of blood with the headline, "Murder suspect may have had help," referring to the driver of the vehicle (1 June 2000).

The public account is conducive to identity formation because it reflects a prevailing epistemology, predicating how and what people can know. This account—the talk of the common good, tranquility, American life, a universal body—is always marked by the other that haunts every turn of phrase with an allusion to danger, confusion, or something else of an entirely different order.

OIL

When Eva said that she wanted to "get [her] house in order," she referred to something else that escapes popular speech but nevertheless manifests through signs—the Sacred Heart of Jesus, for example. Eva's compassion did not end with a trip to Saint Lucy's but extended beyond my wildest dreams. She belonged to the Universal Living Rosary Association, which had brought her into an online network of acquaintances throughout the world.[33] She told many of them—one in Germany, another in England, and yet another in Turkey—about Alejandro's eye. They expressed their sympathies through emails, passed the message on to others, and prayed rosaries for Alejandro. After a daily Mass, Maria Flores, one of the "rosary women" Eva referred to, asked about Alejandro. I told her about the contact lens, and she told me that she and her friends had been praying the rosary for him. Señora Paz, one of Saint Anthony's matriarchs, approached me, asked about Alejandro, and said that she had been praying for him. One day in late May, Eva said, "We can do more for him," and asked me to bring Alejandro to a healing Mass on Wednesday the following evening.[34]

Gabriela; our daughter, Claudia; Alejandro; and I went to the evening healing Mass, where the priest requested special prayers for the sick. After the Mass ended, several members of the Wednesday night prayer group, who were known for their charisma, or gift, of healing, lined up before the altar, making themselves available for those who needed prayers. Holding Alejandro in my arms, I filed out of the pew into the side aisle. Gabriela and Claudia followed behind. And Eva and her friend Juan approached from the altar. Juan placed his hand on Alejandro's forehead, said the Lord's Prayer, a Hail Mary, and, among petitions for the eye, repeated these prayers several times. Then Juan took a small vial of oil, unscrewed the lid, dabbed his thumb, and placed it on Alejandro's forehead, leaving a small, glistening smudge. The whole process took about five minutes; Alejandro lay in my arms, unusually calm.

Oil serves many purposes, its use dating back to at least the fourth century, as documented in the "Prayer Book of Serapion," and in another Syriac document of the fifth and sixth centuries, "Testamentum Domini Nostri Jesu Christi." The latter contains a formula for the blessing of oil and chrism for those who received baptism and, as was customary, for confirmation, a formal rite recognizing full membership in the church. The same document also identifies a special blessing of oil for the sick; it is "an invocation to Christ to give His creatures power to cure the sick, to purify the soul, to drive away impure spirits, and to wipe out sins."[35] Juan may have used an oil of saints, which flows from saints' relics or burial places. Or, as is often the case, the oil may have been mixed with water that has had contact with relics or been found near the burial places. This oil marks the intercession of saints, instrumental in curing bodily and spiritual ailments.[36]

FIRE

At Chartres the Virgin's tunic and the well's water have been the focal point of pilgrims for centuries. Like us on our trip to the healing Mass for Alejandro, where we brought our pain and that of others—of Eva, Alfredo the caretaker, and the children, parents, and relatives who had visited the Sacred Heart of Jesus—the pilgrims have brought the troubles of their worlds, expressing direction toward and belief in this sacred place, the center that galvanizes various components of their lives, at once single and collective. The event that brought this clear vision and direction occurred in 1194, when a fire nearly destroyed the entire cathedral and many buildings of the surrounding village; all that remained were parts of Chartres' southern tower and the crypt containing the Virgin's tunic (James 1988).

In January 2002, long after having attended the healing Mass, Gabriela took Alejandro to a pediatric ophthalmologist in Austin, Texas. We had recently moved from Fresno to Austin, where I would complete my work at the university there. The appointment was an introduction to Alejandro's new doctor, who would assess his vision and prescribe new contact lenses whenever necessary. A medical assistant took Gabriela and Alejandro to a small dark room for a preliminary eye exam. He sat Alejandro on a high chair, patched his left (good) eye, and directed his attention toward symbols projected on the wall. Gabriela took tissues from her purse and began to wipe tears from her eyes, turning away from Alejandro and pretending not to watch the eye exam. The assistant saw Gabriela crying and asked, "Señora, why are you crying?"

"Don't you know?" Gabriela responded. "He had an accident and lost his sight."

"Don't cry," the assistant said. "He sees fine. Look, he recognizes all of the symbols like any other child."[37]

It was true. Alejandro could see without the lens like any other child. The doctor speculated that "perhaps" the hard contact lens previously prescribed had changed the shape of the cornea in the area with the scar tissue, allowing sufficient light to process images entering the eye. Despite this plausible explanation and affirmation of faith in science, the doctor could not say for certain.

When everything seemed better, I asked Alejandro how he hurt his eye.

"Daddy," he said, "I was under the slide rubbing two sticks together, and one went into my eye. I was trying to make fire."

These things do happen, I thought. Eva's El Niño de Prague rose from the ashes of the fire that had destroyed her mother's house in Mesa, Arizona. El Niño "allowed her [Eva's mother] to find him," Eva had explained. Eva had indicated an agency, not of the figurine but of elsewhere, in the ashes. There, like Mary Magdalene when she went to Jesus's tomb, Eva's mother had searched for the living, some trace of her former life, where there was death. El Niño had been passed down to another generation, recalling all of the traces of Eva's life that gave it meaning, accounting for who she was, all of the things she had done for others.

THE ROSE

Except when he participated in the annual nacimiento, El Niño de Prague sat prominently in the center of the dashboard of Eva's blue Ford minivan, reminding her of the purpose of her journey. After having lunch one day, Eva reminded me of that purpose by asking if I'd like to visit her mother. I said that I would, and we proceeded to a nearby cemetery. We pulled up to what Eva called the "Mexican section," got out, and started to make our way through the gravesites toward a large mound of dirt. A funeral service was about to begin, and Eva said tentatively, "I think that they have covered up my mother's gravesite. Should we go there?"

"Let's just see," I said, and we pushed on.

As we approached, Eva said, "Let me warn you about something. My mother doesn't have a tombstone. We couldn't afford one."[38]

Our journey toward the grave was laden with anxiety springing from several social conditions and some personal ones, too: racial segregation; Eva's inability to be like everybody else by erecting a tombstone and fulfilling her obligations to negotiate difference and value, ensuring her self-value according to the logic of commodity exchange; a feeling of loss, her mother's grave having been covered up by careless gravediggers; and a prevailing feeling of us not belonging there among the dead. Could these conditions have been the specter of the Minotaur, rearing up his head for one final gasp of air before falling to his death, however provisional that death may have been? If so, then Eva's feeling of not belonging was appropriate, pushing her toward another place where the madness of this world has been pushed out by a seemingly rare, pivotal moment of harmony.

The gravesite was clear of the mound. A small rosebush with one red rose in bloom marked the space where Eva's mother was buried.

The rose was extraordinary, its hue similar to that of the blood that oozed from the Sacred Heart of Jesus, filtered through the stained-glass windows that opened to the convent's garden. At Chartres the cathedral boasts rose-wheel windows on the west façade that symbolize the turn of fortune and the duplicity of the medieval mind. With an exterior facing the outside world and an interior illuminating a sacred, divine space, the windows remind us that the outside world is mutable. John Leyerle (1977) suggests that their visibility from both outside and inside indicates that, whether understood in human or divine terms, one is a coincidence of the other. This duplicity, Leyerle suggests further, is most apparent in the rose-wheel's function as "*specula*," optical lenses, a "means for transmitting light with special effects," not unlike hard contact lenses under certain circumstances (294). The rose-wheel windows reflect a metaphysical view of light and optics. At the same time they show, through experimentation with instruments, a scientific view of light and optics. The metaphysical and scientific views are two sides of the same subject, often marked by differences and, more important, connections.

EVA AND I EMERGED FROM THE LABYRINTH AND OUR MORNING of contemplative prayer by recognizing the connections indicated by distinct signs—the tomb, heart, and rose. These signs refer to stories that circulate through a social landscape and provide inhabitants with objects of desire, exchange, shock, and horror—the logic of a commoditized world—that outline the contours of the ineffable or, as Father James Alberione recognized, an interior life and obligation "to do something for God and . . . people." The signs, in other words, refer to stories that represented one's interaction with that interior life. When we resist, we witness horrors—racism, murder, and death, for example—that sustain through contrast the logic of a social order: the system of wage labor and a literal and paradigmatic basis of production and consumption in California's San Joaquin Valley. When we embrace this interior life as a mother might embrace a child, or as Eva embraced the lives of others, we gain critical insight into that system and learn about compassion for its victims, including the migrant workers, the fathers, mothers, and children who visit the Sacred Heart of Jesus. Eva's cousin, who murdered her aunt and uncle, is also among the victims. Eva has taught us through her journey how to liberate ourselves from that system and its epistemological and behavioral constraints, or, recalling Sister Mary's instructions, how to leave our "obligations and schedules outside," to not let "them control us," and in Eva's words, to "live and have what we need."

This transition, which is ethical and spiritual, appears at those pivotal moments of clarity and direction. Its ramifications are revolutionary, promising to change the current logic of a social system through an infusion of compassion that enables us to assume the place of others, walk in their steps, experience the traces of their past, see through their eyes, and locate a sacred place, the center of the circle, personal and collective—a history. This history is represented metaphorically by the labyrinth, and allegorically by the pilgrims who have walked its path and recognized along the way the parts of life where humanity has been compromised, has become something else, something beastlike, causing immeasurable human suffering.

Eva and I thanked Sister Mary, left a small donation, exited the convent, and made our way through the garden. We climbed into her blue Ford minivan, feeling that we had changed, but not entirely. For the time being, we had to rest uneasily with our contradictions while we headed toward home.

CHAPTER

THE PASSION PLAY

FIVE

The March air was warm in the wake of winter, forecasting hot summer months and the annual harvest in the San Joaquin Valley.

By 9:00 a.m. a few hundred people had gathered in Saint Anthony's parking lot. Many of them had just finished assisting an early Sunday Mass. Other parishioners joined them, still filing out of the sanctuary with palm leaves in their hands. The gospel writer John tells us that the Jews greeted Jesus with palm branches when he entered Jerusalem with Lazarus by his side. Many of them were recent converts to their faith in Jesus, having witnessed him raise Lazarus from the dead. Palms had always been a symbol of victory; these followers adopted it to show the victory of the "faithful over the enemies of the soul."[1] The Jews hailed Jesus, "Hosanna! Blessed is he who comes in the name of the Lord" (John 12:13 RSV).

Within a half hour, several hundred more people had arrived at Saint Anthony's and gathered around a wooden stage constructed in front of the church's rectory and between the sanctuary and the social hall. Parishioners had set up rows of folding chairs, enough for five hundred people. Many people already sat in the chairs; others had left an article of clothing, claiming a space from where they would watch the Passion play scheduled for later that morning.

By 9:45 a.m. hundreds more had come, increasing the size of the crowd to six or seven hundred people. Many took seats. Others remained standing, milling around and talking to friends. Children ate the cotton candy and Mexican sweet breads that their parents had bought from the street vendors who wheeled around on tricycle carts. Some children ventured away from their parents and played in open spaces and on the stage, performing antics despite admonitions about falling off and tumbling four feet to the pavement below.

Javier Martinez and I leaned against a low iron fence near the entrance of the parking lot. The fence protected a bed of spring roses. I had met Javier the previous September at a Wednesday evening prayer group; he played bass for the group's band. Javier recalled how he had come to the church, reeling away from his experiences in Watsonville, California, where the United Farm Workers (UFW) had spent several years trying to persuade workers in the region's strawberry industry to vote for union representation. We watched people coming from all directions up the sidewalks from nearby parking lots and neighborhood streets. We conversed, watched, and smelled the fresh flowers, baked sweet breads, and spun sugar. We listened to the children's laughter, ambient voices, and the sound of hundreds of footsteps. We listened, conversed, and watched some more.

Shortly after 10:00 a.m., congregants of a second Sunday Mass began to exit the sanctuary. Grandparents, parents, children, cousins, nieces, nephews—extended families—gathered by the sanctuary's main double doors. Some were dressed as Roman soldiers, or Mary, or Simon the Cyrenian. One played the role of Jesus himself. They formed two lines side by side and prepared for a procession through the neighborhood to reenact the Way of the Cross, or the Via Dolorosa—Christ's journey toward the Place of the Skull (in Hebrew, Golgotha) for crucifixion. The warm air was conducive to the people circulating in and out of the sanctuary, through the neighborhood, through the church's parking lot, and before the stage, where a troupe of volunteer actors would soon perform the Passion play.

The Passion play evolved among clergy and laity during the medieval period as a part of the Easter celebration.[2] The twelfth-century Passion play at Monte Cassino, Sandro Sticca (1972) argues, is the earliest known version; the Passion play at Oberammergau, which was first performed in 1633 to help relieve the suffering from the plague, is the chief continental survival.[3] The play's popularity in Europe reflects an interest among monastic orders and laity in a humanistic understanding of Christ expressed through his suffering and helplessness in dramatic human episodes (Southern 1953; Sticca 1972).

Richard C. Trexler (2003) argues that despite its popularity on the continent, the Passion play was extremely rare if not nonexistent on the Iberian Peninsula during the sixteenth century and, therefore, played no role in the Spanish missionaries' initial evangelization in the New World.[4] Trexler credits native inhabitants for the Passion play's development. Drawing from their understanding of the liturgy, sermons, pictorial representations of Christ's passion, and experiences of flagellation, native inhabitants developed the drama that came to fruition in the late seventeenth century. In the Americas, the Passion play has always been a means by which laity—members of peasant and Indian populations—expressed their solidarity in Christ's suffering. This expression, it is important to recognize, came about amid abject natural and social conditions, including the widespread loss of human life to disease and the systemic privation of property, goods (*bona*), actions, liberty, and even control of one's own body. In his discussion of the sixteenth-century juridical language of the Spanish conquest, Anthony Pagden (1987) identifies people's loss of control over their own bodies as the systemic privation of dominium, the basis of a civil society.[5]

The Passion play's history in the Americas provides insight into the meaning of dominium. The Passion play is about empathy, enabling actors and audiences to connect with Christ's life, in his suffering and crucifixion. The connection entails orientation to a way of being that stands in the face of oppression, which for Christ would have been Jewish authorities and Roman oversight. The connection also entails self-sacrifice, a giving up of one's self for another, or a psychological adjustment that shows in external identification with signs of death. One sign is Jesus's walk with Lazarus, and another, his actual crucifixion; each creates ground for expansion to other times and places, as in the decimation of indigenous people in the Americas. The Passion play, then, involves empathy as a way of mediating abjection—a helpless condition often followed by death that comes about when the powerful deny the powerless their dominium. People experience this mediation by transcending their individuality to become a part of a collective body that people claim as their own, effectively resisting oppression to restore dominium.

In this chapter, I address this process of restoring dominium. Saint Anthony's parishioners walked the Via Dolorosa, and others watched a performance of the Passion play. Javier and I observed the Via Dolorosa procession depart on its route through the neighborhood and then return to the church grounds about an hour later. We also watched the Passion play as audience members at our location near the parking lot entrance, leaning against the iron fence that protected a bed of roses. From this position, Javier told his story about Watsonville, trials with union organizers and regional growers, and his eventual arrival to Fresno and Saint Anthony's church. One might see the first two events as staged and the third, Javier's story, as a coincidence. But then one would overlook why people walk the Via Dolorosa and watch the Passion play; that is, because these events from the past and their reenactments in the present create parallels to contemporary life. They provide a frame that helps people conceptualize the course of their lives and of their stories, giving insight into particular events and meaning to how one comes to be in the present. The Via Dolorosa and Passion play are parallels, I argue. They make up an imaginary universe that encircles people's lives. They reference times, places, people, and events where an individual can go and participate alongside others, transforming individual experience of one's own life, often fraught with feelings of detachment and isolation, into a collective journey to claim as one's own.

It is here, then, that I take up the theme of dominium. I reenact the Via Dolorosa and Passion play as performed on Palm Sunday at Saint Anthony's with a cast of actors in the roles of Jesus, Roman soldiers, chief priests, Pharisees, and the disciple Judas. I also reenact Javier's story. The reenactments address the way that Jesus became deprived of dominium only to become a means for people to realize it in their lives. They establish a basis for civil society in contrast to a society that falls short of this objective.

THE PARKING LOT WAS FULL, AND ABOUT ONE HUNDRED participants began the procession through the neighborhood west of Saint Anthony's. Each walked in the footsteps of another, the pace slow and constant behind one participant carrying a plain wooden cross, another carrying a banner of Our Lady of Guadalupe, and another dressed as Jesus. Their journey would take them about a quarter mile west on East Byrd Avenue, a quarter mile south on South Whitney Avenue, and about a half mile east by northeast on Garrett Avenue, which veers back to Saint Anthony's. The procession would stop periodically along the way, allowing the participants to meditate upon the signs of the crucifixion—betrayal, condemnation, trial, torture, compassion, and death.

BETRAYAL

The Passion play began with Jesus and his disciples eating bread. Jesus said, "This is my body which is given for you. Do this as a remembrance of me." Then, Jesus reminded his followers of his imminent betrayal: "Woe to the man by whom he is betrayed" (Luke 22:19, 22 RSV).[6]

JAVIER HAD TRAVELED ALL OVER CALIFORNIA, FOLLOWING the migratory labor circuit until he settled in Watsonville, where he worked "with the companies primarily in agriculture." He said that he was "a kind of human resources person," who drew from his experience of the labor circuit to represent employers in labor negotiations. The job became most significant in 1996 when the UFW began a campaign for union representation on California's Central Coast. "I used to tell people," Javier explained, "why they might not want to join unions. It's not that I am against unions, but I worked to present the employers' case."[7]

The employers' case came with much precedent that gave Javier a distinct advantage over the UFW's ambitions. The UFW's representation in California had declined since 1977, when the union held over 100 contracts, represented 70,000 farmworkers, and had a dues-paying membership of more than 50,000.[8] In those days, the UFW was most recognized by California residents for having secured the enactment of the 1975 Agricultural Labor Relations Act (ALRA), which guaranteed collective bargaining rights for agricultural workers and established a five-member Agricultural Labor Relations Board (ALRB) to arbitrate disputes between growers and employees (Ganz 2000; Mooney and Majka 1995).[9] One of the ALRB's key rulings enabled union representatives to access farm property, where they could solicit support from employees (Mooney and Majka 1995).

These achievements came under the leadership of César Chávez, who had been working on behalf of agricultural workers since 1958 and cultivating union representation since 1962 with the founding of the *Asociación de campesinos*, or Farm Workers Association.[10] Chávez combined social and political networking, nonviolent protest, religious devotion, and an ability to speak persuasively to garner support and build a social movement on behalf of farmworkers. Chávez's movement coincided with others, including the civil rights and peace movements. These movements produced leaders who spoke for Native Americans, Mexican Americans, Puerto Ricans, teachers, and blue-collar workers, constituting a political agenda aimed at changing the way people perceived and treated marginalized people.[11]

Politicians, growers, and affiliated business leaders interested in preserving the status quo in California agribusiness curbed whatever changes might have been underway. A coalition of Republicans and rural Democrats blocked the appropriation of emergency funds to the ALRB, forcing the board in February 1976 to close its offices, lay off staff, and end its operations in upholding the law. The state legislature approved funds the following December, and the ALRB was able to resume operations.[12]

To preclude future actions of this kind, the UFW sponsored a ballot initiative, Proposition 14, which guaranteed the ALRB funding and wrote into law the board's ruling, allowing union access to farm property. Governor Jerry Brown, Democratic presidential candidate Jimmy Carter, Democratic elected officials, and former ALRB members all endorsed Proposition 14. Polls indicated public support.

However, supporters of agribusiness, including the California Farm Bureau Federation, mounted a well-financed campaign against the initiative. They claimed that the ALRB's access ruling violated private property rights. They generally portrayed the ALRB as an example of the government's excessive involvement in people's private lives. California voters defeated Proposition 14 by a 20-percent margin, indicating a change in popular attitudes toward labor. Governor George Deuk-mejian, the Republican, who took office in January 1983 with the sup-port of "hundreds of thousands of dollars of campaign contributions from growers," appointed ALRB members who were unsympathetic and, on occasion, hostile to the UFW and farmworkers. The governor's general counsel appointee, David Stirling, epitomized the board mem-bers' hostility to the UFW, claiming on one occasion that the UFW suf-fered from a "victims' complex" (*Wall Street Journal*, 9 September 1986, 1, 20). With the appointments and the funding limits, Deukmejian dis-abled the ALRB.[13]

Since 1970, strawberry growers on the Central Coast have trans-formed their industry. They began as family farms serving local con-sumers and became high-yield, capital-intensive operations with international distribution.[14] The transformation accompanied changes in management and employee relations to circumvent possible union elections. Strawberries are unique because of their seasonality and fra-gility, and because of harvest requirements related to timing, amount, and skill of labor.[15] To ensure a supply of semiskilled, cost-effective labor, large growers (accounting for 40 to 50 percent of the total straw-berry acreage) established in the middle 1960s a sharecropping system, which delegates labor negotiations to primarily Mexican immigrants who manage from three to five acres each.[16] Small growers have ensured their compliance with labor requirements by cultivating "bonds of inter-personal obligations," including "intangible and material benefits" that project the "image of a generous patron": on-the-job flexibility (breaks, time off); voluntary improvements in work conditions (knee pads, over-shoes, gloves); benefits (health insurance, overtime pay); and access to supplemental resources (housing, legal assistance, translation) (Wells 1981, 697). In addition, growers have adopted strategies of buttressing employer-labor relations. The Salinas Valley Independent Growers Association, founded in the summer of 1970, and the Pajaro Valley Strawberry Growers Association, founded in the spring of 1971, manage the growers' public relations and offer health, accident, and life insur-ance plans for their members' employees (Wells 1981).[17]

In July 1996, the *New York Times* reported that the UFW had begun arguably "the biggest organizing campaign . . . under way in American labor: a drive to unionize all the region's 15,000 strawberry pickers" (3 July 1996, 14). The campaign was also the UFW's first under Arturo Rodriguez, the union's leader since César Chávez's death in 1993 in San Luis, Arizona (near his birthplace), where he had been fasting in the home of a farm-worker family (Griswold del Castillo and Garcia 1995, 173). At the time of Chávez's death, UFW contracts covered approximately 5,000 workers; and the Salinas Valley, once a union stronghold, amounted to one contract (Mooney and Majka 1995, 184).

In his human resources work in Watsonville, Javier represented the relatively new relationships between growers and employees that justified, it appeared, the decline in union representation. "I wanted to educate the workers," Javier said, "about why they might not be better off with the union. The union comes and says all of the things that they are going to give to the workers. It's not that the union representatives have a million dollars in their pockets that they can give to the workers. They have to negotiate contracts with the growers; it's a process that can take time. And in the end, it doesn't necessarily benefit the workers. My aim has always been to try to work out the best arrangement for the workers and the employers. The employers are most concerned about profits and the workers, about wages and work conditions."

These concerns had defined local politics, sorting out winners from losers for decades. Since 1983, farmworkers had suffered a "continuing slide in real wages . . . a drop of more than 10 percent." Farmworkers employed by labor contractors had seen their "earnings cut by 25 percent" (*Los Angeles Times*, 29 April 1993, 24). Low wages accompanied a surplus in labor provided by the constant immigration of primarily Mexican people to California (*San Francisco Chronicle*, 15 December 1996, 1, Z1; 12 April 1997, A1).

Low wages translated into a decline in living conditions. Susan Ferriss and Ricardo Sandoval reported an extreme case on a hillside north of Salinas, which they suggested was "emblematic of the inhuman living conditions [that] were on the rise among farmworkers." They cited "coffin-shaped caves, . . . just big enough for a man to crawl into; some of them had been reinforced with corrugated tin and furnished with decaying mattresses." The grower and property owner subtracted 25 cents from the employees' $3.50 hourly wage for rent (1997, 239–40).

Ferriss and Sandoval's report of these conditions highlighted the farmworkers as expendable. Any "bonds of interpersonal obligations" and "intangible and material benefits" might have been stopgap measures to forestall an inevitable outcome as suggested by signs of decay and death (Wells 1981, 697).

Javier was aware of such conditions that brought contrast to the smell of roses. He'd certainly experienced them when he worked on the labor circuit. He'd seen them in the Pajaro Valley, where rents far exceeded farmworkers' ability to pay. And yet, he told his story, confident in his recollection and his actions that helped prevent the UFW from achieving success. Did he betray the people, César Chávez, and a legacy? His confidence indicated something more at stake than appearances, asking me to suspend judgment.

CONDEMNATION

Jesus turned toward the audience, which had grown to over a thousand, and said, "Why are you sleeping? Wake up, and pray that you may not be subjected to the trial."

Roman soldiers, chief priests, Pharisees, and the betrayer Judas approached Jesus, who asked, "Whom do you seek?" They replied that they were looking for Jesus the Nazarene. When Jesus told them that he was the one, his questioners appeared confused, as if they didn't see clearly whom they sought. Jesus told them again that he was the one. At this, they seized him and formed a tribunal (John 18:4–12 RSV).

THE EMPLOYER-EMPLOYEE RELATIONS AND LIVING CONDITIONS sent mixed messages. The relations neither provided farmworkers with clear insight into their predicament nor directed them toward political organization. Their position between the growers and the union was at best ambiguous, characterized by temporary liaisons and doubt about the future.

"Do you remember when the UFW wanted to unionize all of the workers in the strawberry and packing industry?" Javier asked. "I helped organize a march against the union." The march that Javier organized was a counterblow to another march four months earlier that had been the culmination of an increasingly aggressive union campaign. In the *Santa Cruz County Sentinel*, Tracy L. Barnett characterized the campaign as "a battle cry that has echoed across the nation, amplified by the national labor movement in search of a cause that will mobilize a populace disenchanted with unions" (13 April 1997, 1). The UFW's forces converged in Watsonville on Sunday, 13 April 1997, when organizers brought together an estimated thirty thousand people, including "delegations from locals in 38 states," for a march on Main Street. UFW president Arturo Rodriguez, cofounder Dolores Huerta, AFL-CIO president John Sweeny, Teamsters president John Carey, the Reverend Jesse Jackson, and the actor Martin Sheen walked "arm in arm" and led the "procession of marchers." The procession included unionized teachers, ironworkers, firefighters, nurses, carpenters, Mexican flags, banners of Our Lady of Guadalupe and of César Chávez, "a troupe of befeathered Aztec dancers," and berry pickers (*San Francisco Chronicle*, 14 April 1997, A13).

"This is wonderful, just wonderful," said Dolores Huerta. "I hope these crowds show the growers how much support there is for the union" (*San Francisco Chronicle*, 14 April 1997, A13).

"It's pretty phenomenal what they're doing now," said Miles Reiter of Reiter Berry Farms, reflecting upon the march and the union's nationwide campaign, which included leafleting consumers, sending mailers to millions, and attracting the attention of major media outlets (*Santa Cruz County Sentinel*, 13 April 1997, A6).

"This represents the unity of the labor movement," said John Sweeny (*New York Times*, 14 April 1997, A14). The unity gave the UFW, *New York Times* writer Carey Goldberg observed, "a new dynamism" after the death of the "legendary farm labor organizer" César Chávez (3 July 1996, A14).

Sweeny's word "unity" was most apposite because it referred to a combination of religious, national, and folkloric symbols. "Unity" also referred to people—consumers, farmworkers, union leaders, political activists, and a Hollywood celebrity—who helped galvanize the UFW's public image, widespread appeal, and credibility. At any given moment, the march could have been about anything or anybody, depending on how onlookers focused their attention.

Or the march could have been about nothing at all. The problem resided in the UFW's strategy for reinventing itself. Instead of organizing in the fields and then calling for outside support from consumers, supermarket chains, other union leaders, politicians, and celebrities, the UFW called for outside support before asking the farmworkers about their needs and union representation. The UFW was not, as one local social worker commented, "a grassroots organization anymore" (*San Francisco Chronicle*, 12 April 1997, A1).

Locals participated but with uncertainty about the grounds. Perhaps the most insightful assessment of the UFW's march came from a group of schoolchildren from the Pajaro Valley Unified School District's Migrant Head Start Program who stood by the sidelines and watched the marchers with "muted hope and apprehension." The schoolchildren asked, "What's going to happen after they're all gone?" (*Santa Cruz County Sentinel*, 14 April 1997, A1, A7).

"Something had to be done," Javier said. "The people didn't need the UFW. I wanted to help them with what they needed."

JUDGMENT

Pilate didn't know what to make of Jesus. Jesus had committed no crime, and the chief priests had surely accused him out of envy. According to those priests, who stood before Pilate impatiently, Jesus claimed to be a king; in any case, he was a rabble-rouser who would surely bring on the wrath of Caesar. And nobody wanted that. But Pilate needed something to go on, some kind of crime that justified whatever the people had in store for Jesus. He asked, "Are you the king of the Jews?"

"You have said so," Jesus responded.

The chief priests stepped in and accused Jesus of many things. Pilate asked, "Have you no answer to make?"

Jesus said nothing, indifferent to the accusations (Mark 15:2–5 RSV).

IN HIS TESTIMONY ABOUT THE WATSONVILLE MARCH AGAINST the UFW, Javier made a point about his position in relation to growers. "We didn't represent the growers," Javier said. "That would have been illegal."[18]

The growers had plenty of support without direct representation. An estimated one thousand to three thousand pickers, packers, and drivers had gathered under an unofficial umbrella organization, the Agricultural Workers Committee. As they marched down Main Street, they denounced the UFW by yelling, "*Fuera*," that is, "Get out" (*Santa Cruz County Sentinel*, 11 August 1997, A1).

Newspaper reporters canvassed the crowd in search of the true story about what people thought of the UFW. "We are the true workers," said Leticia Fernandez. "The marchers a few months ago were paid. We are the true field workers" (*Santa Cruz County Sentinel*, 11 August 1997, A12). Other workers echoed Fernandez, saying, "They marched because they wanted to march. And they don't believe they need a union to mediate between them and their employers" (*Santa Cruz County Sentinel*, 11 August 1997, A12).

The reporters had been persistent in their efforts to get the true story. About a year before the August countermarch in Watsonville, reporters had canvassed people in their homes, asking for opinions about the UFW. They found Marco García in a four-room Salinas home that he shared with eleven other young men, all of them from the Mexican state of Hidalgo. The men "lounged around the living room, redolent of frying tortillas, in the languor of after-work fatigue—some leaning against the wall because there were not enough chairs for all of them in the house, for which they [paid] rent of $1,000 a month." García suffered from headaches and impaired vision related to a head injury; a steel bar on the side of a truck carrying strawberry crates had struck him. He had no medical insurance. A housemate pulled up a pant leg and showed the reporter his rash, "a collage of pustules and blotches," that appeared after he had been working around pesticides.

Their opinion about the UFW was unanimous. A housemate pulled out a leaflet that he'd received at work. The leaflet said: "We don't need outsiders to solve our problems" (*New York Times*, 3 July 1996, A14).

The workers had drawn battle lines that separated them from others: their problems from outside problem solvers, their homes from intruders, their volition to act on their own behalf from those paid to act for the union. In these respects, the thousands of farmworkers who supported the August countermarch had become attuned to local interests and prerogatives.

Likewise, Javier had resisted the UFW because he viewed it as an insurgent organization. "I am not anti-union," Javier claimed. "I used to be a member of the UFW. But now, I don't like their attitude. They really follow Emiliano Zapata, you know, that revolutionary during the Mexican revolution. Zapata didn't want better working conditions for Mexicans. He wanted to take over the land. I once heard César Chávez speak, and he said something that has always stayed with me. He said that his goal was not better wages for the workers but to take the land for them."

THE CROSS-BEARER

Nevertheless, Pilate still couldn't hold Jesus responsible for any crime. He suggested letting Jesus go as the one prisoner released according to Passover custom. Instead, the chief priests lobbied the crowd on behalf of Barabbas, another prisoner, who had committed murder in a rebellion. Pilate (turning to the audience) said, "See, I am bringing [Jesus] out to you, that you may know that I find no crime in him." The chief priests and guards, repulsed by Jesus, cried, "Crucify him, crucify him!" (John 19:4, 6 RSV). The guards dressed Jesus in a purple cloak and placed a crown of thorns on his head, mocking pretensions of kingship. They placed a cross on Jesus's shoulders and led him to Golgotha.

CHÁVEZ IDENTIFIED WITH EMILIANO ZAPATA, ENLIGHTENMENT notions of natural rights, and a *campesino* (peasant) heritage rooted in indigenous land claims.[19] Chávez expressed this identification through the name of his original union, *Asociación de campesinos* (Peasant Association), and through a rhetorical act that helped to "unleash . . . a modern social revolution," the Plan of Delano (Quiñones 1990, 106; quoted in Hammerback and Jensen 1994, 53). The plan was written for a pilgrimage that Chávez led from Delano to Sacramento in March 1966. The pilgrimage went through cities in California's fertile San Joaquin Valley—Fresno, Madera, Stockton—where farmworkers had labored for over one hundred years. The plan called the public's attention to farmworkers' rights and called on farmworkers to "rethink their self-identification as second-class citizens" (*Carta Editorial*, 8 April 1966).[20] The plan's messages spread throughout the San Joaquin Valley and the U.S. Southwest by word of mouth "faster than any teletype could have carried them," because they resonated with people who identified with a Mexican history of insurgency (Valdez 1971, 99).

Many plans or proclamations have defined Mexico's history in such a way that the oppressed formally declare "before a civilized world" and "nation to which [they] belong" their pursuit of "social justice" against politicians, landowners, and an entire system that has become rich at the expense of the poor (Jensen and Hammerback 2002, 16).[21] Emiliano Zapata's Plan de Ayala, for example, declared on 28 November 1911, "solemnly on behalf of the civilized world and . . . nation," according to the motto "Liberty, Justice, and Law," a national movement to seize federal authority and restore the fields to the *pueblos* (people and villages) (Hammerback and Jensen 1994, 59; Womack 1970, 397, 399). Zapata's plan echoed Miguel Hidalgo's decree of 29 November 1810, which called for the "reconquest" of Mexico by taking up arms and throwing off "the heavy yoke that pressed down on her for close to three centuries" (Hamill 1966, 149, 195). Francisco Severo Maldonado, editor of the insurgent newspaper *El Despertador Americano*, wrote with reference to the Hidalgo decree: "We believe we are authorized by the Supreme Being, from whom we receive the same natural rights as all other men, openly to aspire to independence" (*El Despertador Americano*, 20 December 1810; quoted in Hamill 1966, 192). The decree came in the midst of a rebellion initiated on 16 September 1810, when Hidalgo called his followers to action. American Creoles, after having been subservient to Spanish colonial policy, galvanized their national identity into a military force in small villages and the countryside outside Mexico City, in Veracruz, and in other major provincial towns. Indians joined the rebellion and provided practical support before transforming its objectives from a Creole coup d'état into a popular uprising aimed at relieving centuries of privation.

Miguel Hidalgo was an American Creole and an intellectual indebted to Europe for part of his cultural heritage. From 1767 to 1792, he was enrolled as a student in the Colegio de San Nicolás Obispo and earned degrees, scholarships, and a faculty position in theology. Under the influence of Francisco Javier Clavigero, Hidalgo's studies included mathematics, natural history, physics, geography, history, philosophy, theology, law, and rhetoric. He became president of literary societies organized by philosophy and law students. He befriended colleagues with interests in literature and social reform. When he became a parish priest in 1792 (he served first in Colima, then San Felipe, and finally Dolores), he cultivated a public life defined by musical, literary, and social activity. He frequented private libraries, where he had access to Cicero, Buffon, and Rousseau among other works from the classical to the Enlightenment periods. And he corresponded with friends outside Mexico and gained a perspective of life in other parts of the Americas (Hamill 1966).

One correspondent, who had "a probable revolutionary influence," was Juan Antonio Rojas (Hamill 1966, 102). Rojas was a professor of mathematics who had fled to New Orleans to escape the Inquisition. There, Rojas published his observations and sent them to friends in Mexico:

> I find myself in the fortunate [country of] North America where dwells Liberty. . . . Here the land is divided in small lots. The busy hand of the industrious farmer is seen working and he is provided with an abundant surplus. [In Mexico] the land is not cared for by those who hold immense expanses of it. . . . Here the Government provides by means of equitable taxation, roads, rivers, canals and as much as can aid the exportation of national produce and the importation of goods from the entire world. Here, if individual riches are not so great, the sum of the parts is greater, larger quantities [of goods] are consumed and no one is aware of that ghastly poverty and unclothed squalor [known in Mexico]. (Hamill 1966, 103)

Rojas's observations reflect more the model of an ideal society formulated in the writings of Locke, Paine, and Jefferson than the realities of the plantation South.[22] Nevertheless, the observations fueled rhetoric against the Inquisition and Spanish hegemony.

The plans defining Mexican and farmworker insurgency drew from the political writings of Europe and the Americas. They included customary arrangement of phrases, literary memory, stylistic flourishes, and delivery to account for the oppression of country people by hands of others—Spaniards, politicians, plantation owners, and growers—who resided most often in urban centers. For Hidalgo, Zapata, Chávez, and scores of campesinos, the plans were as much a reflection of self-awareness as they were models for civil society.

The plans provided campesinos and their leaders with a universally recognized public face. The face, once providing social elites with political footholds, now provided the same to country people. Octavio Paz (1985) calls the face a mask that has served as a defense against a long history of betrayal, disastrous events, and hegemony in colonial New Spain, independent Mexico, and the U.S. Southwest; it has served, as Marco García and his eleven housemates in Salinas reminded us, as a defense against the intrusion of outsiders (Hammerback and Jensen 1994; A. González 1990). This mask is full of "metaphors and allusions" and at the same time, Paz continues, "of reticences . . . of tints, folds, thunderheads, sudden rainbows, indecipherable threats" (1985, 29). The mask represents a paradox of people not being always as they appear, of presence and invisibility, of clear positions and drives of impassioned hearts that disguise sorrow.

On 16 March 1966, César Chávez organized a twenty-five-day, 250-mile pilgrimage from Delano to Sacramento, California. As the pilgrimage made its way through farm country and towns in the San Joaquin Valley, hundreds of workers applauded and many joined (Griswold del Castillo and Garcia 1995). A Catholic priest, Eugene Boyle, recalled his meeting Chávez: ". . . walking with a cane, his feet burning with blisters, one of his legs severely swollen . . . He greeted me graciously, obviously pleased that a priest had connected with the march, fascinating eyes capturing me forever" (1993, 4). A barefoot campesino carried "a plain wooden cross," and another, a "banner of Our Lady of Guadalupe"

(Boyle 1993, 4). "This was an excellent way of training ourselves," Chávez recalled, "to endure a long, long struggle" (Griswold del Castillo and Garcia 1995, 51).

Javier had taken these words to heart. With them, he'd put on a mask to play out his role among union organizers and growers. And herein lies the rub; on wearing a mask, one covers a persona with another persona, obfuscating one's self-presence and replacing it with that of another with a different perspective of matters at hand. Javier in one instance appeared in the image of Judas and then in another, of Pilate. He took on, by most accounts, roles of the wretched. He also took on their sins and a struggle.

CROSS-BEARING PEOPLE

Jesus had fallen under the weight of his cross while making his way to Golgotha. Blood oozed from his knees where pebbles had scraped him, from his back where soldiers had whipped him, and from his head where thorns had pierced his skin. The soldiers, worried that Jesus would not make it to his crucifixion, solicited help from a passerby. Simon, a Cyrenian who was coming from the country, carried Jesus's cross.

JAVIER NEGOTIATED RELATIONSHIPS BETWEEN EMPLOYERS and farmworkers. "The unions were needed twenty years ago," Javier explained. "But now they aren't always necessary. The growers and employers; they are really only interested in one thing, and that's if they are profitable. . . . When I worked for growers, I would tell them that they had to treat employees like numbers and not people. If they saw them as numbers, they'd recognize them as a valuable asset like a truck or machine, something that has dollar value. They'd realize that they have to take care of that asset. So when they saw a worker, they'd ask him about his family. A grower might give him a raise. He took care of the workers so that [they'd] be happy and productive. In some cases, the employer might learn to know everybody by name. People really like that. If the union came to town, there'd be a good chance that [the workers] would vote against it."

When the union and its supporters went to Watsonville, they met resistance. Many locals, as mentioned above, didn't want "outsiders" to solve their problems. Reporters pushed to identify those "outsiders" who were causing so much trouble in this small working-class town of approximately 70 percent Latino residents, one-third under eighteen years of age. *Santa Cruz County Sentinel* reporter Bob Linneman saw the UFW "licking its chops" at the prospect of a union election. Linneman also saw union representatives as "they trotted out" with a couple of workers from Gargiulo Farms (*Santa Cruz County Sentinel*, 23 July 1997). But surely the outsiders couldn't have been, as Linneman implied, just wolves who were invading farms and feasting on livestock, pitting humanity and industry against nature. At the August countermarch, Linneman noted a participant waving a sign: "Arturo Rodriguez and Dolores Huerta are '*hijos del Diablo*,'" the devil's children (*Santa Cruz County Sentinel*, 11 August 1997, A12). The Santa Cruz radio talk show host Rob Roberts, who attended the UFW's April march, commented: "This is a prime example of union arrogance here. They come into a community and force themselves upon us. . . . We've seen hundreds of people come by here today—all carrying Mexican flags and red [UFW] flags. Whether or not an American flag turns up in this parade will be interesting to see" (*San Francisco Chronicle*, 14 April 1997, A13).

Mexican outsiders had been a burning issue in Watsonville for some time. The "third-generation grower" and "Watsonville resident" Tom AmRhein commented as he stood among his "manicured rows," prodding the "earth with a muddy boot," that "the first big floods (of illegal immigrants) began coming over in the '70s, when the Mexican oil market crashed. . . . There are waves every time the peso dips." AmRhein acknowledged, however, agriculture's "short-term benefit from untrammeled immigration." To cope with an increasing population and seasonal unemployment of 28 percent, city planners had initiated the construction of low-cost housing, schools, and shopping centers where retailers provided alternative employment. This trend, AmRhein commented, "[was] already pushing out farmers" (*San Francisco Chronicle*, 15 December 1996, 1, Z1). AmRhein's views reflected a history of conflicts over the ALRB's access ruling, enabling union organizers to campaign on farms in violation, growers complained, of their property rights. To many in the area, the "outsiders," whether wolves, the children of devils, arrogant union representatives, or Mexicans, were a threat to fundamental American values of home, community, order, and stability embedded in private property and represented symbolically by AmRhein's muddy boot.

THOMAS JEFFERSON WROTE EMPHATICALLY ABOUT THE VALUE of property. During his travels in prerevolutionary France in 1785, Jefferson reflected upon the unequal division of property. "The property of this country," he wrote to James Madison, "is absolutely concentered in a very few hands" that employ servants and support manufacturers and tradesmen but leave the masses without work. "I am conscious," Jefferson continued, "that an equal division of property is impracticable. But the consequences of this enormous inequality producing so much misery to the bulk of mankind, legislators cannot invent too many devices for subdividing property, only taking care to let their subdivisions go hand in hand with the natural affections of the human mind. . . . The earth is given as a common stock for man to labour and live on" (Jefferson 1975, 396–97).

These reflections combined the experience of human misery, pragmatic materialism, and conceptions of human equality and natural rights to forge an understanding of liberty and democracy. Jefferson envisioned an agrarian nation wherein the "permanence of government" and the "virtue" of its citizens lay in humankind's freedom to cultivate a livelihood by working the land (Jefferson 1955, 165).

Jefferson's vision has shaped a history of public policy, social initiatives, and scholarship about Americans and their communities. The Homestead Act of 1862, despite abuses by states, railroads, and speculators, ensured the settlement of the West from Texas north to the plains and the Canadian prairies by enabling settlers to claim 160 acres or more for farming.[23] President Franklin Roosevelt's New Deal housing policies increased opportunities for home ownership (Fusfeld 1956; Tobey, Wetherell, and Brigham 1990). Americanization efforts from the turn of the century to the 1930s aimed at assimilating Mexicans into a mainstream according to notions of hygiene, diet, language, work, productivity, patriotism, and cultural loyalty to forge, presumably, a stable society.[24] And scores of social scientists have devoted their scholarship to family and community studies with the intention of fleshing out why people move versus stay in one place and weave social networks and a sense of belonging.[25] These examples, among many others, have shaped values of property, home, community, and social stability—Americana defined, as Jefferson initially observed, by contrast to the circumstances of less fortunate people.

César Chávez was a beneficiary and victim of such values. His grandfather and grandmother had migrated to the United States in the 1880s to flee the poverty of Porfirio Díaz's hacienda system. They crossed the border in El Paso, settled on a 160-acre homestead in the North Gila Valley near Yuma, Arizona, and made their living from a freight business and subsistence farming. Chávez's father, Librado, who was age two when his parents migrated, became a small businessman and supported his family with a grocery store and an auto repair shop. César was born on 31 March 1927, a few years before the family's good fortune took a turn for the worse (Griswold del Castillo and Garcia 1995).

The early years of the Depression, Griswold del Castillo and Garcia explain, had little impact on the Chávez family. The family saved money made by serving the store's "built-in clientele of small landowners and farmers," independent of industrial employment (1995, 4). Librado borrowed money from a lawyer friend and bought a forty-acre lot adjacent to the store. He made payments for a few years before coming up short and falling behind on his taxes. He had to sell his store to make a partial payment on his property taxes. A few years later, still owing back taxes of $4,080, Librado appealed to the governor for relief with no success. He applied for a loan for which he was qualified under federal guidelines. The local banker and owner of an adjacent lot turned him down. On 29 August 1937, the state took possession of the Chávez property.

The family left Yuma to work on California's migratory labor circuit with hopes of earning enough money to buy back the farm and return home. César, who was age ten, recalled: "When we left the farm, our whole life was upset, turned upside down. We had been part of a very stable community, and we were about to become migrant workers. We had been uprooted" (Griswold del Castillo and Garcia 1995, 7).

THE CHÁVEZ FAMILY'S SITUATION WAS FAMILIAR TO THAT of many Mexicans who had experienced privation; they could have provided Thomas Jefferson with plenty of evidence to support his claims about social unrest and stability. In colonial New Spain, the land was concentrated in the hands of Spaniards, Creole elites, and the church—leaving, according to Alexander von Humboldt (1942), 82 percent of the population to live in misery and bear the burden of social inequality. The burden became most acute when the staple, maize, was insufficient due to agricultural crises, price increases, and, generally, economic decline from 1808 to 1810 and again in 1813. During these years, the price of maize increased from 100 to 300 percent, reflecting a decrease in production and widespread unemployment, causing homelessness, migration to the cities, epidemics, and starvation (Florescano 1969; Anna 1978). It is not surprising that the number of Hidalgo's supporters swelled from a few hundred in 1810 to nearly two million by the time the rebellion was over in 1815 (Anna 1978).

Many Americans observed Mexicans and their struggles as the century progressed; unlike Jefferson in France, they saw with unsympathetic eyes. The travel writer Lansford Hastings described the Mexicans' "ignorance" and their "savoring so strongly of barbarity, cruelty, and indolence" ([1849] 1932, 113, 129). In *Recollections of Mexico*, Waddy Thompson suggested that Mexicans had an "incentive to robbery found . . . in the absence of all restraint in its indulgence" (1846, 23). These characteristics, American writers claimed, showed in a rebuff of John Slidell, the U.S. Army envoy sent to Mexico to negotiate the annexation of Texas. The rebuff was an assault on the United States' "national honor and character" that jeopardized "high and lofty principles" (*Democratic Review* 106, April 1847, 293). In his argument for Texas's annexation, the Democratic politician John L. O'Sullivan observed that Mexicans encumbered the "natural growth" of the nation "allotted by Providence" or "manifest destiny" (*Democratic Review* 17, July–August 1845, 5, 9).[26] Enough was enough; the United States sent armies to Mexico in 1846 and by 1848 claimed Mexico's northern territories for itself, fulfilling moral obligations to the prosperity of its citizens.

This moral agenda translated into American enterprise across the U.S. Southwest and into Mexico in the late nineteenth century. Speculators and entrepreneurs, abusing the Homestead Act of 1862 and usurping Spanish and Mexican land grants, formed large ranches suitable for industrial enterprise (P. Gates 1936; Nugent 1999).[27] In Mexico, Porfirio Díaz, who became president in 1876, expropriated campesino and communal lands as part of his commercialization policies. By 1910, Díaz had expropriated 127,111,824 acres of land, leaving 98 percent of campesinos landless and creating a small landed class of 7,000 hacendados (hacienda owners) and 45,000 rancheros (midlevel landholders).[28] American and other foreign entrepreneurs became part of the Díaz land-tenure system through their capital investments in extraction industries— minerals, timber, and oil—and in plantations and ranches producing rubber, cotton, bananas, coffee, henequen, sugar, and livestock. These ranches were associated, John Mason Hart observes, "with the ports of Salina Cruz, Acapulco, Mananillo, Mazatlán, Guaymas, Campeche, Puerto México, Veracruz, Tuxpam, and Tampico, and with the entrepôts of El Paso, Brownsville, Eagle Pass, and Laredo" that linked Mexican agriculture to markets throughout the world (1998, 73). While American landholdings extended throughout Mexico, the Wheeler Land Company's 1,450,000 acres in Sonora and the Laguna Corporation's 1,350,000 acres in Chiapas being the most exemplary, the largest properties were along the coastal and frontier regions—50 percent of the north— enabling Americans to exercise a measure of power comparable to the Spaniards' in colonial New Spain (Hart 1998).

The campesinos were the object of complaint. Despite their destitution, they didn't easily forgo subsistence farming or even the oppressive peon system and acculturate to a capitalist system that demanded a "fluid and responsive labor market" and "work ethic" (Knight 1998, 59). Mexican and foreign employers, many of them Americans, observed— from their so-called progressive point of view—"indolence" and "vice" in the work force. They accused workers of being untrustworthy, not arriving or staying for work when expected. "Most of the rural poor," including peasants, day laborers, and miners, Alan Knight explains, "showed . . . a perverse list for independence, an itch to find alternatives to steady, unremitting and, above all, dependent toil." They became squatters, sharecroppers, artisans, and even beggars (Knight 1998, 61; Katz 1980; Womack 1970).

On 7 June 1911, Francisco Madero met with Zapata and other revolutionary leaders over dinner in Mexico City to clarify the revolution's objectives. Zapata, speaking for himself and his followers, made his objective clear: "What interests us is that, right away, lands be returned to the pueblos, and the promises, which the revolution made, be carried out" (Womack 1970, 96). Madero demurred, suggesting that property was a complicated issue. He also indicated the tenuousness of a coalition that would soon dissolve into popular regional insurgencies under the leadership of Pascual Orozco and Francisco Villa in the north, of Zapata in the south, and of numerous others among Mexico's rural working class throughout the country. Over a ten-year period, they produced most of the violence, drawn from campesino abjection and hunger and directed at landholding elites.

Revolutionary violence, poverty, and a history of demeaning commentaries about Mexicans guided American perceptions of people south of the border. Purveyors of American agribusiness shared these perceptions on looking to Mexico for a source of labor and in assessments of labor's value. To them, it was only natural that the value of Mexican labor was low. And moreover, Mexicans might benefit from the American labor system, which demanded timeliness, self-discipline, orderly conduct, and a measure of productivity that Mexicans had failed to achieve.

WATSONVILLE INHERITED THESE MENTALITIES AS GROWERS came to depend on Mexican labor to support regional agribusiness. From 1975 to the mid-1990s, the number of migratory farmworkers doubled Watsonville's population. The "peaceful backwater town," where "families had farmed the same land for generations," a *San Francisco Chronicle* reporter wrote, had transformed into "the kind of stuff" that "city leaders . . . had to deal with": "deteriorating schools, increasingly crowded housing, . . . souring unemployment, . . . farmworkers getting drunk on weekends, maybe urinating in public, . . . and a bloody gang war—10 gang-related shootings between June and September [of 1996], one of them, a shotgun attack that killed a 14-year-old boy."

"That kid that got shot? The 14-year-old? It was right behind my house. You've got to crack down there, those kids are there all the time," the waitress Pat Schindler told Police Chief Terry Medina while she served him a BLT sandwich and a vegetable soup in a local coffee shop.

Medina had watched Watsonville transform itself into, he said, "a lawless Wild West," a "Tombstone kind of town." While cruising the streets in his unmarked Mercury Marquis, Medina pointed out the "invisible lines" that marked divisions between local gangs engaged in their own battles reminiscent of Mexico's revolution—"the Sureño 'Poor-siders' and the Norteño 'Northsiders.' This park belongs to the Norteños, [who call themselves] 'City Hall'; [the gang] actually claims the city's civic center and police department as part of its turf." On looking over the divisions, Medina said, "They're fighting over space" (*San Francisco Chronicle*, 15 December 1996, Z1).

Mayor Betty Bobeda commented nostalgically about Watsonville, "Home, community, education, responsibility—it seems that those words are no longer a part of the American language" (*San Francisco Chronicle*, 15 December 1996, Z1).

Those words were still a part of the American language, just as they always had been since the time of Jefferson. Those words, however, lost relevance in places like Watsonville because people replaced them with other words that enabled them to interpret a change in demographics. The other words referenced the frontier and Wild West, where, Frederick Jackson Turner once believed, "out of his wilderness experience, out of the freedom of his opportunities, [the immigrant] fashioned a formula for regeneration—the freedom of the individual to seek his own" (1920, 213). As mentioned in chapter 1, Turner made these comments out of fear that the American frontier as a vast, open wilderness was coming to end. Turner thought that a means of American regeneration was dying. Turner overlooked, however, that Americans had long invested their perceptions of the frontier, its wilderness, in Mexicans. Popular writings on Mexico, congressional debates, and common talk had validated such perceptions; they'd also served to regenerate American self-awareness that accompanied the U.S.-Mexico War, annexation of Mexico's northern territories, and transformation of an arid U.S. Southwest into irrigation-fed, industrial farmland with a largely Mexican working-class population to do the work. And if the words were not enough to justify these conditions, one could look onto the poverty and revolution as evidence of something of the wilderness in Mexicans that precluded Mexican progress and realization of a civilized society.

For Mayor Bobeda, Police Chief Medina, Pat Schindler, and, arguably, other Watsonville residents, home, community, education, and responsibility indexed a civilized society. Mexican immigrants could realize this society as their own through their incorporation into the regional labor system, effectively transforming a natural resource into productivity and social order. But in the eyes of many Watsonville residents, the social experiment had gone bad. Nature had prevailed against the forces of civilization. Police officers now had to travel around in unmarked vehicles, conceding authority to gangs that carved out territories of their own and wasted them with violence.

This violence came in the face of another form of violence. The words that index the Wild West and wilderness—ignorance, barbarity, cruelty, indolence, and vice—have always seemed appropriate for their time, whether for Mexican elites in their understanding of campesinos, for American industrialists in theirs of Mexican labor, or for Watsonville residents in theirs of local youth and gang members. Based on these words, Díaz must have felt justified in his expropriation of peasant lands. Similarly, the Yuma, Arizona, banker who denied a loan to Chávez's father must have felt justified in his decision. And Watsonville residents like Pat Schindler felt justified in thoughts about area youth, the "kind of stuff" that city leaders now had to deal with. These words hold the disenfranchised responsible for their own condition. They elide the power of people who use them, people who have resources and stand to benefit from the economic system. The words also elide the shortcomings of this system, one that ensures a good measure of unemployment and a full labor pool that employers can tap at low wages.

As these words have run the course of time, they've led the powerful to make decisions in support of an economic system that benefits some and disparages many. It's always been a matter of time before such disparagement shows its face in violence. And the words of Jefferson's society—material equity, social equality, natural rights, and virtue of the citizen and democracy—hold real value only among the few who persevere to make life better for everybody despite vulnerability to the powerful.

Javier was one of these few; one could hear as much in his words. He spoke the language of employers, empathizing with their disposition to treat people not as people but as capital with a numerical value that helped produce profits. He showed employers how treatment of people as numbers might become treatment as people in mention of their names, conversation about family, and improvement of wages, reversing the effects of the economic system and restoring human dignity.

"WE ORGANIZED THIS MARCH IN 1997 AGAINST THE UFW," Javier reflected. "And it worked. The union was voted down in the election."

"We thought that it would all stop there. But it didn't; employers and workers in the area wanted us to start a nonprofit that could become active in similar situations. We started to organize. I quit my job at the nursery in Salinas. It looked promising. We were getting calls from all over the country, even as far away as Florida. But the whole thing turned into a political mess. There were employees of growers in the organization. I kept thinking that we needed to maintain a neutral position because the union was claiming that we were run by the growers. And that would have been illegal. There was a case brought against the organization, and I had to testify on behalf of the union against the growers."

DEATH

The Passion play approached the end. Jesus stood high above the audience, mounted on a cross, his hands holding stakes and his feet supported by a small wooden platform. The audience was silent. Children sat still and stared at the spectacle, overwhelmed by the sense of reality that took them back to the biblical period, to the moment when their faith began. Jesus cried out, "Father, forgive them; for they know not what they do" (Luke 23:34 RSV). A few moments passed, and Jesus said that he was thirsty. Some bystanders ran up to Jesus with a sponge soaked with vinegar and tried to make him drink. Weary, Jesus said his final words, "My God, my God, why hast thou forsaken me?" (Matt. 27:46 RSV).

THE TRIAL TAUGHT JAVIER ABOUT HOW POWER WORKS. Whether it is the economic, government, or juridical system, each system is a way for people with status and resources to sacrifice those without these attributes and meet political objectives.

"So we moved to Fresno," Javier said. "I have tried to just leave that work [in Watsonville] alone; just let it rest. I was a little depressed. I didn't know it though. I was just dealing with all of these things of the past three years."

"I am much better now. I bought a yard care business. My wife and I have learned to live with a lot less. I have thought about getting back into human resources. The money would be a lot better. But, then we'd have to move and give up what we have found here."

"What do you mean?" I asked.

"Do you know Juan?" Javier began to explain. "He told me about the [prayer group] a long time ago. I met him, and he asked me what I play. When I said bass, he said, 'Oh, you have to join us. We could really use a bass.' You know that the drums that Juan plays and the bass go together. They are like the walls, and the rest, the melody, it is just decoration. I didn't think about coming to play for a long time. And then, I ran into Juan, and he asked me to come. And my wife, she goes to the group and asked me to come a few times. I had never been a church-going guy. But, I decided to come and have been here ever since. The Lord, I guess, had this in mind for me. Maybe that's why he had me learn to play music a long time ago. So that one day I would end up playing with the prayer group."

Javier's move to Fresno came with novel orientation in relation to people who live there and attend Saint Anthony's. The bass and drums that were "like the walls" suggest the texture of this experience—a feeling of support and rhythm. Javier's comment about having learned to "play music," the Lord's "plan," and events "a long time ago" indicates his awareness of temporal continuity that culminates in the present. Javier underwent a perceptual, attitudinal, or psychological adjustment by changing his focus from circumstances where he could never achieve a neutral position to those where he could. In these new circumstances, he became a part of something free from manipulation and larger than his individuality, always within reach and felt but unseen, which he came to recognize through music and membership in the prayer group.

TO UNDERSTAND THIS CHANGE, I'D LIKE TO RETURN TO Watsonville and the specter that haunted the UFW's campaign. César Chávez had died on 23 April 1993, and his absence was felt among the labor leaders. The newspapers noted his absence with the headline "After Chavez, Farm Union Struggles to Find New Path" and the subtitle "Its Founder Gone, a Union Faces an Identity Crisis" (*New York Times*, 19 July 1993).

But what was this "new path" and "identity"? As suggested above, the path led to a variety of religious, national, and folkloric symbols. The path also led to different kinds of people, including teachers, ironworkers, firefighters, nurses, carpenters, activists, and a Hollywood celebrity. All of these things gave an impression that the union had achieved unity and new life. The new life appeared disconnected from the farmworkers and, at the same time, close to farmworker reality.

The "new path" was an old one that Chávez had struggled against most of his life. The path led to a kind of market. In a market, people buy and sell commodities with an underlying desire for each exchange to breathe new life into the system. Farmworkers knew this market well as they'd had to sell their labor in exchange for low wages that inversely helped other people, including growers and consumers, prosper. Similarly, the UFW asked farmworkers for support in exchange for eventual representation that had little to do with them and, inversely, much to do with the union. The union had become a brand compiled by a variety of labels that lacked substance of the farmworkers themselves, their abjection and struggle. And Chávez, like the ghost of Hamlet's father, reappeared as an admonition of a society gone astray.

One might ask about the nature of Chávez's death to yield a better understanding of its aftermath. Chávez had died after a three-day fast to gain "moral strength" while testifying in the UFW's appeal against a $5.4 million award to Bruce Church, Inc. (Griswold del Castillo and Garcia

1995, 173).[29] Chávez had undertaken many fasts during his lifetime to enrich his personal spirituality and gain clarity of vision as a foundation for his activism (Lloyd-Moffett 2008).

Two long fasts stand out as the most noteworthy. Chávez initiated one in 1968 with two objectives in mind: to "dramatize the pain and suffering of the farm workers," and to deter the movement from violence and encourage nonviolence (D. Gates 1993, 68). Growers had had thugs beat strikers on picket lines. Chávez feared retaliation: "I thought that I had to bring the Movement to a halt, do something that would force [the farmworkers] and me to deal with the whole question of violence and ourselves. We had to stop long enough to take account of what we were doing" (Griswold del Castillo and Garcia 1995, 84). Chávez began a second long fast on 16 July 1988, in the Tehachapi Mountains near Bakersfield to draw attention to farmworkers suffering due in particular to pesticide exposure (Griswold del Castillo and Garcia 1995).

Chávez's concern about pesticides had peaked in 1968, when a crew of farmworkers became violently ill after entering a grape field. The field had been sprayed with the chemical parathion thirty-three days earlier. Parathion was one of a new generation of organophosphates that replaced chlorinated hydrocarbons such as DDT. "Initially developed," Robert Gordon explains, "for use as biological weapons during World War II, organophosphates appealed to growers because of their short life-spans" while ensuring crop productivity (1999, 57; Moses 1993; Namba et al. 1971). Niagara Chemical Company and Chemagro Corporation, with the consent of the California Department of Agriculture, supported the claim about the transience of organophosphates by conducting their own study between May 1970 and March 1971. The study used farmworkers and their families to determine the "safe period" between chemical application and reentry into the fields.[30] As in congressional testimonies supporting the use of DDT (which did not prevail with the Pesticide Control Act of 1971), industry experts and congressional representatives claimed that the danger of pesticides lay in their "misuse" or "reckless" and "improper" application.[31] Niagara and Chemagro's experiments showed farmworkers to be careless and irrational and therefore eligible for treatment that most people would not subject themselves or their families to.[32]

The legacy of organophosphates has persisted to recent times. Federal law requires licensed supervision of application and a waiting period before field reentry. These conditions, however, do not preclude poisoning. The most common form of poisoning is drift: "the movement of pesticides away from the site of application." Drift occurs with approximately "85 to 95 percent of pesticides applied as broadcast sprays" and affects "birds, bees, fish, and . . . human beings" (Moses 1998, 596). In California, physicians received 2,111 reports of poisoning in 1993 and 1,995 in 1994. Respectively, 1,307 and 448 were occupational exposures; the organophosphates phosdrin and parathion were the most predominant contributors (596). "Organophosphates," Marion Moses reports, "are responsible for the majority of occupational poisonings and deaths from pesticides in the United States and throughout the world" (577).

Organophosphates function like nerve gas. They poison humans. Symptoms appear between five minutes and twelve hours after exposure, depending on the route and degree of exposure. The symptoms include fatigue, headache, dizziness, numbness of extremities, nausea, vomiting, tightness in the chest, abdominal cramps, and diarrhea (Brender and Suarez 1990). Severe exposure causes respiratory failure and death (Namba et al. 1971, 481). Government studies have found that parathion causes malignant tumors in laboratory animals (*Los Angeles Times*, 19 August 1988, A1). Franklin M. M. White and fellow researchers (1988) found evidence of a link between agricultural chemicals on the one hand and birth defects and stillbirths on the other. During the 1980s, journalists reported more frequently than in previous decades about cancer clusters in the San Joaquin Valley (Ferriss and Sandoval 1997).

During the 1988 fast, César Chávez remained quiet, in a small room, reading the Bible and books by Gandhi and Martin Luther King Jr. (*Los Angeles Times*, 19 August 1988, A1). He drank only water. His most rapid weight loss occurred during the first few days and ultimately averaged from half a pound to a pound per day. Chávez benefited from a "healing crisis"; fasting enables the body to cleanse itself and eliminate toxins. The process, however, increases toxin levels temporarily and causes fatigue, headaches, aches, swelling, abdominal cramps, and vomiting.[33] Chávez suffered from "escalating bouts" of these symptoms and lost a total of thirty-three pounds (*New York Times*, 22 August 1988, A12). By 10:30 a.m., 21 August, the final day of the fast, more than seven thousand people had gathered outside his room to participate in a silent struggle. At least 80 percent were farmworkers. When Chávez appeared, he requested that nobody applaud. His two sons carried him to a rocking chair, where he sat among his supporters and assisted in a Mass (Hoffman 1988; Plummer 1988).

The fasts marked a change from a verbal to a nonverbal code. Similar to linguistic codes, the fasts consisted of signs, referents, and signification germane to intentions and ostensive circumstances. Chávez endured ailments, atrophy, and enervation to purge toxins that he had internalized. At the same time, he freed himself from dialogue with his detractors, avoiding the trappings such as those that induce thugs to beat farmworkers or farmworkers to retaliate. The fasts accounted for ways of expression that reversed the effects of violence and, most fundamentally, enabled one to claim dominium, as in liberty and control over one's own body.

This act involved a paradox. Chávez claimed control over his body only to sacrifice it for others, galvanizing solidarity necessary for pragmatic objectives. In July and August 1988, thousands gave up work during the peak harvest season to join Chávez in his struggle that was also their struggle, drawing attention to themselves as a collective body in silent prayer and celebration.

On moving to Fresno, Javier undertook a different code, leaving the old one relating to human resources to rest. The new one, like "rhythm" and "walls," helped ensure his integration into what he'd found in Fresno, people at Saint Anthony's whom he now supported, contributing to the quality of their lives, which became his own.

THE RESTING PLACE

Joseph of Arimathea took Jesus and wrapped him in burial cloths with spices according to the Jewish custom. In the place where Jesus was crucified, John informs us, "there was a garden, and in the garden a new tomb where no one had ever been laid. So . . . they laid Jesus there" (John 19:41–42 RSV).

I HAD SPOKEN TO JAVIER VERY LITTLE BEFORE OUR CONVERSATION during the Passion play on Palm Sunday in 2001. Of course, we had greeted each other often in passing, using the familiar term "brother." Apart from these encounters, I knew Javier through his role in the prayer group and, as he said, through "something special" that he "found at Saint Anthony's." Javier appeared every Wednesday evening in the back of the band, playing his bass, setting the beat, and keeping the rhythm.

To Javier, this role came naturally, meaning that he didn't think much about it. That is, until he was reminded of the anguish and horror of undergoing a somatic and subjective transformation that initiates a novel orientation in the world. As he recalled, it happened while he was playing at Fresno State University: "I was just playing, not thinking about anything. And then I heard this screaming; it was really strong, kind of hurt my ears. I looked and saw this woman on the ground. [My friend's] wife was praying over her. She was turning on the ground. She turned maybe three times. . . . The Lord works in powerful ways."

ON 29 APRIL 1993, AN ESTIMATED THIRTY-FIVE THOUSAND people participated in a funeral procession. They formed a line over three miles long and walked one behind another in a steady procession from Memorial Park in Delano, California, to the UFW's office north of town, where they assisted in a Mass. The people walked in memory of the man who had taught them about relentless labor, self-sacrifice, and hope in a better, equitable society.

The day before the funeral, the people kept a vigil over an open casket. An old man approached the casket with a young child. He lifted the child above his head and enabled him to peer down on the "small, grey-haired man who lay inside." He said, "I'm going to tell you about this man someday," and thereby explained the terms of a legacy (Matthiessen 1993, 82). The old man would tell the child about how César Chávez undertook pilgrimages, marches, and fasts to bring people together, keep them from driving each other apart, and fulfill the promise of a better, civil American society.

THE PASSION PLAY ENDED, AND THE PROCESSION REENACTING the Via Dolorosa wound back to Saint Anthony's parking lot, where the participants dispersed to find their families. Children took over the stage and began their own performances, parents glancing over from time to time with warnings about falling off. People milled around, enjoyed the taste of Mexican sweet breads and the company of others. The palm leaves in each person's hand bobbed in open air. Alfredo Reyes, the church's caretaker who had just finished walking the Via Dolorosa, approached, greeted Javier and me, and stood for a moment leaning against the iron fence that protected the rose garden. Alfredo said: "Do you hear that sound?" referring to the myriad of footsteps and of wondering voices. "That's the sound of Jesus."[34]

The day was warm without a hint of summer, just as it should have been.

PILGRIMAGE

SIX

It appears that we have been on a long journey.

The people who open their hearts have led us along the way, showing us their steps forward, backward, and always in procession. Recall how the Matachines rotated in opposite directions and integrated crossovers and exchanges while preparing for their trip to Tepeyac, Mexico, to visit Our Lady of Guadalupe. They gathered in Saint Anthony's parking lot, their parents helping them with suitcases and giving them snacks of tamales, Mexican sweet breads, chips, and Coca-Cola—enough to pass the time amusingly while traveling south by bus through Bakersfield, Los Angeles, and San Bernadino to Mexicali, where they would cross the border, just as their parents, friends, and acquaintances had done when heading north from Sonora, Sinaloa, Guanajuato, and Michoacán.

In anticipation of the trip, the dancers mingled in Saint Anthony's environs and looked at the mural of Juan Diego leading a procession. Many also stood by the fountain with the tile mural of Juan Diego kneeling before the apparition, his mantle full of red roses, the fine image of Our Lady impregnating its coarse fibers. These legendary images are signs of social memory that have directed pilgrims to Our Lady since her apparition in 1531 and have enabled them to see themselves in the image of perfection: a step forward that is also a step backward when one faces another.

Despite the festivity, don't be fooled; these steps represent, as César Chávez said, "a long, long struggle" (Griswold del Castillo and Garcia 1995, 51). To appreciate the magnitude of this struggle, face the Matachines as they have faced me. Flavia Waters Champe (1983) says that I have the "caricature of the white man's way of dress. [My] clothing is old and assembled in a ludicrous manner." I wear a mask that expresses "grotesque facial reproductions." A knotted rope is wrapped around my waist, cinching up a loose coat, "giving the effect of a priest's cassock." And I keep a stick or crude whip handy for El Toro, whom I lead around on a leash. I am familiar with the dance steps, as I have danced alongside the Matachines. Surely, I have gotten some of the steps right. However, when I was so bold in my antics as to give the Matachines direction, they laughed and indicated that I had missed the point so clearly visible in my portrayal of priest; conquistador; *vaquero*, or cowboy; and rancher among other actors who have played leading roles in colonial history.

El Toro represents another prominent actor in colonial history. His name is elusive, and his impressions on people, mixed. Spanish herders first brought cattle from the Iberian Peninsula and the Canary Islands to the New World by way of Española (Dominican Republic and Haiti) (Morrisey 1951). The herders came from rural Spain, where the population had been growing for generations and agricultural resources had become scarce. For them, New Spain meant new opportunities for investing in cattle that could feed the armies enforcing royal policy (Bishko 1952; Butzer 1988). At first, they brought few cattle (far fewer than sheep). But between 1538 and 1540, cattle herds multiplied at an alarming rate, particularly on the central plateau, where herders took advantage of a Castilian custom that held grass to be a gift of nature. Municipal authorities, many of them cattle barons, granted cattlemen *estancias*, or grazing rights, that made pastures and untilled fields into open ranges (Chevalier 1963).[1] Cattlemen first stalked the Toluca Valley, for example, in 1535. Within twenty years, the region consisted of more than sixty estancias and boasted more than 150,000 head of cattle and horses belonging to local dignitaries (Chevalier 1963, 93). The herds overran the countryside and destroyed maize, leaving Indians destitute and forcing them to flee into the mountains. François Chevalier documents similar events near Tepeapulco and Jilotepec, constituting a demographic transformation in the regions around Mexico City. Agrarian communities became vagrant populations; the bull, responsible for the proliferation of vast herds, became a metaphor for claims to place and displacement, settlement and transience, opulence and deprivation.

In 1549, Viceroy Luis de Velasco ordered cattlemen to drive their herds north, thereby removing them from fertile regions around Mexico City; the bull as a metaphor, characterizing the lives of ranchers, Indians, and campesinos, came to fruition. Mexico's northern regions between the infamous mines in Zacatecas and Guanajuato were arid and sparsely populated by Indians. Some of these inhabitants were settled, and most, nomadic. The central government delegated its authority to "private citizens," who paid the costs of colonization in exchange for large tracts of land (Baretta and Markoff 1978, 591; Chevalier 1963). These citizens drove large herds across the countryside and thus assured the "European animals," says Richard J. Morrisey, of a "permanent footing and furnished a link between the wars of conquest and the widespread grazing economy of modern America" (1951, 115).

The cattle herds caused the uprooted Indians to orient their lives around horses. Many Indians, Chevalier comments about sixteenth-century Mexico, "obtained the viceroy's permission to keep, pack, and saddle horses," thereby becoming an integral part of the frontier economy and setting a precedent for future generations (1963, 94). Indians and mestizos had few options—enslavement on encomiendas, peonage on ranches, or vagrancy—because of racial prejudice that dictated public policy. The majority chose vagrancy by becoming horsemen and working in various capacities. Some became vaqueros, working for the cattlemen. Many more became formidable warriors, attacking poorly defended ranches and military outposts. Others became mediators by negotiating peace with Spanish officials and cattle barons, only to fight another day on the side of insurgents (Baretta and Markoff 1978). In the eighteenth century, some horsemen made their living from banditry, smuggling, or serving as frontier police (Baretta and Markoff 1978). Porfirio Díaz recruited horsemen from all parts of Mexico's countryside to serve as police and shore up an economic climate suitable to foreign (American) investment. And during the Mexican revolution, Francisco Villa and Emiliano Zapata recruited horsemen who fought to dismantle

Díaz's autocracy and restore the land to the pueblos (Vanderwood 1992; Nájera-Ramírez 1994). In all cases, the horsemen had plenty of cheap meat for sustenance. Vagrancy translated into fluid identities—vaquero, peacemaker, warrior, bandit, smuggler, police officer, revolutionary— that contrasted with missionary objectives of establishing a sedentary Christian peasantry. The fluid identities also threatened Spanish and Mexican elite hegemony and provided a population with a sense of liberty within systemic oppression.

IN THE PLAZA OUTSIDE THE BASILICA OF OUR LADY OF Guadalupe, twelve Matachines carrying rattles, tridents, and fans separated evenly into two lines and moved forward and backward. One line mirrored the other. And El Toro approached their leader. He told her the policies about going inside to see Our Lady, about the costumes, and about disturbing others. And the dance quickened as it had done for centuries.

REMEMBER ALFREDO REYES, WHOM FATHER ALBA DESCRIBED as a part of the church in body and soul. In church language, such comments mean that he was a part of "us," a member of the faith participating in retreats, the Mass, and meals, "kneeling before the cross in deep prayer," and doing his handyman work. Seeing Alfredo meant seeing a reflection of one's self and calling him "brother"; it meant greeting him with a handshake or a hug. This harmony, however, came to an end when an office manager acknowledged with keen interest a small detail that tapped into more than one hundred years of popular talk: Alfredo hadn't "arranged his papers." The "illegal alien" was capable of turning against his friends, as Mexico had always turned against the United States and as Mexicans had always turned against Americans. This perspective heightens by contrast American identification with work, language, hygiene, property, social stability, and cultural loyalty.

Father Alba let Alfredo go. Alfredo stayed away, holed up in his small apartment, where he was no longer an apparent threat. The parish restored order according to an American cultural grammar that accompanied the faith of its parishioners. Like the bull, faith is a source of universal sustenance that nourishes peaceful coexistence—that is, until faith turns against its bearers, draws its battle lines, and separates insiders from outsiders, us from others.

In the southeast Fresno neighborhood around Saint Anthony's, congregations drew similar battle lines, just as people had drawn them in the cultivation of a California pastoral. For the Californios of the nineteenth century, pastoral California was an ideal conception of the past where diverse members of the population shared a common identity through their experiences with the land, work, language, religion, family, and, most significantly, through a shared understanding of history (R. Sánchez 1995). The Californios who participated in the Bancroft interviews gleaned this conception as an afterthought in a common mental space well fortified against the Anglo insurgents who had migrated to the region by overland routes and made claims to the land and political power in the aftermath of the U.S.-Mexican War. Bancroft himself shared this conception of paradise, but only as it might have existed before the Mexican administration (1821–48) and Californio tenure. To him, Californios wasted the land and caused society's decline because of racial ineptitude. Bancroft's conception of this lost paradise justified the Anglo hegemony of his time—the cultivation of a better California according to a modern economy, and the permanent relegation of Mexican residents (and other people of color) to ensure that they would never waste the land again.

In Fresno, Pastors Alvarez of La Gracia Church, Pérez of the Nazarene Church, Rosales of the Pentecostal Church, and Lopez of the Rapto Divino Church were aware of Bancroft's legacy. They ministered to people with few options in life—gangsters selling drugs and controlling the neighborhood, patrons of a nearby tavern, street kids, "throwaways," the incarcerated—by providing them with a conception of an ideal place where people lived in harmony. They called this place love and went about making it real by telling stories designed to break down barriers separating people and by inducing affection that keeps them together.

The barriers that separate people—Anglos and Mexicans, gangsters and law enforcement, the prosperous and the deprived—are never straightforward. Pastor White of the Assembly of God Church revealed an ambiguity about divisions in his comment about the fence that had enclosed his church for generations: "And yet inside, the property was real run down. The grass was brown. Everything looked bad; it looked seedy. . . . And when I was behind it, I felt like the people who walked past, I felt separated. I felt like, 'O.K. I'm *out* here and you're *in* there.' We had an attitude of, 'Well, you stay *out* there and we'll stay *in* here. We'll have church and we'll be happy.'"[2]

Pastor White's inversion of the prepositions "in" and "out" suggests that a person on the inside is also on the outside. These circumstances show in the way people understand and treat each other. People identify one another according to evaluations that carry over to categories of work, home, institutions of incarceration, and, as in this case, the space of a church. This way of assigning values and allowing them to index areas of experience resembles what people do in a market to create conditions conducive for the exchange of commodities—goods and services, including labor. It is as if markets train people how to treat each other, not for what they are, for whatever history plays a role in their formation as people, but for perceptions of differences in value. And these perceptions are reinforced through ways of speaking along the lines of racial stereotypes, prejudice, and discrimination, distinguishing one person from another, and often justifying claims to wealth and giving reasons for poverty. People's interactions, markets, and ways of speaking account for mutually reinforcing patterns that often culminate in violence—between Mexico and the United States, landholders and revolutionaries, law enforcement and farmworkers, and neighborhood gangs—that leaves everything looking "seedy" and "run down" and everybody "feeling" like each other.

Recall, also, that for Pastor White; his wife, Cory; and the members of the congregation, faith was their means of recognizing this human condition. The fence had wrapped around their hearts, making them feel self-contained and separating them from the rest of the world and their pursuit of happiness. They prayed. They prayed some more for about six months and realized that the fence had to come down.

Like faith, the bull has played a role in human degradation that changes to bonds of affection and hope in the future. After the Revolution of 1910, the Mexican government dismantled the hacienda system and made campesinos into communal and small landowners. The majority of the campesinos remained without prospects in agriculture and migrated to urban centers for work. Likewise, the horsemen, who had transformed the country, had fewer prospects than ever. Olga Nájera-Ramírez reminds us, however, that the Mexican people did not forget the horsemen, or *charros*, and made them into a national symbol that combined nostalgia for "traditional" rural life, "national identity, and democratic ideals" (1994, 5, 6). The charro made a north-of-the-border, 1894 debut in Buffalo Bill's Wild West Show, showcasing Mexican horse life for American consumption. In the 1920s, enthusiasts established the Asociación Nacional (National Association), which, with the Federación Nacional de Charros (National Federation of Horsemen), established in 1933, fashioned standards for public performances and made *charrería* (horse-riding skills) into a national sport. Film, music, and stage productions featured the charro to audiences in Mexico, the U.S. Southwest, or greater Mexico (Nájera-Ramírez 1994).[3] Despite the commercial influence that standardized charrería through a blend of regional distinctions, the charro is a story about bulls and people oppressed under colonialism and united through, as César Chávez said, "a long, long struggle" (Griswold del Castillo and Garcia 1995, 51).[4]

THE MATACHINES FACED EACH OTHER, MOVING FORWARD, sometimes backward, and in procession. They wore a headdress in the shape of a bishop's miter. Two pheasant feathers affixed to the back rose high above their heads. The miter, quite possibly, came from the bishop who led the expulsion-conversion of the Moors on the Iberian Peninsula in the fifteenth century, introduced Christianity to the New World with hopes of harvesting new souls for the kingdom of God, and accompanied Hernando Cortés as a passive and, sometimes, forceful arm of conquest.[5] The feathers, quite possibly, belonged to the feathered serpent called Motecuhzoma or Quetzalcóatl. He was a messiah-like figure who would return after a long exile, defeat the oppressors, and liberate the people. In all cases, the dancers reflected the people whom they had met along the way to Our Lady of Guadalupe, in whose basilica they would rest and gaze at the image of their perfection.

THE JOURNEY HAS PROCEEDED ALONG A PATH WITH SIGNS indicating turns and moments of confusion that give way to clarity.

Recall Eva Gonzales's walk through the labyrinth, through the under-world of a classical and medieval conception, or simply through her life. She passed by many signs—the tomb, heart, and rose—that broached stories about a mother's death, devastating fires, unfulfilled desires, trails of blood, and quiet moments of solace. Consider, for example, the rose. Its hue formed a trail of blood leading from her aunt's and uncle's bodies in the Malaga living room, "35 drops that stretched . . . out to the street, 50 feet to the street corner, and then another 100 feet down Grand Street" (*Fresno Bee*, 1 February 2000). Imagine, as the *Fresno Bee* re-ported, the crime—the "spectacular fight," multiple stabbings—and the victims: "the elderly couple," fifty-year residents on Calvin Street, just across from the Catholic church. The media told the story by drawing on a way of speaking that reflected a social psyche; the ideal, faithful, neigh-borhood matriarch and patriarch called people to self-awareness to be accentuated by a visceral yet elusive brutality, not-self, or other. Abstract yet meaningful enough, the way of speaking is a vehicle for drawing people together into a common frame of mind. Yet, like the market, this frame of mind involves forgetting relationships, how one comes to know friends, neighbors, or, in this case, an aunt and uncle, bringing about terms of endearment. One forfeits memory of the past to become a part of a public persona or image with provisional value, a persona that fits circumstances at hand (Warner 1993). No wonder Eva was quite beside herself when she heard the news about the slain "elderly couple," not able to connect them with her aunt and uncle.

Eva experienced a form of alienation; the public self with all of its predictable manners represented a separation from her past with an aunt, an uncle, and even with the killer, who turned out to be her cousin's son. She knew them through family gatherings, first communions, quin-ceañeras, and stories about children, friends, and past generations in other parts of California, in Arizona, and in Mexico that made up a part of her past, not necessarily understood through words but through the feelings words evoked, an intuitive understanding, making her world cohesive.

To better understand this orientation, its verbal yet intuitive, tacit, and sensual characteristics, recall that Eva's faltering was momentary. Before long she was at the rosary for her aunt and uncle. For her, the rosary was "creepy"; people didn't seem as usual. They exchanged gazes and suspicions, trying desperately with watchful eyes to sort out the good from the bad. Eva's own father was caught up in the evaluation; the rosary women were repulsed by his relation to the victims, his sharing the same bloodline and, quite possibly, his association with the horror that had descended upon the family. The familiar became strange. The sense of community, however provisional it might have been at a rosary, dissipated in an economy of good and evil that determined interpersonal exchanges according to categories of us and them, of comfort and abjection.

Eva found this rosary "creepy" because she identified with a different rosary: the biblical stories about Mary, her son Jesus, and the miracles that defined their lives and their faith. This rosary reflected a hue onto her life that refracted through the convent windows, where we spent our days of contemplative prayer; through the sacred heart of Jesus; through the prayers that lay at his feet; and through Chartres' *specula*, or optical lenses, which became the lenses of Saint Lucy, of my son, Alejandro, and of this book's performance.

The hue also refracted through the rose that marked the place where Eva's mother was buried, indicating its proximity to a maternal place. For Eva, going there meant wheeling back through her life in recollections about her marriage, the dreams of a good life in California, her parents on the migratory labor circuit, the wages they earned, and back even further to her father's home in Michoacán, her mother's in Mesa, Arizona, the fire that burned the house down, and the Bohemian figurine of the Christ Child found in the embers. Each step back meant reliving something—an event, relationship, and object—that Eva identified with before stripping it away to move back even further beyond her life and into the lives of past generations. This process entailed proceeding toward origins, approaching the death of one's self-awareness in small increments and being in the world with others. The rosary was all about being in a place that was "personal" yet "mindful of others," as Sister Mary of the Sister Disciples of the Divine Master reminded us. This place was circular, yet "the circumference was nowhere" and the center, "everywhere."[6]

Gracie Romana Adame also took us to this place. She talked about it figuratively, through stories about her grandfather, whom Pancho

Villa's men saved from assassination; about her grandmother, who would tell a little girl that somebody loved her; about youth who reconciled conflicts with their fathers; and about a young artist who came to her with street affectations and left her with a portrait of Jesus. No matter where these stories went—to a revolutionary Mexico or to children who felt unwanted—they always circled back to Gracie being mindful of others. The stories enabled Gracie to discern social wounds. Through the ritual of telling stories, she brought into relief all of the "tensions and aggressions" of the society's interrelations (V. Turner 1967, 392). She lined up the sides of differences and worked them back and forth in a rhythmic-like motion, creating a stream of affect that flowed toward the center of her life as reflected through other people's lives: the sacred center called love.

We are all familiar with this stream, Gracie assured us. She told us about it when I asked her where she first learned about love. She represented the stream through her description of the drive leading to the orphanage, where she had spent a part of her childhood. It was a "long, long drive," Gracie recalled. "You start going up like that. You see the trees. And there's just one straight road, and you turn around and come out again." This journey entailed pictures of "Mary," "Mary holding the baby," the symbol of all mothers and feelings of intimacy and warmth that Gracie also found in her friend, an Anglo girl; in a splash of warm water; and in a smile.[7]

Ironically, the "long, long drive" that "you start going up" until "you turn and come out again" also led to fear. Gracie represented this emotion through her experience of separation from her mother, the slam of the orphanage door, and the cold water with which the sisters told her to bathe her friend. This irony that juxtaposes intimacy/separation, warmth/cold, or love/fear is precisely the point. The irony defines a space that involves empathy with diverse drives, motives, and mentalities—often, constructed from perceptions of race and class—that express the tensions separating people as well as connecting them. In this position, Gracie was able to work out the tensions by drawing on their linguistic expression, attitudes, and emotional content and incorporating them into stories, which became a means of reflection and understanding.

Indeed, we are all familiar with the stream; most of us have traveled down it at least once. But to travel down this stream once again is altogether a different matter. One can easily miss the stream because the experience of travel down it is indirect. One experiences travel down the stream through the politics of war, property, immigration, labor, or, in the juridical language of the Spanish conquest, the politics of dominium. The people who open their hearts demonstrate a way to recognize this stream. The way entails a counterintuitive move, stepping in the opposite direction from the one that you would think of when the politics get tough, when the union comes to town and clashes with locals, when the wages drop and force campesinos to live in coffin-shaped caves, or when campesino families become random samples for pesticide safety tests.

Javier Martinez demonstrated this step. He retreated to an alternative space that contrasted with the one where he worked in "human resources," where people manipulated others according to assessments of value. Javier showed the way to arrive at this space through his role in the band. He played bass and tapped the beat of parishioners. Many of them were campesinos. They labored daily in the fields. Some had year-round employment in agriculture's satellite industries, and some with their small businesses. He also tapped the ways he'd been in touch with their lives, either directly or indirectly. One way traced his own steps in migratory labor that had led to his union membership under César Chávez. Another way centered on his convictions about property rights, natural rights, and about outsiders solving local problems. He might not have identified these things, as I have done, in view of Enlightenment values. But he did acknowledge how values stir people to take sides as he had done when the UFW came to Watsonville, creating conditions for the powerful to use the powerless and sustain the status quo.

Javier's step became a stream, enabling him to glean the affections of those whom he met along the way. In time, he met me and, I'm sure, my friend Devon Sanders. He heard Devon's hurtful comments, taking them with aplomb as he told his story in a natural and forceful style. This way of telling came from experience of having played many roles and adopted mentalities to work through the differences and emerge seasoned, as a native, a person truly belonging to this region and a role model for the rest.

What makes Javier different from other people—politicians, growers, and valley residents—who might claim native status is accountability. His step back from the events in Watsonville and into the band where he played bass indicated an effort to deal with the politics, the violence, and himself. Whether through intuitive responses, attitudes, racial prejudice, or class affiliation, Javier entertained the positions of others, often unwittingly and often wittingly. And in doing so, he tapped into a structure of feeling necessary to raise the positions of others with all of their intricacies and contradictions to consciousness and raise his understanding of being in the world (Williams 1977).

Indeed, Javier had a long way to go. His journey in many respects had just begun. However, he was in the stream of affect, feeling the structure, moving forward, sometimes backward, and in procession with Eva Gonzales, Juanita Ramirez, Gracie Romana Adame, Alfredo Reyes, and many others who kept the beat, walked in the rhythm of each other, and learned, as César Chávez said, "to endure a long, long struggle" in the name of passion.

INSIDE THE BASILICA OF OUR LADY OF GUADALUPE, THE Matachines stood for a moment in the back, in the aisle between two rows of pews leading to the altar, where Juan Diego's mantle with Our Lady's fine image hung for all to see. El Toro was with them but had sloughed his roles as priest, conquistador, rancher, cattle baron, vaquero, politician, and journalist among others. He had lost the oppression-driven virility that accompanied roles of the powerful. He had become a companion and universal means of sustenance, no longer telling the Matachines what to do or how to do it. He had joined the Matachines in their pilgrimage by making the sign of the cross, lowering himself to his knees, and shuffling forward slowly, head bowed.

Upon arriving to the altar, where they had rails, the Matachines stopped, most remained kneeling, some stood. It was so emotional to see her up there. She came out of the picture and hugged them, a perfect moment, when a perfect being embraced her incarnation. It was beautiful.

Then, the Matachines went outside, in their costumes, with their feathers. And they danced.

CONCLUSION

The Matachines teach us the steps of a procession. The etymology of "procession" references the Latin word *processio*, which means progress. In the twelfth century, people used the word in relation to religious events, indicating a column of marching people, action of proceeding, and emanation of the Holy Spirit. In contemporary times, people define "procession" in relation to going along in an orderly succession as part of a ceremony.[1] The Matachines' steps are always about going along and facing another in orderly succession with moves forward, sometimes backward, as if they were physiological pathways that were also cognitive ones for a journey and apprehension of a full range of possibilities.

Parishioners of Saint Anthony's undertook a similar journey at a parish council meeting in January of 2001. In the back room of a social hall, eight or nine people sat around a table and clasped hands. They took turns praying the Our Father. They prayed the Hail Mary. They traveled back to the time of Jesus in the garden, of Jesus at the pillar, and when he received a crown of thorns, among other events that make up the rosary's sorrowful mysteries. The events also led to others; parishioners announced special intentions in relation to an event or condition— an upcoming retreat, a friend's battle with cancer, and so forth. Parishioners evoked different events involving formal characteristics, which in this case were those of irony as found in the mysteries. Jesus, the innocent, experienced the sins of the world and the scourge of his detractors. And in their proclamation of Jesus as king, Jesus experienced abjection. These instances of persecution highlighted Jesus's individuality and loneliness, only to bring about empathy and unity. Parishioners clasped hands as yet another formal characteristic that helped create a path, a way of proceeding, toward a full range of experiences.

The Matachines and parishioners showed that ritual frames stories. The stories might be about biblical times, experiences of past generations, or recent events. In all cases, the ritual frame constitutes a dynamic structure that helps people align disparate times and places into a cohesive impression endowed with moral and spiritual value. Such is an underlying thesis that I've attempted to support through numerous examples in the preceding chapters.

I've also attempted to support an explicit thesis, something about why people practice religion, their ability to approach origins—mythological, historical, and social—and account for the sacred center of all the stories that define their lives and, unfortunately, social pathology. The rituals provide a conceptual frame that highlights different elements of these stories, including tradition, language, and symbols, for submission to treatment aimed at working out tensions separating people and shoring up bonds holding them together. Like the claim about ritual and stories, this one about approaching origins highlights the role of ritual in cultivating social cohesion with moral and spiritual endowment.

To say what's going on might still fall short of satisfying a reader who turns attention toward the two questions that were most immediate every time I got involved in religious activities: Why do these people practice religion? What is the role of rituals that define their religion? Sometimes short answers aren't good enough because they amount to just information.

In the pages that follow, I take up the questions again with a different approach. I address research participants as if they were dancers and facing others in writings on Latino/a religion. At the same time, I consider participants in view of previous anthropological and philosophical writings. The approach, then, follows the Matachines by acknowledging different kinds of counterparts and moving in step, sometimes forward, sometimes backward, and always in procession. The approach brings into relief and celebrates answers and, moreover, an impression that constitutes the participants' afterlife, something, I believe, they would have liked readers to take away from reading about their lives.

DEVOTIONAL SPACE

The days had become short in anticipation of cool mornings in the San Joaquin Valley, laden with a thick layer of fog. I approached the door of Gracie Romana Adame's white stucco home; the door's black sheet metal perforated with fine holes allowed one to see out but not in. I stood on her porch and heard a soft voice, "Hola, mi hijo," followed by the insertion of a key into a lock, the slide of a dead bolt, the opening of a door, a step into an entryway, and a warm embrace.[2] The entryway led to Gracie's living room, with a window and curtains drawn, allowing heat from the morning sun to penetrate and leaving the light dim. We sat on a sofa and talked about the rosary and a journey that Gracie was so involved in.

I'd been in such a place before, when I had first met Gracie at Saint Anthony's administrative office on a Friday afternoon in mid-May 1999. There, the office lights were low, and the curtains drawn to offer relief from the glare and heat of the late spring sun. Gracie invited me to come and "get involved" that very afternoon by assisting in a 5:30 p.m. Mass.

I assisted in the weekday Mass that day and almost every weekday during the course of research from July 2000 through November 2001. I passed through Saint Anthony's sanctuary and into a short, dark corridor that led to a door and chapel. The chapel was small, having seats for about thirty parishioners, always nearly filled. Parishioners sang, "*Unidos como hermanos, / Venimos a tu altar, / Que llenes nuestras vidas de amor y amistad.*"[3] Their voices resonated as if they were the ball of string Ariadne gave to Theseus. He used the string to mark a path through a labyrinth, to a Minotaur, and on slaying the beast, back to Ariadne.

The enclosed spaces—a living room, office, and chapel—entail adjustments in talk and in visual and other sensory perception, indicating progress toward the center of a universe. One proceeds toward this center as if on a solitary journey only to realize a collective one.

Followers of Mexican and Mexican-American literature and lore have taken similar steps. Consider the space of a home in Rudolfo Anaya's *Bless Me, Ultima* (1972). The home is located on the rocky soil of a hill and at the edge of a llano, an equal distance from the New Mexican town of Guadalupe, farmlands nourished by a river, and pasture lands. This marginal location changes on the arrival of Ultima, an elderly *curandera*, or healer, and mentor to Antonio Márez, the novel's young protagonist and narrator. With Ultima's guidance, Antonio learns that he lives in a space where prairie folk, farmers, and townspeople meet and where the earth meets the sky, coordinating opposing human, geographical, and spiritual orientations into a vision of beauty that becomes his life.

This assimilation of the exterior world's features into a space that becomes a person's life mirrors the progress of pilgrimage. Pilgrims walked, Elaine Peña (2011) explains, from Querétaro and Zitácuaro to Tepeyac, Mexico. They also walked from Chicago neighborhoods toward a second Tepeyac in Des Plaines, Illinois, where parishioners had built a replica of the first. Their steps referenced hardships relating, for example, to migration, family, commercialism, prejudice, and gender. The walking oriented pilgrims' physiological disposition to geographical spaces and secular concerns that culminated on arrival at shrines and devotion to Our Lady of Guadalupe.

These places occur according to precedent as in the site of the 1531 apparition of Our Lady to Juan Diego; they also occur where people identify a need of reconciliation. In Chicago's Pilsen neighborhood, for example, residents enacted the Way of the Cross. They put stations, Karen Mary Davalos explains, at locations to commemorate Jesus's ordeals relating to his crucifixion and recent incidents of social injustice, struggle, and violence. One station was located at a library branch named after Rudy Lozano, a labor leader who'd been murdered allegedly because of his efforts to unionize workers (2002, 55). At two stations, women made temporary altars, filling them with items from their homes. These altars resembled home altars and other devotional art— yard shrines, *nichos* (niches), *capillos* (small chapels), roadside crosses—

that combine references to biblical and contemporary events (2002, 54, 56). The reconciliation involved an alignment of a place with other places.

Mircea Eliade gives insight into the nature of this alignment in a discussion about the "construction of sacred space." The construction is based on a "primeval revelation disclosed [as] the archetype of the sacred space . . . which [people] indefinitely copied and copied again with the erection of every new altar" (1958, 371–72). The archetype is a common feature that enables people to align a place with other places. The archetype also directs the mind's eye from places to their origins in space.

Without the archetype, there would be no means of identifying space. Space, Susanne Langer reminds us, "has no shape . . . even in science, though it has 'logical form,'" that resides in a "substrate of all our experience, gradually discovered by the collaboration of our several senses—now seen, now felt, now realized as a factor in our moving and doing—a limit to our hearing, a defiance to our reach" (1953, 71–72). And herein lies the issue at hand. That is whether apprehension of this space through an archetype, or "logical form," as if it were a fleeting certainty, always central yet not quite within grasp, comes from the interior of being or the exterior world.

Should it derive from the interior of being, apprehension involves approaching an abyss. To be clear, I wouldn't identify this abyss with Freud's (or Lacan's symbolic representation) because there is nothing entirely restrictive about it.[4] Rather just the opposite as indicated by representation in religious activity, the abyss greets one as if it were an open door, the resonance of words, "Hola, mi hijo," or a warm embrace that accompanies, the Matachines know well, "the perfection of being. . . in the inclination to consider the perfect or near perfect beings of our existence as mirrors themselves" (J. Fernandez 1986, 165). These activities characterize a space that Julia Kristeva calls *chora*, a "receptacle" one enters in defiance of narcissism and that allows self-awareness to merge into a perception of "the Other," undergoing death, mourning for its own loss, and abjection for (re)birth as a different being with "new significance" (1982, 14, 15).

Kristeva's insight comes from Plato's explanation of an exterior, virtual world. One apprehends this world through a breakdown of two kinds of nature or vitality essential to self-awareness. One kind accompanies reason. It is identifiable through a "form, which is always the same, . . . never receiving anything into itself from without." The other kind comes with "sense, . . . always in motion, becoming in place and again vanishing out of place." This vanishing point marks a juncture where a "kind of spurious reason" takes hold for entry into another nature, "a third nature." The third nature "is space and is eternal, and . . . provides a home for all created things, . . . all of existence." Like Kristeva's conception of chora, this space is "hardly real," and one can behold it only as if in a dream, in an image (*Timaeus* 51e–52c).

This thought recalls the images that parishioners evoked on saying the rosary: Jesus in the garden, at the pillar, and with a crown of thorns. These images characterize Jesus's path toward crucifixion. They also express a predicament of the rosary. People make their way through this ritual according to the images, each, Plato would have said, modeled after a reality to which it doesn't belong, a reality that "exists ever as a fleeting shadow" (*Timaeus* 52c). Whether in the interior of being or the exterior world, this reality sustains its status as sacred by being, Sister Mary suggested in reference to the labyrinth, at the center, which is everywhere and with a circumference that is nowhere.

Despite this ambiguity, people find their way according to signs that indicate where to go. Theseus saw a sign in the string that showed him where to turn away from death and proceed through the labyrinth to Ariadne. For Antonio Márez, Ultima is his Ariadne; and Ultima's guidance, the string. The people in Karen Mary Davalos's study saw signs in a library and labor leader that became stations of the cross, showing them where to turn away from hardship and toward something better and unified—a community. The people in Elaine Peña's study indicated that these signs were as much in their environments as they were embodied, directing each step of a pilgrimage and assisting an amalgamation of many individual lives into a life of devotion. The signs, whether in images or embodied, share a common characteristic—an "archetype," "logical form," or "kind of spurious reason" as in irony. This characteristic marks the path through the rosary and a garden for the cultivation of life that casts an allusive shadow onto sacred space.

DEVOTIONAL TIME

Alfredo, the caretaker, said another Our Father. Words referenced trespasses, forgiveness, and delivery from evil, bringing to mind the fourth sorrowful mystery. Simon from Cyrene was traveling from the countryside and came across Jesus and the soldiers on route to Golgotha. The soldiers made Simon carry the cross and walk behind Jesus.

Parishioners of Saint Anthony's came across Jesus in this way, just as I'd done on a Thursday in April 2001. My son, Alejandro, had had an accident that caused loss of vision in his right eye. I wanted him to be as he had been before the accident. In the back of the sanctuary, I found an image of Jesus, his heart exposed and blood pooled on a table with a glass top below his feet. People had left notes on scraps of paper, expressing feelings similar to my own.

Alfredo approached and stood by my side. He asked if I knew this Jesus. He explained the heart, how Jesus receives people with an open heart, taking on their wants, hardships, pains, and other bad things.

Soon afterward others joined in—Eva, Juanita, a few friends. They followed Alfredo's lead, assuring that they could do something on Alejandro's behalf. And so a journey began that led to other places, including Saint Lucy's Church in Fowler, a town in Sicily of the fourth century, a nearby town of Malaga in more recent times, and a Wednesday night prayer group meeting, among other places. Each person followed in the steps of another. Like Simon, each took on another's burden as if to be the other person for a time sufficient to understand where that person might have been and might be going.

The image of Simon in the role of Jesus provides insight into the nature of this journey; it comes by way of a metaphor that, in this instance, shows a person as another person by sharing a characteristic—a burden, weightiness, or feeling and compulsion to move as another moves.

In a study of Our Lady of the Rosary Parish, New York City, Alyshia Gálvez provides further insight into such movement by indicating what people achieve. She recalls meeting Marco, the caretaker, who was sweeping around the feet of an image of Our Lady of Guadalupe (Gálvez 2010, 1). Sweeping, Gálvez comments, is a "devotional practice" that has been around for a long time. Philip II of Spain (1527–98) was known to regularly sweep the shrine at Guadalupe in Extremadura. The activity expressed "his power over his subjects and his humility to the Virgin Mary" at a turning point in Spain's history. The *Reconquista* (Reconquest) of Spain from Muslims came to an end, while the conquest of the New World began. Sweeping was also a part of a Mexica ritual in Mesoamerica that marked a change in calendric cycles. In the *Florentine Codex*, Fray Bernardino de Sahagún documented Coatlicue's conception of a principal deity, Huitzilopochtli, while sweeping as a form of penance.[5] Gálvez notes that Sahagún's mention of penance was a religious gloss of Iberian origin (Gálvez 2010, 8). The activity, nevertheless, accompanied a dramatic subversion in the Aztec pantheon involving the fall of rival siblings, birth of a god, and creation of the cosmos (*Historia de los Mexicanos* [1888–92] 1941–44; Sahagún [1590] 1975, 3:1–5; Graulich 1997). Whether called penance, devotional practice, caretaking, or just sweeping, the ritual movement entails undertaking a burden for another that accompanies changes of small and large proportion. Marco's vantage point in all of this was one of doing; he swept just as others had done before.

He also took on other responsibilities. Marco attended Guadalupano committee meetings and those of other groups. He was "often simply around," involved in almost every aspect of parish life. He supported "communitarian cooperation" as one of the most "eloquent spokespeople," only to acknowledge a painful reality—an inability to support his family, to make something more of his life (Gálvez 2010, 58). It was as if his life were at a crossroads, as indicated in comments about parish life: "To grow together, and just as we live together in poverty, to grow together in wealth. Well, I think it's a very important goal, to arrive at this with every Mexican. It's a sad reality when I look at my own position, just as I felt alone and could have sunk into drugs. . . . I have found people who've fallen into vice: alcoholism, drugs, sex. That is not good. For a good image of Mexicans we have to grow together and at the same pace" (Gálvez 2010, 59).

An admixture of isolation, nationalism, vice, image, and growth reflects multiple life trajectories that hinge on conceptions of wealth. Marco said "wealth," in contrast to poverty, indicating material accumulation to focus on social disposition that allows people to "grow together" and prevail over isolation, vice, and stigma. Marco swept and, in doing so, performed a social alchemy that created social prosperity out of want of material wealth and out of despair.

In a study of devotion to Our Lady of Guadalupe, Jeanette Rodriguez shows how women in San Francisco made similar changes out of their "assumptive world" (1994, 115). They created this world by combining a psychological orientation, defined by their faith, and a historical orientation. They derived the latter from their understanding of biblical times as applied to more recent and contemporary times.

"She's always been there," Yolanda comments about Our Lady. "Not in the sense of just the painting, . . . but we all feel that we need to imitate her, and being a mother, how would she do, how would she handle it" (J. Rodriguez 1994, 128).

"She must have been strong," Catalina reflects. "All the punishment, the talk, just everything that happened to Jesus. And she had to [handle all that]" (J. Rodriguez 1994, 129).

"When I see the image," Carolina says, "I feel a lot of pain. She's got that expression on her face. . . . Mothers always try to encourage their children to look towards her as a protector for the family. I guess they identify with her because she understands everything that they are going through. . . . Our Lady of Guadalupe knows what they are going through and what their goals are: trying to raise a family and trying to accomplish something" (J. Rodriguez 1994, 134).

Yolanda, Catalina, and Carolina thought and acted as Our Lady of Guadalupe might have thought and acted in relation to Jesus and Juan Diego to reveal values of motherhood, loyalty, protection of children, and accomplishment. They expressed a subordinate disposition of struggle, "punishment," and "pain," which became one of strength.

Devotion enables people to transform ordinary experiences into an extraordinary one. Marco swept and transformed isolation and dejection into inclusion and community. Yolanda, Catalina, and Carolina imitated Our Lady of Guadalupe and coordinated elements of myth, legend, history, and spirituality into an experience of faith. These people followed predecessors, who in biblical, precolonial, and colonial times, respectively, did things on behalf of others to bring celestial and human worlds together for visions of new possibilities. People do things that take them, Victor Turner explains, to "liminality," that is, to where the past meets the present, selfhood meets otherness, and an interior life meets an exterior one, combining innumerable characteristics for creating the world anew and as it should be (1974).

This creativity involves playing the role of others and acting as a metaphor. Marco, Yolanda, Catalina, and Carolina drew out—to borrow Aristotle's language concerning metaphor—their "similarity" to predecessors "in dissimilars," and created a link between two or more semantic domains, between those of biblical, mythical, and/or historical times on the one hand and those of the present on the other (*Poetics* 1459a8). The similarity might be in instances "as they were or are, or as they are said or thought to be or to have been, or as they ought to be," configuring content into a conception of time (*Poetics* 1460b8–11).

More recent philosophers identify this conception of time as poetic and sacred. "In a lyric," Susanne Langer suggests, "the whole creation . . . is an awareness of a subjective experience, and *the tense of subjectivity is the 'timeless' present*" (1953, 268; emphasis original). "Sacred time," Mircea Eliade explains, "is circular, reversible and recoverable, a sort of mythical present that is periodically reintegrated by means of rites" (1959, 69). A lyric, then, is a rite; a lyric and a rite have a characteristic in common. Each has formal features that orient people to a conception of time that is exceptional due to having no beginning or end—just being ever-present.

No wonder: people undertake rituals that become journeys with poetic features choreographing movement from one place to another. Alfredo said another Our Father and arrived at my side and before the image of Jesus with blood at his feet. Others had left signs of being there also in small scraps of paper slipped under glass. Eva, Juanita, and a few friends went to Fowler to find Saint Lucy because she, like Jesus and Simon before, had suffered afflictions. She had lost her vision. The friends went to ask Saint Lucy if she could help Alejandro as God had helped her, restoring her vision with light, radiance, and apprehension. Each followed in the path of another, taking on another's burden because they grasped what Aristotle had explained long ago: that movement is time without a beginning or an end. Movement just is, "circular" and "continuous"—sacred (*Metaphysics* 1071b12).

TROPE, RITUAL, STORY

Words about the kingdom, earth, and how it will be as it is in heaven brought to mind parallel worlds. In one of them, Mary the mother of Jesus, her sister Mary the wife of Clopas, and Mary Magdalene stood by Jesus while he hung on the cross (John 19:25). In the other, eight or nine of us sat around a table, our hands clasped, and our thoughts meandering in and out of each other's life.

"This is what anthropologists do," I thought.

This kind of meandering is also what other people did. Alfredo meandered from Guanajuato, Mexico, to California and Washington, and to Saint Anthony's, where he continued to do so around the parish. Eva meandered, as was evident in her journey through the labyrinth, which characterized much of her life. So did Gracie; she meandered from parish council meetings to catechism classes, and to youth group meetings where she gave something of herself and received something in return, the impetus of a journey that is a rosary.

Gracie focused (as I do) on the sorrowful mysteries. Her life hadn't been easy. Her childhood travels with parents on the labor circuit, facing a judgmental priest on her return from Wyoming, and being left at the door of an orphanage: these instances, among many others, made her feel unworthy and want to keep moving.

Gracie's steps involved an encounter that brought relief from any hardship she might have felt. On the labor circuit, letters followed Gracie, catching up on occasion. Some letters were from her grandmother and "protector," who wrote about love. The priest told Gracie that ordinary parishioners shouldn't administer the Eucharist. She had an idea, instead, of "something to offer," "a community." In the orphanage, Gracie knew a girl who, she explained, "was beautiful." The girl wet her bed, and a nun told Gracie to take the girl to a shower and give her cold water. When the nun left, Gracie turned on hot water. The girl "started smiling."[6] Gracie stood before hardship as the three Marys had stood before Jesus on the cross, each one in the image of another, to form a symbol of beauty out of loss.

In a discussion about religious symbols, Clifford Geertz suggests that they make up a system. The system enables people to bring their experiences into focus and grasp their meaning. A part of this focus involves "tone," "character," "order," "aesthetic style," and "moral," among other features, composing people's "ethos" and "mood" (1973, 89). Another part is "motivation," or direction for a course of action (1973, 97). On recalling the three Marys, one acknowledges the symbol of the three Marys before Jesus in relation to other symbols that coordinate a bifurcated experience of mood and motivation, articulating where depth of feeling meets reason to act.

Sherry Ortner adds to Geertz's observations by showing how people apprehend symbols in terms of spatial relationships. In one respect, people conceive symbols in terms of "summing up," representing in an "emotionally powerful and relatively undifferentiated way, what the system means to them" (Ortner 1973, 1340). Such a symbol directs one to proceed vertically from a place like the one featuring Jesus on the cross. There, people acknowledge a part-to-whole relationship that, in this case, involves transcendence. Jesus sacrificed himself to relieve people of their sins and enable them to have a place in heaven. The symbol of Jesus on the cross, then, directs emotive and cognitive behavior according to metonymy.

In another respect, people proceed horizontally, through "elaborating symbols." People rely on elaborating symbols as "vehicles for sorting out complex . . . feelings and ideas, making them comprehensible." Elaborating symbols hold a "central status" in a culture, giving "order to the world" and dramatizing "key scenarios" for "successful social action" (Ortner 1973, 1340, 1342). The elaboration, whether used as a "vehicle," to give "order," or to guide "social action," entails reasoning across a social landscape. In this instance, the elaboration entails sorting out similarities in dissimilarities or metaphor: three Marys, each the same in name and experience of loss but different according to position in kinship and social status.

A metaphor derives meaning from context that entails present circumstances as much as historical ones. A metaphor, Stephen C. Pepper explains, references a point of origin in historical events. People sustain historical events when evoking a metaphor, effectively "*re-presenting* events, to make them in some way alive again." An awareness of a historical event being alive is what makes it real to people: "an event in its actuality, it is going on *now*, the dynamic dramatic active event" that "we may call an act" (1942, 232).

This reasoning came across as common sense for Gracie—three Marys before Jesus on the cross, each the same despite differences. Her grandmother wrote letters about love, and Gracie turned on hot water, each having something to offer—protection of a child in the formation of a virtual world made out of space endowed with time, historical in depth yet transcendent and ever-present.

So when life felt as if it were falling apart, Gracie said the rosary. Her friend Helen joined Gracie when she was worried about her son in prison. And so did I when feeling as if I'd lost something in my son or were missing something about the people at Saint Anthony's and other congregations in the neighborhood. One says the rosary, Gracie explained, "to see what happens," to feel for others as Christ felt for humankind, allowing for isolation and loss to "grow" or "become something" whole, as in a group or community.[7]

Anthropologists have long observed that ritual helps people do this kind of thing. M. N. Srivinas observed something similar among South India's Coorgs (1952). And A. R. Radcliffe-Brown (1948, 1952) and, before him, Emile Durkheim (2001) observed it of people in different settings such as the Andaman Islands, South Africa, and Western Australia. For these scholars, religious ritual expresses a structure of moral and social order that reflects individual feelings and imaginings of the same. On performing a ritual, individuals assert their places in a society and reinforce social homogeneity and stability, which is particularly helpful in the event of adverse circumstances such as illness or encounters with outsiders.

Marshal Sahlins documents the role of ritual in a famous encounter with an outsider: the Hawaiians' with Captain Cook in January 1789 (1981). The Hawaiians saw Cook's arrival through the lens of a myth. To them, Cook was a god who had returned to the islands, his identity confirmed by a ritual circumnavigation and landing. The return initiated rituals relating to calendric cycles, god alternation, suspension of hostilities, fishing practices, fertility of nature and gardens, adoration, and the restoration of kingship, which culminated in Cook being put to death. The rituals enabled the Hawaiians to sort out familiar and unfamiliar signs—Cook the god versus Cook the captain—and form a perspective that sustained continuity between a mythical and historical past and the present. For the Hawaiians, myth and history came to being through ritual movements directed by Cook as a god and metaphor. The metaphor channeled a course of elaboration, revealing multiple features—spiritual, natural, social—of Hawaiian life. At the same time, the ritual movements focused on Cook as metonymy, his death standing for fecundity and renewal of Hawaiian culture.

Gananath Obeyesekere (1992) disputes Sahlins's representation of Cook's demise on the islands. He argues instead that the Hawaiians reasoned practically about Cook, identified his foreign credentials and intensions, and dealt with him accordingly. If Obeyesekere's representation of what the Hawaiians thought is as credible as Sahlins's, then the Hawaiians might have played out Cook's demise according to irony without certainty of which side of irony's opposition were true.

Whether as metaphor, metonymy, or irony, Cook referenced an underlying form of cultural production, inherently open to foreign influences. The Hawaiians incorporated such an influence, Cook the captain and British subject, into a social body through ritual. The movements broached the spatial and temporal dimensions of a virtual world endowed with sufficient emotive and rational qualities for the Hawaiians to create stories that made this world apprehensible, tangible, and their own.

Trope, ritual, and story account for a scale that ranges from narrow to wide and transcendent. On the one end, a trope, such as metaphor, metonymy, and irony, provides people with direction for how they talk about things. Gracie told stories about a child's deprivation, the labor circuit, and a priest's rebuke of ordinary people administering the Eucharist. These stories turned into ones about warmth, protection, and companionship. Her orphan friend smiled. Her grandmother said that somebody loved Gracie, and the community showed Gracie that this was true. Gracie demonstrated how irony helped her transform dire circumstances into fortunate ones, suggesting a duality in faith as if hardship and evil were always at hand for making something better and spiritual.

This perspective of duality, however, might overlook the point of ritual, the second part of a tripartite account of scale. Ritual involves formal movements with the body and mind, an amalgamation of physiological and cognitive faculties. The movements create a space that draws into purview disparate signs of power, strife, and abjection such as cold water, wage labor, and the door of an orphanage for treatment and integration into an imitation "of one thing," "one action," a "complete whole" as much material as immaterial, natural as forceful, moved as loved, balanced, and beautiful (Aristotle, *Poetics* 1451a30–34).

GRACIE ASKED ME TO COME AND "GET INVOLVED" JUST AS she'd asked many others before my time. I said the rosary that day in mid-May 1999 unaware of a journey that would ensue. The journey took me along the parameters of the place where I'd grown up, my old neighborhood with friends whose lives had helped define my own—resources and choices accompanied on occasion by feelings of entitlement.

With my parents gone and a deep sense of loss, I came to realize that these things mattered only as an indication of asymmetry. Modern development had made farmland out of desert and provided a bountiful life for some, leaving most to languish, their struggles further troubled by prejudice, substance abuse, family dissolution, and violence among other features that often accompany poverty. The world had lost its luster.

Eva sat behind me in the chapel and waited to assist in the daily Mass. She too had entered through a short, dark corridor that led to the chapel's door. She had opened the door to the call inside, *"Que llenes nuestras vidas de amor y de amistad."*[8] Eva's sister, Juanita, and her children were there also, each to learn about the liturgy or about a call to "perform a public duty," a message that gave the journey ethical endowment.[9]

"Do you know who this is?" Alfredo the caretaker asked, referring to the image of Jesus with an open heart.[10] Alfredo stood by my side, and shortly after, others joined us: Eva, Juanita, and a few friends.

They went to Saint Lucy's in Fowler in a blue Ford minivan with a Christlike figurine, El Niño de Prague, mounted on the dashboard. They followed the course of Saint Lucy's life, which included her loss of vision by the hands of power. They made this journey on Alejandro's behalf only to say, "We can do more for him."[11]

My wife, Gabriela; our daughter, Claudia; Alejandro; and I went to a Wednesday night prayer group known for people with the charisma, or gift, of healing powers. The prayer group met in Saint Anthony's sanctuary. Hundreds of people filled the pews. They filed out, lined up, and walked toward the altar, each one following another. I held Alejandro in my arms with Gabriela and Claudia behind, taking steps. People said the Our Father and Hail Mary.

The steps led to remarkable places—Chartres, France, of the twelfth century and Mesa, Arizona, and Fresno in more recent times. Each place, I discovered, became known through fire. Like Mary Magdalene at Jesus's tomb, people had gone to these places in search of the living, some trace of a former life, where there was death.

Children, Eva suggested in reference to El Niño de Prague, have a way of bringing about this kind of irony. Parents take them places—in their arms, hand in hand, by their side, or in vehicles. Children learn from their parents by absorbing the rhythm of steps, the clasp of hands, their joys and sorrows. And eventually, parents allow children to separate from immediate care and become their own generation. At this juncture, parents look at their children to see traces of their former lives, only to be reminded of age and mortality.

Children also show signs to reverse this outcome. Gabriela took Alejandro to an ophthalmologist in Austin, Texas, and cried. She wanted to protect him from harm. She felt his loss of vision as if it were her own. Then an assistant said, "He sees fine. Look, he recognizes all of the symbols like any other child."[12] Gabriela saw hope where she'd seen sadness.

A change of circumstances begins with learning how to read signs or symbols that, Geertz explains, set a mood and motivation for a course of action. Gracie traveled down "one straight road" where "you turn around and come out again," describing a driveway that led to the orphanage. Inside, Gracie saw pictures of "Mary, Mary holding a baby." She had "an expression on her face," Carolina explained. The expression showed that "she understands everything . . . trying to raise a family and trying to accomplish something." She must have "been strong," Catalina said. "All the punishment, the talk, just everything that happened to Jesus."

"Mothers know their sons," Gracie explained further. "It's a part of the journey."

Other people became a part of the journey. Some came from Querétaro and Zitácuaro, Mexico, and some, from Chicago neighborhoods. Some were children who'd written prayers about families without love on scraps of paper slipped under glass. Alfredo had come from Guanajuato, wandering from place to place out of a need for work. Marco swept around the feet of Our Lady of Guadalupe, producing a rhythm that helped people "grow together and at the same pace."

"Mothers know their sons," Gracie said. And people learn to know each other. They follow each other's steps, meandering across a landscape as Gregorio Cortez once did on a mare or as Antonio Márez did to define a home and life. They do so to take on hardship as opposed to escaping it. They receive each other's burdens to become like one another and emerge as something better, nurturing and expansive in body and mind, balanced—the "more" people can do.

NOTES

Introduction

1. Sister Mary Tiziana, interview with the author, telephone, 3 March 2003. Sister Tiziana requested that I identify her by her name. Unless indicated otherwise, I have changed the names of the people who participated in this research.

2. Hereafter I will often refer to this church as Saint Anthony's Church and follow a customary reference of parishioners.

3. Gracie R. Adame, interview with the author, Fresno, California, 3 February 2001. Ms. Adame requested that I identify her by name.

4. See Tambiah's 1985 discussion of ritual in the terms of a refrain.

5. At the time of the research, the rosary consisted of meditations upon three sets of mysteries—the joyful, sorrowful, and glorious. In 2002, Pope John Paul II inaugurated the "Year of the Rosary" in the *Rosarium Virginis Mariae* with the proposal of an additional five, luminous mysteries. The mysteries include Jesus's baptism and the events of his public life that show the kingdom of God in his person. See http://www.vatican.va/holy_father/john_paul_ii/apost_letters/documents/hf_jp-ii_apl_20021016_rosarium-virginis-mariae_en.html (accessed 24 May 2007).

6. James Fernandez (1986) reviews the scholarship that treats symbolism of wholes and the experience of relatedness, citing in particular Durkheim and Mauss (1963), Cassirer ([1944] 1962), and Lévi-Strauss (1966).

7. See Ronald Grimes's 2006 discussion of ritual space and agency in response to Jonathan Smith's 1980 and 1987 work about ritual place.

8. See Bourdieu's 1977 discussion of *habitus*, Merleau-Ponty's 1962 discussion of the phenomenal body, and Csordas's 1994 articulation of the sacred self.

9. The sacred should be understood, as Edith Turner suggests, as something that "has always been so," experienced as a sense of connectedness, the "consciousness of spiritual power" that passes through everything—matter and all living things, animals and humans—but doesn't necessarily stay still for empirical investigation (2006, 54–55).

10. See José E. Limón's 2007 and 2012 discussions of Américo Paredes's methods.

11. See José E. Limón's 2012 discussion of Américo Paredes and three generations of scholars out of Texas.

12. A *manda* is a promise to fulfill an act of devotion, sometimes to reciprocate for a miraculous event like recovery from economic hardship or a serious illness and sometimes as a plea for a miraculous event.

13. This literature review would be amiss without acknowledgment of numerous Latina/o scholars and writers, some from Fresno, who journeyed from humble circumstances to achieve leadership in their fields—music, drama, history, literature, and political science. The review also acknowledges the many teachers, social workers, neighborhood organizers, and activists among other people of past and present times whose performances have contributed to the tradition and its by-product in academic achievements.

14. See in Sandell 2014 a similar discussion of Aristotle in relation to Mexican *retablos*.

15. See Marx's discussion of the labor process ([1967] 1987).

16. *Oxford English Dictionary*, 2nd ed., s.v. "Allegory."

ONE.   The Dance

1. I conducted exploratory research in Fresno, California, from May through June 1999. I returned in July 2000 and stayed until November 2001. I met Antonio Estrada in August 2000 at the Claretians' provincial headquarters in San Gabriel, California, where I attended a retreat. Antonio began a year's internship at Saint Anthony's in September.

2. Gracie R. Adame, interview with the author, Fresno, California, 4 October 2001. A *compadre* is a godfather of another adult's child. The title indicates a special relationship between the two adults reinforced by the exchange of favors and gifts. Gracie mentioned that her compadre did not reveal his manda to the group until after they had danced on several occasions, attracting a growing audience.

3. *Diccionario de la lengua castellana*, s.v. "Matachini"; *Supplément aux Diccionaires Arabes*, s.v. "Matachine."

4. My representation of the Matachines dance draws from several sources. Flavia Waters Champe (1983), whose work is based in New Mexico, gives the most detailed account of the dance, its characters, and its history, constituting an instruction manual suitable for the dance's production (and preservation). J. D. Robb's research is based on observations of the performance in Mexico and New Mexico, or "old and New Mexico," from 1902 to 1955. He notes the most common characteristics, which include a dedication to the Virgin of Guadalupe, the cast of characters—El Monarca, La Malinche, El Abuelo, El Toro, and the "two lines of dancers, each ranging in number from six to twelve or even larger numbers" (1961, 94–95). And Sylvia Rodriguez (1991, 1994, 1996) provides a detailed com

parison of performances among the Pueblos and Hispanics in the Upper Río Grande Valley, New Mexico.

5. Contrary to Paz's account, it is important to acknowledge, as does Harris, that recent scholarship portrays La Malinche, otherwise known by her Spanish Christian name Doña Marina, in a redeeming light. I use Paz's caricature of La Malinche as a foil to advance an argument for a complex and proactive identity formation that complements Chicana scholarship. See Moraga and Anzaldúa (1981), J. Martin (1990), Cypess (1991), and Alarcón (1999).

6. Robb (1961) and Spicer (1962) identify La Malinche with Cortés's mistress and translator. Toor (1947) raises doubts about this identification because of La Malinche's intimate role with Moctezuma, indicating her role in overcoming European dominance. Treviño and Gilles (1994), Ichon (1969), Champe (1983), and S. Rodriguez (1991) mention the allusion to Cortés's Malinche and opt for Toor's position. Harris (1996) supports Toor's claim with a detailed account of Aztec mythology. My point, which I flesh out farther along, is that the mere mention of La Malinche always raises the specter of her double.

7. The dancers do not necessarily conceive the dance according to acts and scenes; they follow a sequence of events with names. "To one familiar with the stage production of opera, drama, and ballet," Champe suggests, "these various [events] easily fall into a standard pattern" (1983, 21).

8. Champe (1983) notes that the music is played on a violin and guitar. S. Rodriguez (1991) notes a fiddle, drum, and guitar. When I watched Saint Anthony's Matachines dance in December 2000, the dancers grasped tambourines, wore bells on their feet, and were accompanied by no other instruments.

9. The Catholic Church's Jubilee 2000, commemorating 2000 years of Christianity, began when Pope John Paul II opened the doors of St. Peter's Basilica on Christmas Eve in 1999 and ended with their closure on the Epiphany, 6 January 2001.

10. See Sahagún's account of calendar festivals in *A History of Ancient Mexico* (1976).

11. Susan Gillespie remarks that our understanding of Quetzalcóatl's saga relies upon early documents provided by Aztec elites and Spanish missionaries (1989, 173–74). See Lafaye (1976), León-Portilla (1963), and Wagner (1944) for accounts of Quetzalcóatl drawn from early documentation.

12. The Guadalupana ministry organizes special events for Our Lady of Guadalupe. The most common are processions and *novenas* for the Virgin before and on her day of December 12. The ministry sponsors an annual raffle for fundraising. Candidates for the queen sell tickets, and the candidate who sells the most wins the role. A *novena* is a Christmas ritual, consisting of nine days of consecutive prayer that shows devotion to Jesus and preparation for his birth.

13. See note 4 and Robb's 1961 coinage "the old and New Mexico."

14. The farm towns, often called *colonias*, are the homes of primarily Latino residents, 80 percent or more, in contrast to only 23 percent in the 1950s (the other 77 percent being primarily Anglo). This change in population reflects the recent history of agribusiness and immigration. Since the 1970s, immigrants have accommodated the growers' demands for cheap labor. The growers have exchanged low-value crops (wheat and cotton) for high-value crops (fruits and nuts), the latter being much more lucrative and labor-intensive, especially during the harvest season. Seasonal jobs, high poverty levels, and a low percentage of high school graduations induce people to leave the *colonias* for urban centers, like Fresno, once they acquire English-language skills and long-term employment opportunities, leaving the lower-paying farm jobs to recent immigrants (Allensworth and Rochín 1995). See Lopez (1995) and J. Taylor, Martin, and Fix (1997) for their discussion of California's *colonias*.

15. Estimates of the number of people migrating annually from Mexico to the United States are always speculative. Segal (1993) states 1.2 million. Clark (1998) estimates that each year between 1985 and 1995 1.5 million migrants made California their home. In recent years leading to the present in 2014, the number of migrants who cross the border has lowered due to border patrol vigilance and increased risk in relation to safety with and the price of *coyotes* (escorts), who often collaborate with narco-traffickers. This observation is based on reports related to the author in Mexican villages near the cities of Silao and León, Guanajuato, in June and July 2014.

16. The terms "migrant" and "immigrant" indicate different social positions. The people who come from Mexico and parts of Central America to work, live, and, sometimes, stay in the United States tend to call themselves "migrants." "Immigrant" signifies the perspective of a native U.S. resident. In this book, I use these terms accordingly.

17. Gracie R. Adame, interview with the author, Fresno, California, 30 November 2000.

18. For discussions of American nativism, see Bodnar (1996), Feagin (1997), and Nether (1996). See Acuña (1972), Almaguer (1994), Menchaca (1993), and Griswold del Castillo (1990) for a review of the Treaty of Guadalupe of Hidalgo (which brought an end to the U.S.-Mexican War) and for an account of the denial of constitutional rights to Mexican and indigenous people. George Sánchez (1993) provides a comprehensive review of nativism and, in particular, its influence on domestic institutions and policies.

19. See in particular Sánchez's discussion of Dr. S. Bogardus, who was trained under Robert Park at the University of Chicago. Bogardus, appointed the first chairman of USC's Department of Sociology (then organized under the School of Social Work), devoted his work to the social conditions of Los Angeles's Mexican immigrants and produced generations of social workers, teachers, and

public administrators, who played a role in shaping California's public policies under auspices of various public and private institutions (1993, 97–107).

20. See discussion about Porfirio Díaz in chapter 5.

21. See Timothy Dunn's discussion of border enforcement and labor control since their initiation during the recession of 1920–22, when Mexican workers on farms in the Southwest were "scapegoated for allegedly causing unemployment among U.S. workers." The U.S. Border Patrol was established in 1924 (1996, 11).

22. See Chavez (2001); Cornelius (1989); Cornelius, Martin, and Hollifield (1994); Crane, Asch, Heilbrunn, and Cullinane (1990); and Dunn (1996).

23. See Leonel Sanchez's "2 Agents Face Civil Suit in Alleged Beating," *San Diego Union-Tribune*, 4 September 2002, sec. B, addressing the civil suit filed on behalf of a San Diego man who was detained by border agents in a holding cell and beaten. Regarding prostitution, see Jeff McDonald and Leonel Sanchez, "Prostitution-Ring Arrangements Expected in Federal Court Today," *San Diego Union-Tribune*, 5 December 2001, sec. B. Read also Scott Gold's article "Suit Targets U.S. Border Vigilantes," *Los Angeles Times*, 30 May 2003, sec. A, about a case in Texas filed on behalf of six immigrants who were detained at gunpoint, threatened with death, and beaten by self-appointed border vigilantes carrying assault rifles and accompanied by dogs. The vigilantes claimed that they were "citizens" and "taxpayers" losing their rights to "trespassers." They were "merely doing what the United States has failed to do." For accounts of what immigrants face upon crossing the U.S.-Mexican border, see Chavez (1998, 2001) and Dunn (1996).

24. See *New Catholic Encyclopedia*, s.v. "Guadalupe, Our Lady of," and de la Torre Villar and Navarro de Anda (1982).

25. Bernardino de Sahagún addresses a connection between the Aztec goddess Tonantzin and "*nuestra madre Eva*" (our mother Eva) (1969, 1:46). Sahagún also critiques a connection between Tonantzin and Mary, saying that devotion to Tonantzin reflects a "*falsedad antigua*" (old falsehood) (1969, 3:354). Alonso de Montúfar, a Dominican and Mexico's second archbishop (1551–72), adopted a conciliatory position regarding the natives' devotion to the Aztec goddess Tonantzin in the same conceptual framework as Our Lady of Guadalupe (Poole 1995). De la Torre Villar and Navarro de Anda (1982) and Nutini and Bell (1980) focus on the Franciscan opposition to the dual devotion and highlight the politics among religious orders. Eric Wolf (1958) recalls Echánove Trujillo's 1948 mention of Fray Martín de León's identification of the Guadalupe and Tonantzin connection, presumably a popular view. Mexican writers, Miguel Leatham (1989) observes, most likely cultivated the perception of indigenous Guadalupan devotion by posting the original name for the image in Nahuatl, which Spaniards translated to "Guadalupe." This claim finds support in the 1666 writings of Luis Becerra Tanco ([1675] 1979). Leatham also distinguishes exegetic treatments that support sixteenth-century indigenous conversion: Behrens (1966), Elizondo (1980), and

Rojas Sánchez and Hernández Illescas (1983). See also William B. Taylor's 1987 discussion of the rationale for early indigenous devotion.

26. The *encomienda*, whose name derives from the Spanish verb *encomendar*, "to trust," was a system of tributary labor in the American colonies. It was originally applied as a means of exacting tribute from Muslims and Jews during the reconquest of the Iberian Peninsula, then exported to the New World, where it became a form of enslavement. The *encomienda* consisted of a grant by the crown to a conquistador, soldier, official, or deserving Spanish subject of a number of Indians living in a particular area. The receiver of the grant, the *encomendero*, could extract tribute from the Indians in the form of gold and labor. In return, the encomendero, in theory, provided protection and instruction in the Christian faith. The encomienda did not include a grant of land; however, an encomendaro, in practice, took land as compensation, he claimed, for the Indians' failure to fulfill their obligations. See *The New Encyclopaedia Britannica*, s.v. "Encomienda."

27. The debate at Valladolid, which was summoned by Charles V, began in mid-August 1550 and lasted for about a month. A second session took place from mid-April to mid-May 1551. The debate addressed, Lewis Hanke comments, whether or not it was lawful for "the King of Spain to wage war on the Indians, before preaching the faith to them, in order to subject them to this rule, so that afterward they may be more easily instructed in the faith" (1974, 67). This debate focused on the Indians' capacity to be Christian, become Spanish subjects, and assume dominium. The debate was unique because it accounted for the culmination of five decades of arguments that took place generally in writing.

28. See Anthony Pagden's 1987 discussion of dominium, its nuanced definition stemming from classical origins and juridical language during the sixteenth and seventeenth centuries. See also Lewis Hanke's 1974 analysis of Las Casas, Sepúlveda, the Valladolid debate, and generally, the intellectual history that influenced the Spanish conquest of the New World.

29. William B. Taylor (1987) argues that the sixteenth-century veneration of the Virgin of Guadalupe was most widespread among the "non-Indian" population. Indigenous veneration became more predominant in the seventeenth century. Nevertheless, see early testimonies of indigenous devotion in Fernandez, Sánchez, and Rosado (1999).

30. On 12 October 1976, a new basilica was completed to house Juan Diego's mantle bearing the image of Our Lady of Guadalupe. The old basilica was unsafe for visitors because, like many structures around Mexico City, it is sinking in the sandy soil left by the draining of many lakes in the region. See Johnston's 1981 explanation of the structures.

31. Eva Gonzales, interview with the author, Fresno, California, 10 March 2001.

32. See a discussion of Eva Gonzales's family in chapter 4.

33. Alfonso Suárez, interview with the author, Fresno, California, 5 May 2001. The translation from Spanish is mine.

34. Ana Rodríguez, interview with the author, Fresno, California, 14 October 2001.

35. See Deverell (1994) and Wrobel (1996) for a discussion of Frederick Jackson Turner's conception of the American frontier and his fear that the American identity would lose its uniqueness.

36. The 1986 Immigration Reform and Control Act (IRCA) combined legalization and employer sanctions. Undocumented immigrants who had arrived before 1 January 1982 were eligible for a general legalization program. Immigrants who had arrived later were subject to arrest and deportation. The act did not include an immigrant worker program for agriculture (Chavez, Flores, and Lopez-Garza 1990). Such a reform, introduced by Representative Leon Panetta (D-California) and Representative Sid Morrison (R-Washington), passed the House in 1984. A similar reform, introduced by Senator Pete Wilson (R-California), passed the Senate in 1985, and indicated that growers could exact special provisions for labor. These reforms were the Special Agricultural Worker and Replenishment Agricultural Worker programs (SAW and RAW, respectively). The SAW program, Philip L. Martin explains, "permitted illegal aliens who had done at least 90 days of work in Seasonal Agricultural Services (SAS) to become legal U.S. residents. If newly legalized SAWs left agriculture, RAW immigrants could replace them" (1990, 70). In addition, the employer sanctions, as stated in the *Immigration Reform and Control Act of 1986*, Public Law 99-603, 99th Cong., 2nd sess. (6 November 1986), entailed "civil and criminal penalties for the knowing employment or recruitment of illegal aliens." "Knowing" is the operative word, enabling growers to escape criminal charges either by claiming ignorance or, as is often the case, by following a standard legal verification procedure: the request of a Social Security number and driver's license, documents widely available to anybody regardless of legal status. For a thorough discussion of the IRCA's ramifications, see Baker (1990); Bean, Edmonston, and Passel (1990); and Rivera-Batiz, Sechzer, and Gang (1991).

37. Senate Committee on the Judiciary, Subcommittee on Immigration and Refugee Policy, *Immigration Reform and Control Act: Hearings on S. 529*, 98th Cong., 1st sess. (7 March 1983), 506.

38. Alfredo Reyes, interview with the author, Fresno, California, 1 October 2001. The translation from Spanish is mine. See further representation of Alfredo in chapters 2 and 4.

39. Gracie R. Adame, interview with the author, Fresno, California, 4 October 2001.

40. Gracie R. Adame, interview with the author, Fresno, California, 4 October 2001.

TWO.   The Daily Service

1. These verses are from the final stanza of the entrance hymn, "*Vamos cantando al señor*" (*Flor y canto* 1989). They translate as follows: "United as brothers and sisters, / We come to your altar, / That you may fill our lives with love and friendship" (my translation).

2. *The Catholic Encyclopedia*, s.v. "Liturgy."

3. Several historians document Charles G. Briggs's role in the settlement of Malaga, but with some confusion about his name and origin. In *History of Fresno County* (1882), the author notes that "Charles G. Briggs" was a "celebrated fruit producer" from Yolo County. Hanna (1946) identifies Charles Briggs, the namesake of Briggston, Yolo County, who settled in Benecia and organized the lumber company of Briggs and Russell. Hanna further notes that "G. G. Briggs" founded the Malaga Colony. Thickens (1939) credits "F. G. Briggs" for establishing the colony of Malaga. I rely on *History of Fresno County*, where the author discusses "Charles G. Briggs," noting that Charles G. Briggs's first initial "C" became "G" in later publications.

4. See Ines M. Miyares's 1997 study of the Southeast Asian refugees in the San Joaquin Valley.

5. William Secrest, email correspondence with the author, 1 May 2002. The historian William Secrest informed me that Jensen Avenue was named after Chris P. Jensen, a civil engineer and resident of the Central California Colony. In *History of Fresno County* (1882), the author states that the firm of E. Hughes & Sons created the Fresno Colony, an original tract of 2,880 acres, from the estate of "E Jansen." The colonies were subdivisions consisting of twenty-acre tracts that developers sold to settlers.

6. Juan Ramirez, interview with the author, Fresno, California, 23 February 2001.

7. The California Wine Association was formed during the depression of 1894, or 1892 according to Carosso (1951), and ended in 1936. Maynard Amerine (1969) notes that the association consisted of five companies. Mike Dunne (2001) notes seven companies with the main office in San Francisco. The association was designed to pool resources and marketing strategies, which was particularly useful during the prohibition years. By 1914, the association controlled 84 percent of California wine. See also Haraszthy (1978), Peninou and Greenleaf (1954), and Verdier (1933). See Mike Dunne's article, "Book Recalls How San Francisco Once Held Vital Role in Viticulture," in *Sacramento Bee*, 18 July 2001.

8. Jorge Cruz, interview with the author, Fresno, California, 9 March 2001.

9. *Oxford English Dictionary*, 2nd ed., s.v. "Religion."

10. Rosaura Sánchez (1995) highlights the roles of property, political power, language, religion, family, national origin, and most significantly, a shared history

in the Californios' formation of an identity. She stresses that Californios exhibited no single political vision and multiple affiliations, precluding an essential identity. During this era, elite or ruling members of the California population identified with the Catholic religion and, for political reasons, lobbied for the secularization of the missions. Liberalism was a political philosophy introduced through the administration of Governor José María Echeandía (1825–31), and professed ideas of liberty, equality, and republicanism. See Hale (1968).

11. See Rosaura Sánchez's discussion of an emerging ethnic talk in the context of the Californios' interviews with Bancroft's agents. She describes these interviews as an "umbrella construct that often subsumed a number of economic, political, and social antagonisms that also call for disarticulation" (1995, 269).

12. Foreign immigration by land after 1841, Doyce B. Nunis Jr. explains, was a "more daunting and difficult challenge to the Californios than [was] welcoming and absorbing those who arrived by ship" (1997, 311).

13. Mariano Guadalupe Vallejo called overland immigrants "industrious individuals" whose talents for agriculture were needed in the territory (Vallejo n.d., 3:384; quoted in Rosenus 1995, 41). See recent scholarship that focuses on an amalgamation of Frederick Jackson Turner's (1920) ideological understanding of the frontier and Walter Prescott Webb's (1931, 1952) regional social histories: Aron (1994); Cronon, Miles, and Gitlin (1992); Deverell (1994); Steiner (1995); Wrobel (1996); and most notably, Slotkin (1992).

14. See Bancroft's discussion of the "plan of the *pronunciamiento*," written upon deposing the Mexican ruler Nicolás Gutiérrez, 3 November 1836 (1886, 3:466–69). See also Castillo Negrete's comments about the state of affairs following Gutiérrez's withdrawal (Bancroft 1886, 3:486–87).

15. Leonard Pitt suggests turning to the following sources for examples of this phraseology: *Daily Alta California*, 18 January, 25 June, and 23 August 1853. See also Governor John Bigler's message of 1856, cited in Cleland (1951, 123–24).

16. See Albert K. Weinberg's (1935) and Gene M. Brack's (1975) studies of Manifest Destiny.

17. Pastor Marc Rosales, interview with the author, Fresno, California, 11 October 2001.

18. Pastor Aurelio Lopez, interview with the author, Fresno, California, 1 October 2001.

19. See George Sánchez's (1993) and Rodolfo Acuña's (1972) discussions of Mexico's modernization under Porfirio Díaz and foreign investors, which left Mexico and its labor force an economic appendage of the United States and other European nations.

20. See Andrew Nether's (1996) discussion of labor and ethnic identification.

21. While LULAC advocated "love [for] the men of your race, pride in your origins," and learning the Spanish language, their understanding of the "purist form of Americanism" translated into the assimilation of the American ethos I

discuss in the body of this chapter. As LULAC's president-general suggested in 1932, Mexican Americans should "fuse" with Americans, "known to be members of a vigorous and masterful race.... Such co-mingling ... in the end tends to bring out the force and character and the fertility of intellect that create and perpetuate a leading nation" (Gonzales 1932; quoted in Gutiérrez 1995, 83). The Bracero Program was a federal program that allowed seasonal employment for hundreds of thousands of Mexicans in American agriculture. Initiated in 1942, it assured growers of adequate, cheap labor and contributed to, as its proponents proclaimed, the war effort. The Bracero Program lasted until 1964 (Gutiérrez 1995). See also Gutiérrez's discussion of other organizations—Order of the Sons of America and Order of the Knights of America. See similar discussions in Acuña (1972) and G. Sánchez (1993).

22. See George Sánchez's (1993) discussion of the California State Department of Education, Commission of Immigration and Housing of California, Daughters of the American Revolution, Herbert Gutman, Robert Park, and the University of Southern California's Department of Sociology and School of Social Work.

23. Glazer and Moynihan's argument about "black pathology" is similar to Oscar Lewis's (1961) notion of a "culture of poverty." The latter stipulates that impoverishment, disenfranchisement, and other forms of social marginality are the result of conditions created by the people who are subject to these conditions. See United States Department of Labor (1965).

24. Pastor Jorge Alvarez, interview with the author, Fresno, California, 10 October 2001.

25. Pastors Dan White and Cory White, interview with the author, Fresno, California, 24 September 2001.

26. Pastor César Pérez, interview with the author, Fresno, California, 20 October 2001.

27. Pastor Marc Rosales, interview with the author, Fresno, California, 11 October 2001.

28. Since the 1880s, the development in Fresno has moved from the south, the location of railroad yards and "downtown," toward the north, showing increasingly higher levels of material investment. Currently, Shaw Avenue, which runs east and west, demarcates a sharp division between opulent neighborhoods (to the north) and deteriorating, older neighborhoods (to the south). Mayor Alan Autry often referred to the distinction and its history as the "tale of two cities."

29. According to the Central California Appellate Program, there are thirty-four state prisons and four California Youth Authority facilities. The Federal Bureau of Prisons lists eleven federal prisons in California. See, respectively, http://www.cdcr.ca.gov/Prisons/ and http://www.bop.gov/locations/list.jsp.

30. Pastor Dan White and Cory White, interview with the author, Fresno, California, 24 September 2001.

·

31. In the election of November 2002, San Joaquin Valley voters approved a $161 million bond measure for the renovation and new construction of community colleges. Of this amount, $25 million was allocated for renovating Fresno City College's historic Old Administration Building.

32. These quotations came from the "Principal's Message" and the school's "History," which on 10 December 2002 were available on Fresno High School's website.

33. Devon Sanders, interview with the author, Fresno, California, 13 April 2001.

34. The spelling of names is reproduced as published in newspaper articles, often dropping an accent.

35. Gracie R. Adame, interview with the author, Fresno, California, 29 February 2001.

36. Alfredo Reyes, interview with the author, Fresno, California, 28 January 2002.

37. The verses are from the exit hymn "*Caminando unidos*" (*Flor y canto* 1989). They translate as follows: "Walking together to become united as one, / Walking together with our Lord, / Walking together to become united as one, / Walking together to be with our Redeemer" (my translation).

THREE.   The Journey Home

An earlier version of this chapter was published as "Ritual, Stories, and the Poetics of a Journey Home," *Anthropology of Consciousness* 20 (1): 53–80.

1. A *posada* is a Christmas ritual in which participants reenact Mary and Joseph's search for shelter the night before Jesus's birth.

2. Anne Winston-Allen (1998) provides a thorough discussion of the rosary's medieval origin and notes the unsubstantiated allusion to Saint Dominic.

3. The interview with Gracie R. Adame that I recall in this chapter took place on 4 October 2001. I also draw into this event conversations on other occasions during my stay in Fresno, California.

4. Gracie R. Adame, interview with the author, Fresno, California, 3 February 2001.

5. Gracie R. Adame, interview with the author, Fresno, California, 6 April 2001.

6. See the discussion of my return to Fresno, California, in the introduction.

7. During my stay, Saint Anthony's had two youth groups, one English-speaking and the other Spanish-speaking. Most of the youth (if not all) were bilingual, simply privileging one language over the other. The two youth groups have united since my departure in November 2001.

8. Gracie R. Adame, interview with the author, Fresno, California, 3 February 2001.

9. On 29 January 1973, the Congregation of Divine Worship issued a statement that allowed fit persons to assist ordinary ministers—priests, deacons, and acolytes—in the celebration of communion, limiting their duties to the distribution of the Eucharist. A fit person suffered from no grave sins such as divorce. See "Immensae Caritatis—On Facilitating Reception of Communion in Certain Circumstances," http://www.ewtn.com/library/CURIA/CDWIMCAR.htm.

10. Father Rick Alba, interview with the author, Fresno, California, 15 October 2001.

11. See Carlos G. Vélez-Ibáñez's 1996 discussion of the structural conditions that contribute to neighborhood social marginalization and dissolution, substance abuse, gang violence, and incarceration.

12. Gracie addressed the relationship between mothers, sons, and prison on several occasions. This passage accounts for interviews with the author, Fresno, California, 3 February 2001 and 4 October 2001.

13. See in particular Parenti's 1999 chapter entitled "Balkans in a Box: Rape, Race War, and Other Forms of Management." Parenti discusses at length how prison officials pair particularly irascible inmates with violent serial rapists, turning the former into submissive and docile "punks."

14. Gracie R. Adame, interview with the author, Fresno, California, 3 February 2001.

15. Gracie R. Adame, interview with the author, Fresno, California, 4 October 2001.

16. Gracie discussed this drawing on two occasions: 3 February 2001 and 4 October 2001. The comments that I document in this chapter are from the February meeting.

17. Gracie R. Adame, interview with the author, Fresno, California, 3 February 2001.

18. See Mary Douglas's 1966 treatment of rituals of purity and impurity. See also Julia Kristeva's 1982 treatment of filth and defilement, where she identifies this paradox of ego and non-ego.

19. Gracie R. Adame, interview with the author, Fresno, California, 28 September 2001.

20. This interpretation of Gracie's separation from her mother and entry into the orphanage draws from Jacques Lacan's understanding of the Symbolic order (1977, 64–67). See also Geertz's "concept of culture" and in particular his elaboration of culture's semiotics (1973, 5).

21. See George Sánchez's (1993) discussion of the California State Department of Education, Commission of Immigration and Housing of California,

Daughters of the American Revolution, Herbert Gutman, Robert Park, and the University of Southern California's Department of Sociology and School of Social Work.

22. While notions of the "deserving" and "undeserving poor" were most prevalent in the 1800s, they lingered on through the Great Depression (1930s). See Hacsi (1997).

23. The passage translates as follows: "'You give her cold water, don't give her hot water.' And I thought 'Ooh, cold water'" (my translation).

24. See Lacan's discussion of love and the *"Fort-Da"* (1977, 102–4).

25. Gracie R. Adame, interview with the author, Fresno, California, 3 February 2001.

26. See Edith Turner's 2006 discussion of Roy Willis's 1999 documentation of the entry of spirits in ritual. This experience, which takes place among the Lungu in eastern Zambia, entails a provisional loss of self and acquisition of healing properties. In this chapter, I suggest an attitudinal and ethical change involving a sustained and flexible conception of the self that hinges upon involvement with others.

27. Kristeva notes the Virgin's identification as symbolic and experiential. She represents the "Word" of God, and also the experience of childbirth or the creation of a subjectivity that accounts for a fluid exchange between the real, or the mother, and the Symbolic order. In her discussion of the Virgin, Kristeva advises, "Take a chance with meaning under the veil of words. WORD FLESH" (Kristeva 1976, 262–63; quoted in Oliver 1993, 53).

28. See Kelly Oliver (1993), and in particular her discussion of scars.

FOUR.   The Sacred Circle

An earlier version of this chapter was published as "Poetics, Politics, and the Life of Latino Catholics in California," *Aztlán: A Journal of Chicano Studies* 34 (1): 125–54. © Regents of the University of California. Published by the UCLA Chicano Studies Research Center Press. Reprinted with permission.

1. See the link to Blessed James Alberione on the Sister Disciples of the Divine Master website: http://www.pddm.us/. For an explanation of Father Alberione's enlightenment, refer to his biography at http://www.alberione.org/.

2. Sister Mary Tiziana, interview with the author, Fresno, California, 3 March 2003.

3. In contrast, a multicursal labyrinth has many paths, multiple internal entrances, and dead ends. See Penelope Reed Doob (1990) for a comprehensive discussion of the labyrinth and its primary classical references in Virgil (70–19 BC), Ovid (43 BC–AD 17), and Pliny the Elder (AD 23–79).

4. For a discussion of Marian devotion and the tunic at Chartres, see Katzenellenbogen (1959) and the *Encyclopedia of the Middle Ages*, s.v. "Chartres" (Vauchez 2000).

5. *The Catholic Encyclopedia*, s.v. "Lent" (Herbermann 1913–14).

6. *The Catholic Encyclopedia*, s.v. "Ash Wednesday."

7. *The Catholic Encyclopedia*, s.v. "Ashes."

8. Juanita Ramirez and Eva Gonzales, interview with the author, Fresno, California, 6 March 2001.

9. A *nacimiento* is a Christmas tradition of Mexican origin celebrating the birth of Jesus. Celebrants construct a nacimiento and display it prominently, as in a living room. It features a nativity scene and personal mementoes.

10. Despite a college education and training as a pharmaceutical technician, Juanita had an unsteady employment history, working primarily wage-labor jobs in the retail industry. These types of jobs enabled her to adjust her schedule according to those of her children, whom she raised alone.

11. Migration scholarship is vast; key figures include Anderson (1976), Galarza (1964), García y Griego (1996), Lázaro Salinas (1955), and Monto (1994).

12. These oral histories, Ruiz notes, are housed in archives at California State University, Long Beach. All the women, with one exception, were U.S. citizens and attended Southwestern schools. Ten were born between 1913 and 1929. All considered themselves working class, their fathers' occupations ranging from farmworker and butcher to small family farmer. See also Emory S. Bogardus (1934), who interviewed migrants about their concerns about and aspirations of life in the United States.

13. Eva Gonzales, interview with the author, Fresno, California, 2 October 2001.

14. See Griswold del Castillo (1980), Sandos (1998), and Sagarena (2002) for a comprehensive review of the revitalization of Spanish architecture at the turn of the century. See also the *Fresno Bee* (10 May 2001) article entitled "Historic Homes Revisit the Elegance of Days Gone by via La Paloma's Tour," describing the homes' styles, their architects, and owners who were connected with local government and the region's agribusiness.

15. Eva Gonzales, interview with the author, Fresno, California, 2 February 2001.

16. See Hanke (1959) and Pagden (1987, 1982) for a review of classical ideas in American prejudice. See also R. Lewis (1955) and H. Smith (1950).

17. This historical trajectory can be traced through conceptions of the American frontier, Manifest Destiny, and ideologies of progress justifying the U.S.-Mexican War (1846–48) and the U.S. annexation of northern Mexico. See V. Turner (1962), Webb (1931, 1952), and Slotkin (1992). For constructions of whiteness and Anglo-Mexican relations, see Acuña (1972), Montejano (1987),

D. Weber (1982), Almaguer (1994), Camarillo (1979), Monroy (1990), Pitt (1971), Griswold del Castillo (1990), and G. Sánchez (1993).

18. Mike and Kyle Jameson, interview with the author, Fresno County, California, 15 November 2000.

19. Mike and Kyle Jameson, interview with the author, Fresno County, California, 15 November 2000.

20. The California Secretary of State provides election results for past propositions through its search window at http://www.sos.ca.gov/.

21. The media's representation of these economic conditions is standard news content, appearing periodically throughout the year and in particular during the winter months, when unemployment rates rise due to seasonal layoffs. See, for example, Robert Rodriguez, "Jobless Rate Hits 16 Percent in Fresno County, California, amid Seasonal Slump," *Fresno Bee*, 23 February 2002, and Dale Kasler, "Economy of Mendota, California, Area Is Chronically Depressed," *Sacramento Bee*, 19 December 2002. And for a report about bankruptcies, see Sanford Nax, "Bankruptcy Filings Mount in Fresno, California," *Fresno Bee*, 11 April 2001.

22. See John Ellis, "Council Turns Down Resolution on Unemployment," *Fresno Bee*, 13 March 2003.

23. The program is entitled Fresno County's More Opportunity for Viable Employment. See Ron Trujillo's article, "Fresno County, California, Joins Jobs Program," *Fresno Bee*, 5 July 2001.

24. Mendota's Mayer Riofrio provided this unique insight into the residents' conduct. See Dale Kasler, "Economy of Mendota, California, Area Is Chronically Depressed," *Sacramento Bee*, 19 December 2002.

25. See Virgil, *Aeneid* 6.3–47, and Ovid, *Metamorphoses* 8.140–74.

26. Chance (1994) provides a comprehensive study of medieval mythography and neoplatonism, focusing in particular on the Chartres school.

27. See *Oxford English Dictionary*, 2nd ed., s.v. "Religion."

28. Eva Gonzales, interview with the author, Fresno, California, 23 January 2001.

29. Alfredo Reyes, interview with the author, Fresno, California, 21 March 2001.

30. Periodically the petitions were removed, making space for new ones. Saint Anthony's pastor enabled me to see and record the petitions I had seen upon my visit to the Sacred Heart of Jesus. I represent them unedited. The petition in Spanish says: "I pray for my children's welfare and that everything in my house goes well with your blessing" (my translation).

31. See *The Catholic Encyclopedia*, s.v. "Saint Lucy."

32. Papal instruction says, despite the lack of historical record, that Saint Dominic had used the rosary in the early thirteenth century as the "invincible sword to destroy the nefarious heresy of the Albigensians who threatened the

peace and tranquility of Christendom" (Pius IX 1980, 37). Winston-Allen (1998) discusses the rosary's medieval origin and the unsubstantiated allusions to Saint Dominic.

33. Living Rosary associations enlist members to say a rosary daily and ensure its perpetual recitation. Eva Gonzales is a member of the Universal Living Rosary Association of Saint Philomena, based in Dickinson, Texas.

34. Eva Gonzales, interview with the author, Fresno, California, 28 May 2001.

35. See *The Catholic Encyclopedia*, s.v. "Holy Oils."

36. See *The Catholic Encyclopedia*, s.v. "Oil of Saints."

37. Gabriela Gándara, interview with the author, Austin, Texas, 17 January 2001. Gabriela recalled the conversation with the assistant and doctor. Her conversation with the assistant was in Spanish, which she translated for me in English.

38. Eva Gonzales, interview with the author, Fresno, California, 1 November 2001.

FIVE.   The Passion Play

1. *The Catholic Encyclopedia*, s.v. "Palm."

2. Current scholarship of the Passion play highlights earlier debates about whether this drama evolved among clergy or laity, suggesting that both played a role, one often competing with the other over who could represent the life of Christ (Drumbl 1981; Sticca 1972; Trexler 2003).

3. According to *The Catholic Encyclopedia*, the Passion play evolved with the Easter Play in the medieval period and was the outcome of the church's liturgy. Originally performed in Latin and then in German, the play incorporated "popular [secular] ideas" until the fifteenth century, when the play became clearly "religious." The Passion play of Oberammergau, first mentioned in 1633, was the most renowned. See *The Catholic Encyclopedia*, s.v. "Passion play."

4. The Passion play, therefore, does not stem from Spain's Golden Age as do other religious dramas—Los Pastores and Autos de Reyes Magos, for example— that were instrumental in the Spanish missionaries' evangelization in the New World (Flores 1994; Marie 1948).

5. See a discussion of *dominium* in chapter 1.

6. All Passion play quotations are from a script entitled "La pasión de nuestro señor Jesucristo," or "The Passion of the Lord," which was performed on Sunday, 8 April 2001, Saint Anthony Mary Claret Church, Fresno, California. See also the biblical references. For reflections on the stations of the cross, I am indebted to *Way of the Cross* (1992), edited by Virgil Elizondo.

7. Javier Martinez, interview with the author, Fresno, California, 8 April 2001. All subsequent quotations of Javier Martinez are from the same interview.

8. The estimates of the UFW's representation vary according to different sources. The *San Francisco Chronicle* reports a peak representation of 80,000 farmworkers in the early 1970s (12 April 1997, 1). David Gates (1993), writing for *Newsweek*, reports 100,000 farmworkers.

9. The Agricultural Labor Relations Act was initiated in a legislative proposal drafted by UFW attorney Jerry Cohen and cosponsored by California Assembly Members Richard Alatorre and Richard Burton, both Democrats. The bill's focus on the right to a secret vote on union representation follows the right provided by the National Labor Relations Act of 1935, which excludes farmworkers. The California Assembly approved the bill late in the legislative session, and the bill never arrived to the Senate for a vote. In any case, the bill faced a veto by Governor Ronald Reagan. Jerry Brown, elected governor in November 1974, fulfilled a campaign promise to support secret-ballot union elections and introduced a modified version of the Alatorre-Burton bill on 10 April. The UFW endorsed Governor Brown's bill on 8 May. The bill passed the state Senate and Assembly and was signed into law by Brown in early June. The law took effect on 28 August 1975 (Mooney and Majka 1995, 173–74).

10. See Richard Griswold del Castillo and Richard A. Garcia's 1995 discussion of Chávez's early training. Chávez first worked with Fred Ross as an organizer in Saul Alinsky's Community Service Organization (CSO), which helped organize Mexican Americans politically in Los Angeles and San Jose. The CSO sent Chávez to Oxnard, California, in 1958 to support a local labor strike among lemon workers. The Farm Workers Association, later known as the UFW, was officially called the National Farm Workers Association and was established on 30 September 1962, with César Chávez elected president and executive officer, Dolores Huerta and Gilbert Padilla, vice-presidents, and Antonio Orendain, secretary treasurer (Griswold del Castillo and Garcia 1995, 31, 37). Within three years, the FWA established a death benefit, social service program, credit union, and newspaper (*El Malcriado*) and had its own flag, a small treasury, two paid staff, and fifteen hundred members (Ganz 2000, 1024).

11. J. Craig Jenkins and Charles Perrow (1977) credit this social and political climate for the UFW's success. In response to this and similar claims (Brown 1972; Majka and Makja 1982; Jenkins 1985), Marshall Ganz attributes the UFW's success to Chávez's "strategic [leadership] capacity" (2000, 1005).

12. In 1976 the ALRB received hundreds of election petitions, straining the board and staff and depleting its original $1.3 million appropriation. The ALRB requested $3.8 million for fiscal year 1976, which ended in June. Approval of emergency funds requires a two-thirds majority vote instead of the simple majority required for regular appropriations. A Democratic caucus forced progrower Democrats to support the funding, and the legislature approved $2.6 million by a 54–24 vote. The ALRB resumed operations with a reduced staff on 1 December 1976. The legislature attached modifications to the funding: no more than two

union representatives could access farm property one hour before work, during the lunch break, and anytime after work (Arce Decierdo 1980; *Wall Street Journal,* 12 October 1976, 7).

13. See Daniel (1987), Griswold del Castillo and Garcia (1995), Griswold del Castillo (1996), and Mooney and Majka (1995) for discussions of changes in California politics that affected the UFW and farm labor.

14. Miriam J. Wells reports, "by 1979, there were 11,500 acres of strawberry fields in California, cultivated by about 900 growers averaging 13 acres each" (1981, 682). This number of acres increased to 33,000 by 2004 (Borris, Brunke, and Kreith 2006). The California Strawberry Commission shows that the number of acres increased to 39,073 by 2014, accounting for 88 percent of national production valued at 2.5 billion dollars. According to the Commission's 2014 survey, California's Central Coast, including Santa Cruz and Monterey counties, provided 44.1 percent of the state's strawberry production (http://www.californiastrawberries .com/). In the mid-1990s, the time when the UFW was attempting to persuade workers to join the union, there were "270 growers in the Pajaro and Salinas valleys, more than 100 of whom [were] small growers with about 20 to 60 acres." Midsize farms consisted of up to 200 acres. Large operations, such as the Monsanto-controlled Gargiulo, Inc., farmed more than 500 acres and employed a thousand or more people (*Santa Cruz County Sentinel,* 13 April 1997, 7).

15. The planting and cultivation months require an estimated 35 person-hours per acre; the harvest months require from 300 to 1,200 person-hours per acre. The labor must be skilled in fruit picking and packing and available for relatively short harvest cycles—every 4 to 5 days for fresh berries and 7 to 10 days for freezer berries. These conditions make the strawberry industry extremely vulnerable to work stoppages (Wells 1981, 683; 2000).

16. Sharecroppers accounted for half of the production in the 1980s and declined to a mere 10 percent in the 1990s due to the dynamics of regional social relations defined along the lines of class and politics. See Wells's discussion of the sharecropping (1981, 1996, 2000).

17. In April 2001, Assembly Member Dean Florez (D-Shafter) sponsored Assembly Bill 883, which mirrored these collective Central-Coast strategies. Bill 883 pooled money from growers, the state, and nonprofit groups to provide "low-cost health insurance for California farm workers and their families. . . . 'Surveys show,'" Florez reported, "'more than two-thirds of farm workers lack any form of health coverage, making them one of the largest groups of the uninsured employees in the state'" (*Fresno Bee,* 21 April 2001). Bill 883 died 30 November 2002. See a discussion on Dean Florez in chapter 2.

18. The Agricultural Labor Relations Act of 1975 prohibits organized grower representation.

19. The term "indigenous" refers to people who carry on a Mesoamerican peasant tradition. For the meaning of campesino political identification, see Boyer (2003).

20. The *Carta Editorial* article is reproduced in "Walkout in Albuquerque: The Chicano Movement Becomes Nationwide" and quoted in Hammerback and Jensen 1994, 53.

21. Davis and Virulegio (1987) compiled and examined the complete texts of more than two hundred such "plans." See in particular the Plan of San Diego, which in 1914 revealed Mexican Americans' hope of reclaiming for Mexico land taken by the United States in the formation of the U.S. Southwest.

22. See in particular John Locke's *Two Treatises of Government* (1988), Thomas Paine's *Rights of Man* (1984) and *Common Sense* (1986), and Thomas Jefferson's *Notes on the State of Virginia* (1955).

23. The Homestead Act of 1862 enabled settlers to claim at least 160 acres. Under each provision of a preemption law, which included the commutation clause of the Homestead Act, the Timber and Stone Act, and the Desert Land Act, settlers could claim 160 acres, for a total of 480 acres. The Desert Land Act permitted an additional 640 acres, enabling an individual to claim up to a total of 1,120 acres. It is important to note that while 160 acres was often more than sufficient for a single family-farm in the well-watered states of Iowa, Kansas, Nebraska, and Minnesota, it was hardly sufficient for survival in arid regions. California promoted capitalist-style farming over subsistence farming, never undergoing the impact of homesteading (Nugent 1999; P. Gates 1975). See also Pitt (1971) and McWilliams (1990) for explanations about the Spanish and Mexican land grants in the U.S. Southwest under the Homestead Act and, generally, about a systemic bias toward Anglo settlement. For information about the Homestead Act's ethos, claims filed, and abuses, especially at the expense of Indian populations, see P. Gates (1936) and Nugent (1999).

24. See Bogardus (1934), Drachsler (1920), Ellis (1929), Mahoney and Herlihy (1918), Park and Miller (1921), *Proceedings: Americanization Conference* (1919), and Sharlip and Owens (1925). For critiques, see Entrikin (1980), Gaziano (1996), Cicourel and Kitsuse (1963), G. González (1974), and Van Nuys (2002).

25. For classic community studies, see Lynd and Lynd (1929, 1937). The literature on urban history, Tobey, Wetherell, and Brigham comment, "is immense" (1990, 1396). Noteworthy works include Rossi (1955), Chudacoff (1972), Ebner (1981), Knights (1971), Perin (1977), Thernstrom (1964), and Thernstrom and Sennett (1969). Katz, Doucet, and Stern (1982) focus on modernization's influence on a mobile proletariat. Fairbanks (1988) reviews the public policy and sentiments of the 1920s and 1930s that culminated in the Federal Housing Act of 1949. See also Rossi and Shlay (1982) for a scholarship review. Family studies include Hayden (1984) and Shorter (1975).

26. The *Democratic Review*, as is commonly known and cited, was published as *The United States Magazine and Democratic Review*. Historians attribute the 1845 article, "Annexation," to John L. O'Sullivan, the magazine's editor (Johannsen 1997; Sampson 2003).

27. See Acuña (1972), McWilliams (1990), Monroy (1990), and Pitt (1971) for accounts of the various machinations by which Anglo Americans usurped Spanish and Mexican land grants and acquired large ranches. In Texas, see Montejano (1987).

28. Despite these impressive landholdings, of which Hart (1998) provides a thorough account, Knight (1998) argues that they paled in comparison to American investment in the extraction industries. Real estate accounted for approximately 4 percent of the total U.S. investments in Mexico in 1910. During the Porfirian and revolutionary periods, U.S. foreign policy focused on protecting capital investment in those industries.

29. The suit charged that the UFW had used illegal tactics in the boycott of the company's lettuce. The initial award to Bruce Church, Inc., was $5.4 million. Upon appeal, a jury ruled again in favor of Bruce Church, Inc., in June 1993 and awarded the company $2,898,280 in compensatory damages and $1,000 in punitive damages. For a brief description of this case and César Chávez's testimony, see the *New York Times*, 12 June 1993, section 1, 11.

30. Company representatives of Niagara Corporation and of Chemagro Corporation recruited farmworkers through their crew leaders to participate in an experiment whereby the farmworkers, including women and children, entered a field seven days after the application of the products Ethion and Guthion. Niagara conducted blood tests four days after reentry, and Chemagro, twenty-one days after. The workers showed critical declines in plasma content and red blood cell counts. Both companies provided evidence, apparently contrived with no ethical discussion, supporting their claims of safe reentry seven days after application. This event, among others, provided impetus to H.R. 10729, which amended the Pesticide Control Act of 1971. For details regarding this incident, see Senate Committee on Agriculture and Forestry, Subcommittee on Agricultural Research and General Legislation, *Federal Environmental Pesticide Control Act: Hearings on H.R. 10729*, 92nd Cong., 2nd sess. (7 and 8 March 1972), 332–45.

31. See in particular the statement of Senator Gaylord Nelson (D-Wisconsin) on pages 66–80 of the document cited in the note above. See the testimonies of other congressional representatives and industry experts in the same document. With reference to the Pesticide Control Act of 1971, see Senate Committee on Agriculture and Forestry, Subcommittee on Agricultural Research and General Legislation, *Federal Environmental Pesticide Control Act: Hearings on S. 232, S. 272, S. 660, and S. 745*, 92nd Cong., 1st sess. (23, 24, 25, and 26 March 1971). See George Hoberg's 1992 review of pesticide regulation between 1969 and 1975.

32. Other pesticides, including fungicides (e.g., captan) and herbicides (e.g., dinoseb), also contribute to the number of reported poisonings in California. Under pesticide law, all incidents of poisoning in California must be reported. In 1990, California became the first state to require that the use of all pesticides be reported monthly to county agricultural commissioners. County agriculture commissioners report data to the California Department of Pesticide Regulation. See the *Los Angeles Times* (19 August 1988, A1) for a brief description of pesticides used in California. See the California Department of Pesticide Regulation website for an account of past and present pesticide use: http://www.cdpr.ca.gov/docs/pur/purmain.htm.

33. See *The Gale Encyclopedia of Medicine*, s.v. "Fasting" (Longe and Blanchfield 2002).

34. Alfredo Reyes, interview with the author, Fresno, California, 8 April 2001.

SIX. Pilgrimage

1. Chevalier comments that Ferdinand and Isabella wanted to "avoid the splitting up of pasture to the benefit of individuals." They preferred a "system of common grazing" that existed in Spain before the erection of barriers. Municipal authorities compromised this policy by granting cattlemen grazing rights, or *estancias*, that established exclusive areas but without title. The *estancias* often followed the cattlemen's use of the land, effectively endorsing squatting rights and setting a precedent for ownership (1963, 88).

2. Pastor Dan White, interview by the author, Fresno, California, 24 September 2001.

3. See discussion of Greater Mexico in the introduction.

4. Drawing from Monsiváis (1976), Olga Nájera-Ramiriz (1994) comments about the standardization of the *charro* image.

5. The church's role in the conquest took many forms. Lewis Hanke (1959, 1964, 1974) and Ursula Lamb (1956) discuss the legacy the sixteenth-century racial and theological ideologies that substantiated the Crown's authority in the New World. Arnold J. Bauer (1983) accounts for the church's acquisition of material resources. In the context of California, which has been the focus of recent debates about Fray Junipero Serra, see Costo and Costo (1987), Cook (1976), Heizer (1978), R. Jackson (1994), R. Jackson and Castillo (1995), and Monroy (1990) for documentation of missionary coercion and conversion. See Hackel (1997) for a review of Indian cooptation and leadership in the missions' systematic oppression.

6. Sister Mary Tiziana, interview with the author, Fresno, California, 3 March 2003.

7. Gracie R. Adame, interview with the author, Fresno, California, 28 September 2001.

Conclusion

1. *Oxford English Dictionary*, 2nd ed., s.v. "Procession."

2. Gracie R. Adame, interview with the author, Fresno, California, 4 October 2001.

3. As indicated in chapter 2, these verses are from the final stanza of the entrance hymn, "*Vamos cantando al señor*" (*Flor y canto* 1989). They translate as follows: "United as brothers and sisters, / We come to your altar, / That you may fill our lives with love and friendship" (my translation).

4. See Freud's discussion of the unconscious and id, which are instrumental in defining the ego according to stricture and prohibition. Freud acknowledges that such strictures could be injurious, and therefore an objective of psychoanalysis is to remove them (1961). Lacan takes up a similar line of reasoning in his allocation of order and stricture to language and the unconscious's representation in the symbolic order (1977).

5. Coatlicue appears as Cihuacóatl, who is also known as Tonantzin (mentioned in chapter 1). To see these gods as one and the same or different ignores doubling and referral that characterize relationships among gods in the Aztec pantheon.

6. Gracie R. Adame, interview with the author, Fresno, California, 3 February 2001.

7. Gracie R. Adame, interview with the author, Fresno, California, 4 October 2001.

8. The verse translates as follows: "That you may fill our lives with love and friendship."

9. *The Catholic Encyclopedia*, s.v. "Liturgy." See also Lebbe 1949.

10. Alfredo Reyes, interview with the author, Fresno, California, 21 March 2001.

11. Eva Gonzales, interview with the author, Fresno, California, 28 May 2001.

12. Gabriela Gándara, interview with the author, Austin, Texas, 17 January 2001.

WORKS CITED

Acuña, Rodolfo. 1972. *Occupied America: A History of Chicanos*. San Francisco: Canfield Press.

Alarcón, Norma. 1999. "Chicana Feminism: In the Tracks of 'the' Native Woman." In *Between Woman and Nation*, edited by Caren Kaplan, Norma Alarcón, and Mino Moallem, 63–71. Durham, NC: Duke University Press.

Allensworth, Elaine M., and Refugio I. Rochín. 1995. *Rural California Communities: Trends in Latino Population and Community Life*. East Lansing: Julian Samora Research Institute, Michigan State University.

Almaguer, Tomás. 1994. *Racial Fault Lines: The Historical Origins of White Supremacy in California*. Berkeley and Los Angeles: University of California Press.

Amerine, Maynard A. 1969. "An Introduction to Pre-repeal History of Grapes." *Agricultural History* 43 (2): 259–68.

Anaya, Rudolfo. 1972. *Bless Me, Ultima*. New York: Grand Central Publishing.

Anderson, Henry P. 1976. *The Bracero Program in California*. New York: Arno Press.

Anna, Timothy E. 1978. *The Fall of the Royal Government in Mexico City*. Lincoln: University of Nebraska Press.

Arce Decierdo, Margarita. 1980. "The Struggle Within: Mediating Conflict in California Fields, 1975–1977." Chicano Political Economy Collective, Working Paper Series no. 106. Berkeley: Department of Sociology, University of California.

Aristotle. 1984. *The Complete Works of Aristotle*. Edited by Jonathan Barnes. 2 vols. Bollingen Series 71. Princeton: Princeton University Press.

Aron, Stephen. 1994. "Lessons in Conquest: Towards a Greater Western History." *Pacific Historical Review* 63 (2): 125–47.

Baker, Susan González. 1990. *The Cautious Welcome: The Legalization Programs of the Immigration Reform and Control Act*. Santa Monica: Rand Corporation/ Washington, DC: Urban Institute.

Bakhtin, Mikhail M. 1981. *The Dialogic Imagination*. Edited by Michael Holquist. Austin: University of Texas Press.

———. 1986. "The Problem of Speech Genres." In *Speech Genres, and Other Late Essays*, translated by Vern W. McGee, edited by Caryl Emerson and Michael Holquist, 60–102. Austin: University of Texas Press.

Bancroft, Hubert Howe. 1886. *History of California*. 7 vols. San Francisco: History Company Publishers.

———. 1888. *California Pastoral*. Vol. 34 of *The Works of Hubert Howe Bancroft*. San Francisco: History Company Publishers.

Baquedano-López, Patricia. 1997. "Creating Social Identities through *La Doctrina*." *Issues in Applied Linguistics* 8 (1): 27–45.

Baretta, Silvio, R. Duncan, and John Markoff. 1978. "Civilization and Barbarism: Cattle Frontiers in Latin America." *Comparative Studies in Society and History* 20 (4): 587–620.

Basso, Keith H. 1996. *Wisdom Sits in Places: Landscape and Language among the Western Apache*. Albuquerque: University of New Mexico Press.

Bauer, Arnold J. 1983. "The Church in the Economy of Spanish America: *Censos* and *Depósitos* in the Eighteenth and Nineteenth Centuries." *Hispanic American Historical Review* 63 (4): 707–33.

Bauman, Richard. 1977. *Verbal Art as Performance*. Long Grove, IL: Waveland Press.

Bauman, Richard, and Charles L. Briggs. 1990. "Poetics and Performances as Critical Perspectives on Language and Social Life." *Annual Review of Anthropology* 19:59–88.

Bean, Frank D., Barry Edmonston, and Jeffrey S. Passel. 1990. *Undocumented Migration to the United States: IRCA and the Experience of the 1980s*. Santa Monica: Rand Corporation / Washington, DC: Urban Institute.

Becerra Tanco, Luis. [1675] 1979. *Felicidad de México en el principio, y milagroso origen, que tubo el Santuario de la Viren María Nuestra Señora de Guadalupe*. 3rd ed. (facsimile). México City: Editorial Jus.

Behar, Ruth. 1995. "Rage and Redemption: Reading the Life Story of a Mexican Marketing Woman." In *The Dialogic Emergence of Culture*, edited by Dennis Tedlock and Bruce Mannheim, 148–78. Urbana: University of Illinois Press.

Behrens, Helen. 1966. *The Virgin and the Serpent God*. México City: Editorial Progreso.

Benjamin, Walter. 1968a. "The Storyteller." In *Illuminations*, translated by Harry Zohn, 83–109. New York: Harcourt, Brace & World.

———. 1968b. "The Task of the Translator." In *Illuminations*, translated by Harry Zohn, 69–82. New York: Harcourt, Brace & World.

Berger, Harris M., and Giovanna P. Del Negro. 2002. "Bauman's *Verbal Art* and the Social Organization of Attention: The Role of Reflexivity in the Aesthetics of Performance." *Journal of American Folklore* 115 (455): 62–91.

Bishko, Charles Julian. 1952. "The Peninsular Background of Latin American Cattle Ranching." *Hispanic American Historical Review* 32 (4): 491–515.

Bodnar, John. 1996. "Introduction: The Attractions of Patriotism." In *Bonds of Affection: Americans Define Their Patriotism*, edited by John Bodnar, 3–18. Princeton: Princeton University Press.

Bogardus, Emory S. 1934. *The Mexican in the United States*. University of Southern California School of Research Studies Number 5, Social Science Series. Los Angeles: University of Southern California Press.

Boriss, Hayley, Henrich Brunke, and Marcia Kreith. 2006. "Commodity Profile: Strawberries." Davis, CA: Agricultural Issues Center, University of California.

Bourdieu, Pierre. 1977. *Outline of a Theory of Practice*. Translated by Richard Nice. Cambridge: Cambridge University Press.

———. 1990. *The Logic of Practice*. Translated by Richard Nice. Stanford: Stanford University Press.

Boyer, Christopher R. 2003. *Becoming Campesinos: Politics, Identity, and Agrarian Struggle in Postrevolutionary Michoacán, 1920–1935*. Stanford: Stanford University Press.

Boyle, Eugene J. 1993. "¡Viva la Causa!" *America* 168 (18): 4.

Brack, Gene M. 1975. *Mexico Views Manifest Destiny, 1821–1846: An Essay on the Origins of the Mexican War*. Albuquerque: University of New Mexico Press.

Bradford, William. 1898. *Bradford's History "Of Plimoth Plantation."* Boston: Wright & Potter Printing Co.

Brading, David A. 2001. *Mexican Phoenix*. Cambridge: Cambridge University Press.

Brender, Jean D., and Lucina Suarez. 1990. "Paternal Occupation and Anencephaly." *American Journal of Epidemiology* 131 (9): 517–21.

Briggs, Charles L. 1993a. "Generic versus Metapragmatic Dimensions of Warao Narratives: Who Regiments Performance?" In *Reflexive Language: Reported Speech and Metapragmatics*, edited by John A. Lucy, 179–212. Cambridge: Cambridge University Press.

———. 1993b. "Metadiscursive Practices and Scholarly Authority in Folkloristics." *Journal of American Folklore* 106 (422): 387–434.

Brown, Jerald. 1972. "The United Farm Workers Grape Strike and Boycott, 1965–70." PhD diss., Cornell University, Department of Anthropology.

Broyles-González, Yolanda. 2002. "Indianizing Catholicism: Chicana/India/Mexicana Indigenous Spiritual Practices in Our Image." In *Chicana Traditions: Continuity and Change*, edited by Norma E. Cantú and Olga Nájera-Ramírez, 117–32. Urbana: University of Illinois Press.

Burkhart, Louise M. 1993. "The Cult of the Virgin of Guadalupe in Mexico." In *South and Meso-American Native Spirituality: From the Cult of the Feathered Serpent to the Theology of Liberation*, edited by Gary H. Gossen and Miguel León-Portilla, 198–227. New York: Crossroad.

Butzer, Karl W. 1988. "Cattle and Sheep from Old to New Spain: Historical Antecedents." *Annals of the Association of American Geographers* 78 (1): 29–56.

Camarillo, Albert. 1979. *Chicanos in a Changing Society: From Mexican Pueblos to American Barrios in Santa Barbara and Southern California, 1848–1930*. Cambridge, MA: Harvard University Press.

Campbell, Ena. 1982. "The Virgin of Guadalupe and Female Self-Image: A Mexican Case History." In *Mother Worship: Theme and Variations,* edited by James J. Preston, 5–24. Chapel Hill: University of North Carolina Press.

Carosso, Vincent P. 1951. *The California Wine Industry, 1830–1895: A Study of the Formative Years.* Berkeley and Los Angeles: University of California Press.

Cassirer, Ernst. [1944] 1962. *An Essay on Man: An Introduction to a Philosophy of Human Culture.* New Haven: Yale University Press.

Castoriadis, Cornelius. 1988. *The Imaginary Institution of Society.* Translated by Kathleen Blamey. Cambridge: Polity Press.

Champe, Flavia Waters. 1983. *The Matachines Dance of the Upper Rio Grande: History, Music, and Choreography.* Lincoln: University of Nebraska Press.

Chance, Jane. 1994. *Medieval Mythography: From Roman North America to the School of Chartres, A.D. 433–1177.* Gainesville: University Press of Florida.

Chauvet, Fidel de Jesús. 1978. *El culto Guadalupano del Tepeyac: Sus orígenes y sus críticos en el siglo XVI.* Mexico City: Centro de Estudios Bernardino de Sahagún, A.C.

Chavez, Leo R. 1998. *Shadowed Lives: Undocumented Immigrants in American Society.* Fort Worth: Harcourt Brace College Publishers.

———. 2001. *Covering Immigration: Popular Images and the Politics of the Nation.* Berkeley and Los Angeles: University of California Press.

Chavez, Leo R., Estevan T. Flores, and Marta Lopez-Garza. 1990. "Here Today, Gone Tomorrow? Undocumented Settlers and Immigration Reform." *Human Organization* 49 (3): 193–205.

Chevalier, François. 1963. *Land and Society in Colonial Mexico: The Great Hacienda.* Translated by Alvin Eustis. Berkeley and Los Angeles: University of California Press.

Chudacoff, Howard P. 1972. *Mobile Americans: Residential and Social Mobility in Omaha, 1880–1920.* New York: Oxford University Press.

Cicourel, Aaron V. 1985. "Text and Discourse." *Annual Review of Anthropology* 14:159–85.

Cicourel, Aaron V., and John I. Kitsuse. 1963. *The Educational Decision-Makers.* Indianapolis: Bobbs-Merrill.

Clark, William A. V. 1998. *The California Cauldron: Immigration and the Fortunes of Local Communities.* New York: Guilford Press.

Cleland, Robert Glass. 1951. *The Cattle on a Thousand Hills.* San Marino, CA: Huntington Library Publications.

Clifford, James. 1986. "On Ethnographic Allegory." In *Writing Culture: The Poetics and Politics of Ethnography,* edited by James Clifford and George E. Marcus, 90–121. Berkeley and Los Angeles: University of California Press.

Comaroff, John, and Jean Comaroff. 1992. *Ethnography and the Historical Imagination.* Boulder, CO: Westview Press.

Cook, Sherburne R. 1976. *The Conflict between the California Indian and White Civilization.* Berkeley and Los Angeles: University of California Press.

Cornelius, Wayne A. 1989. "Impacts of the 1986 U.S. Immigration Law on Emigration from Rural Mexican Sending Communities." *Population and Development Review* 15 (4): 689–705.

Cornelius, Wayne A., Philip L. Martin, and James F. Hollifield. 1994. "Introduction: The Ambivalent Quest for Immigration Control." In *Controlling Immigration: A Global Perspective,* edited by Wayne A. Cornelius, Philip L. Martin, and James Hollifield, 3–42. Stanford: Stanford University Press.

Costo, Rubert, and Jeannette Henry Costo, eds. 1987. *The Missions of California: A Legacy of Genocide.* San Francisco: American Indian Historical Society / Indian Historian Press.

Crane, Keith, Beth J. Asch, Joanna Zorn Heilbrunn, and Danielle C. Cullinane. 1990. *The Effect of Employer Sanctions on the Flow of Undocumented Immigrants to the United States.* Santa Monica: Rand Corporation.

Cronon, William, George Miles, and Jay Gitlin. 1992. "Becoming West: Toward a New Meaning for Western History." In *Under an Open Sky: Rethinking America's Western Past,* edited by William Cronon, George Miles, and Jay Gitlin, 3–27. New York: W. W. Norton.

Csordas, Thomas J. 1994. *The Sacred Self: A Cultural Phenomenology of Charismatic Healing.* Berkeley and Los Angeles: University of California Press.

Cypess, Sandra Messinger. 1991. *La Malinche in Mexican Literature: From History to Myth.* Austin: University of Texas Press.

Daniel, Cletus E. 1987. "Cesar Chavez and the Unionization of California Farm Workers." In *Labor Leaders in America,* edited by Melvyn Dubofsky and Warren Van Tine, 350–82. Urbana: University of Illinois Press.

Davalos, Karen Mary. 2002. "'The Real Way of Praying': The Via Crucis, Mexicano Sacred Space, and the Architecture of Domination." In *Horizons of the Sacred: Mexican Traditions in U.S. Catholicism,* edited by Timothy Matovina and Gary Riebe-Estrella, SVD, 41–68. Ithaca, NY: Cornell University Press.

Davis, Angela Y. 1999. Foreword to *Behind the Razor Wire: Portrait of a Contemporary American Prison System,* ix–xviii. New York: New York University Press.

Davis, Thomas B., and Amado Ricon Virulegio. 1987. *The Political Plans of Mexico.* Lanham, MD: University Press of America.

de Man, Paul. 1979. *Allegories of Reading: Figural Language in Rousseau, Nietzsche, Rilke, and Proust.* New Haven: Yale University Press.

Derrida, Jacques. 1974. "'. . . That Dangerous Supplement. . .'" In *Of Grammatology,* translated by Gayatri Chakravorty Spivak, 141–64. Baltimore: Johns Hopkins University Press.

Deverell, William. 1994. "Fighting Words: The Significance of the American West in the History of the United States." *Western Historical Quarterly* 25 (2): 185–206.

Diccionario de la lengua castellana. 1914. Madrid: Impresores de los Sucesores de Hernando.

Doob, Penelope Reed. 1990. *The Idea of the Labyrinth from Classical Antiquity through the Middle Ages.* Ithaca, NY: Cornell University Press.

Douglas, Mary. 1966. *Purity and Danger: An Analysis of the Concepts of Pollution and Taboo.* New York: Routledge.

Dozier, Edward P. 1958. "Spanish-Catholic Influences on Rio Grande Pueblo Religion." *American Anthropologist* 60 (3): 441–48.

Drachsler, Julius. 1920. *Democracy and Assimilation: The Blending of Immigrant Heritages in America.* New York: Macmillan.

Drumbl, Johann. 1981. *Quem quaeritis: Teatro sacro dell'alto mediovo.* Rome: Bulzoni.

Dunn, Timothy J. 1996. *The Militarization of the U.S.–Mexican Border, 1978–1992: Low-Intensity Conflict Doctrine Comes Home.* Austin: Center for Mexican American Studies, University of Texas.

Durand, Jorge, and Douglas S. Massey. 1992. "Mexican Migration to the United States: A Critical Review." *Latin American Research Review* 27 (2): 3–42.

Durkheim, Emile, and Marcel Mauss. 1963. *Primitive Classification.* Chicago: University of Chicago Press.

———. 2001. *The Elementary Forms of Religious Life.* Translated by Carol Cosman. Oxford: Oxford University Press.

Ebner, Michael H. 1981. "Urban History: Retrospect and Prospect." *Journal of American History* 68 (1): 69–84.

Eliade, Mircea. 1958. *Patterns in Comparative Religion.* Translated by Rosemary Sheed. New York: Sheed & Ward.

———. 1959. *The Sacred and the Profane.* Translated by Willard R. Trask. New York: Harcourt, Brace and Company.

Elizondo, Virgilio. 1980. *La Morenita: Evangelizer of the Americas.* San Antonio: Mexican American Cultural Center.

———. 1983. *Galilean Journey: The Mexican-American Promise.* Maryknoll, NY: Orbis Books.

———. 2001. *Guadalupe: Mother of the New Creation.* Maryknoll, NY: Orbis Books.

Ellis, Pearle Idelia. 1929. *Americanization through Homemaking.* Los Angeles: Wetzel Publishing Company.

Emerson, Ralph Waldo. [1841] 1945. *Essays of Ralph Waldo Emerson.* New York: Literary Classics Inc.

Entrikin, Nicholas J. 1980. "Robert Park's Human Ecology and Human Geography." *Annals of the Association of American Geographers* 70 (1): 43–58.

Fairbanks, Robert B. 1988. *Making Better Citizens: Housing Reform and the Community Development Strategy in Cincinnati, 1890–1960.* Urbana and Chicago: University of Illinois Press.

Feagin, Joe R. 1997. "Old Poison in New Bottles: The Deep Roots of Modern Nativism." In *Immigrants Out! The New Nativism and the Anti-immigrant Impulse in the United States,* edited by Juan F. Perea, 14–43. New York: New York University Press.

Fernandez, Fidel González, Eduardo Chávez Sánchez, and José Luis Guerrero Rosado. 1999. *El encuentro de la Virgin de Guadalupe y Juan Diego.* Mexico City: Editorial Porrúa.

Fernandez, James W. 1986. *Persuasions and Performances: The Play of Tropes in Culture.* Bloomington: Indiana University Press.

Ferriss, Susan, and Ricardo Sandoval. 1997. *The Fight in the Fields: Cesar Chavez and the Farmworkers Movement.* New York: Harcourt Brace & Company.

Flor y canto. 1989. Portland: OCP Publications.

Flores, Richard R. 1994. "*Los Pastores* and the Gifting of Performance." *American Ethnologist* 21 (2): 270–85.

———. 1995. "*Los Pastores*": *History and Performance in the Mexican Shepherd's Play of South Texas.* Washington, DC: Smithsonian Institution Press.

———. 2002. *Remembering the Alamo: Memory, Modernity, and the Master Symbol.* Austin: University of Texas Press.

Florescano, Enrique. 1969. *Precios del maíz y crisis agrícolas en México (1708–1810).* Mexico City: Colegio de México.

Forrest, John. 1984. *Morris and Matachin.* Sheffield, UK: Cectal Publications.

Foucault, Michel. 1977. *Discipline & Punish: The Birth of the Prison.* Translated by Alan Sheridan. New York: Vintage Books.

Freud, Sigmund. 1961. *The Standard Edition of the Complete Psychological Works of Sigmund Freud.* Translated by James Strachey. 24 vols. London: Hogarth Press / Institute of Psychoanalysis.

Friedrich, Paul. 1991. "Polytropy." In *Beyond Metaphor: The Theory of Tropes in Anthropology,* edited by James W. Fernandez, 17–55. Stanford: Stanford University Press.

Friedricks, William B. 1990. "Capital and Labor in Los Angeles: Henry E. Huntington vs. Organized Labor, 1900–1920." *Pacific Historical Review* 59 (3): 375–95.

Fusfeld, Daniel R. 1956. *The Economic Thought of Franklin D. Roosevelt and the Origins of the New Deal.* New York: Columbia University Press.

Galarza, Ernesto. 1964. *Merchants of Labor: The Mexican Bracero Story.* Charlotte: McNally & Loftin.

Gálvez, Alyshia. 2010. *Guadalupe in New York.* New York: New York University Press.

Gamio, Manuel. 1930. *The Mexican Immigrant: His Life Story*. Chicago: University of Chicago Press.

———. 1931. *Mexican Immigration to the United States*. Chicago: University of Chicago Press.

Ganz, Marshall. 2000. "Resources and Resourcefulness: Strategic Capacity in the Unionization of California Agriculture, 1959–1966." *American Journal of Sociology* 105 (4): 1003–62.

García y Griego, Manuel. 1996. "The Importation of Mexican Contract Laborers to the United States, 1942–1964." In *Between Two Worlds: Mexican Immigrants in the United States*, edited by David G. Gutiérrez, 45–85. Wilmington: Jaguar Books on Latin America.

Gates, David. 1993. "A Secular Saint of the '60s." *Newsweek* 121 (May): 68.

Gates, Paul Wallace. 1936. "The Homestead Law in an Incongruous Land System." *American Historical Review* 41 (4): 652–81.

———. 1975. "Public Land Disposal in California." In *Agriculture in the Development of the Far West*, edited by James Shideler, 158–78. Washington DC: Agricultural History Society.

Gaziano, Emanuel. 1996. "Ecological Metaphors as Scientific Boundary Work: Innovation and Authority in Interwar Sociology and Biology." *American Journal of Sociology* 101 (4): 874–907.

Geertz, Clifford. 1973. *The Interpretation of Cultures*. New York: Basic Books.

Gillespie, Susan D. 1989. *The Aztec Kings: The Construction of Rulership in Mexica History*. Tucson: University of Arizona Press.

Glazer, Nathan, and Daniel Patrick Moynihan. 1970. *Beyond the Melting Pot: The Negroes, Puerto Ricans, Jews, Italians, and Irish of New York City*. Cambridge, MA: MIT Press.

Gonzales, M. C. 1932. "The Aim of LULAC." *LULAC News* 1 (March): 3, 7.

González, Alberto. 1990. "Mexican 'Otherness' in the Rhetoric of Mexican Americans." *Southern Communication Journal* 55 (3): 276–91.

González, Gilbert C. 1974. "Racism, Education, and the Mexican Community in Los Angeles, 1920–30." *Societas* 4:287–301.

Gordon, Robert. 1999. "Poisons in the Fields: The United Farm Workers, Pesticides, and Environmental Politics." *Pacific Historical Review* 68 (1): 51–77.

Graulich, Michel R. 1997. *Myths of Ancient Mexico*. Translated by Bernard R. Ortiz de Montellano and Thelma Ortiz de Montellano. Norman: University of Oklahoma Press.

Grimes, Ronald L. 2006. *Rite Out of Place: Ritual, Media, and the Arts*. Oxford: Oxford University Press.

Griswold del Castillo, Richard. 1980. "The del Valle Family and the Fantasy Heritage." *California History* 59 (1): 2–15.

———. 1990. *The Treaty of Guadalupe Hidalgo: A Legacy of Conflict*. Norman: University of Oklahoma Press.

———. 1996. "Cesar Chavez: The Final Struggle." *Southern California Quarterly* 78 (2): 199–214.

Griswold del Castillo, Richard, and Richard A. Garcia. 1995. *César Chávez: A Triumph of Spirit.* Norman: University of Oklahoma Press.

Gudde, Erwin G. 1960. *California Place Names: The Origin and Etymology of Current Geographical Names.* Berkeley and Los Angeles: University of California Press.

Gutiérrez, David R. 1995. *Walls and Mirrors: Mexican Americans, Mexican Immigrants, and the Politics of Ethnicity.* Berkeley and Los Angeles: University of California Press.

Habermas, Jürgen. 1991. *The Structural Transformation of the Public Sphere: An Inquiry into a Category of Bourgeois Society.* Translated by Thomas Burger. Cambridge, MA: MIT Press.

Hackel, Steven W. 1997. "The Staff of Leadership: Indian Authority in the Missions of Alta California." *William and Mary Quarterly* 54 (2): 347–76.

Hacsi, Timothy A. 1997. *Second Home: Orphan Asylums and Poor Families in America.* Cambridge, MA: Harvard University Press.

Hale, Charles. 1968. *Mexican Liberalism in the Age of Mora, 1821–1853.* New Haven: Yale University Press.

Hamill, Hugh M. 1966. *The Hidalgo Revolt: Prelude to Mexican Independence.* Gainesville: University Press of Florida.

Hamman, André, OFM, ed. 1967. *The Mass: Ancient Liturgies and Patristic Texts.* Translated by Thomas Halton. Staten Island, NY: Alba House.

Hammerback, John C., and Richard J. Jensen. 1994. "Ethnic Heritage as Rhetorical Legacy: The Plan of Delano." *Quarterly Journal of Speech* 80 (1): 53–70.

Hammond, Michael, Jane Howarth, and Russell Keat. 1991. *Understanding Phenomenology.* Oxford: Blackwell.

Hanke, Lewis. 1959. *Aristotle and the American Indians: A Study in Race Prejudice in the Modern World.* London: Hollis and Carter.

———. 1964. "More Heat and Some Light on the Spanish Struggle for Justice in the Conquest of America." *Hispanic American Historical Review* 44 (3): 293–340.

———. 1974. *All Mankind Is One: A Study of the Disputation between Bartolomé de las Casas and Juan Ginés de Sepúlveda in 1550 on the Intellectual and Religious Capacity of the American Indians.* DeKalb: Northern Illinois University Press.

Hanks, William F. 1989. "Text and Textuality." *Annual Review of Anthropology* 18:95–127.

———. 1993. "Metalanguage and Pragmatics of Deixis." In *Reflexive Language: Reported Speech and Metapragmatics,* edited by John A. Lucy, 127–58. Cambridge: Cambridge University Press.

Hanna, Phil T. 1946. *The Dictionary of California Land Names.* Los Angeles: Automobile Club of Southern California.

Haraszthy, Arpad. 1978. *Wine-Making in California*. San Francisco: Book Club of California.

Harris, Max. 1996. "Moctezuma's Daughter: The Role of La Malinche in Meso-american Dance." *Journal of American Folklore* 109 (432): 149–77.

Hart, John Mason. 1998. "Social Unrest, Nationalism, and American Capital." In *Rural Revolt in Mexico: U.S. Intervention and the Domain of Southern Politics*, edited by Daniel Nugent, 72–88. Durham, NC: Duke University Press.

Hastings, Lansford W. [1849] 1932. *Narratives of the Trans-Mississippi Frontier: The Emigrants' Guide to Oregon and California*. Princeton: Princeton University Press.

Hayden, Dolores. 1984. *Redesigning the American Dream: The Future of Housing, Work, and Family Life*. New York: W.W. Norton & Company.

Heizer, Robert F. 1978. "Impact of Colonization on the Native California Societies." *Journal of San Diego History* 24 (1): 121–39.

Herbermann, Charles G. 1913–14. *The Catholic Encyclopedia*. New York: Encyclopedia Press.

Historia de los mexicanos por sus pinturas. [1888–1892] 1941–44. In *Nueva colección de documentos para la historia de México*, edited by Joaquín Garcia Icazbalceta, 3:209–40. México City: Salvador Chávez Hayhoe.

History of Fresno County, California. 1882. San Francisco: Wallace W. Elliott & Co.

Hoberg, George. 1992. *Pluralism by Design: Environmental Policy and the American Regulatory State*. New York: Praeger.

Hoffman, Pat. 1988. "Cesar Chavez's 'Fast for Life.'" *Christian Century* 105 (29): 895–97.

Humboldt, Alexander von. 1942. *Ensayo político sobre Nueva España*. Santiago: Ediciones Ercilla.

Husserl, Edmund. 1960. *Cartesian Meditations*. Translated by Dorion Cairns. The Hague: Martinus Nijhoff.

Ichon, Alain. 1969. *La religion des Totonaques de la sierra*. Paris: Editions du Centre National de la Recherche Scientifique.

Iser, Wolfgang. 1980. "The Reading Progress: A Phenomenological Approach." In *Reader-Response Criticism: From Formalism to Post-Structuralism*, edited by Jane P. Tompkins, 50–69. Baltimore: Johns Hopkins University Press.

Jackson, Michael. 1989. *Paths toward a Clearing: Radical Empiricism and Ethnographic Inquiry*. Bloomington: Indiana University Press.

———. 2002. *The Politics of Storytelling: Violence, Transgression and Intersubjectivity*. Copenhagen: Museum Tusculanum Press.

Jackson, Robert H. 1994. *Indian Population Decline: The Missions of Northwestern New Spain, 1687–1840*. Albuquerque: University of New Mexico Press.

Jackson, Robert H., and Edward D. Castillo. 1995. *Indians, Franciscans, and Spanish Colonization: The Impact of the Mission System on California Indians*. Albuquerque: University of New Mexico Press.

Jakobson, Roman. 1960. "Concluding Statement: Linguistics and Poetics." In *Style in Language*, edited by Thomas A. Sebeok, 350–77. New York: Technology Press of Massachusetts Institute of Technology.

———. 1987. *Language in Literature*. Edited by Krystyna Pomorska and Stephen Rudy. Cambridge, MA: Harvard University Press.

James, John. 1979. *The Contractors of Chartres*. Dooralong, NSW: Mandorla.

———. 1988. *The World of Chartres*. New York: Harry N. Abrams.

Jaramillo, Cleofas M. 1941. *Shadows of the Past (Sombras del pasado)*. Santa Fe: Seton Village Press.

Jefferson, Thomas. 1955. *Notes on the State of Virginia*. Chapel Hill: University of North Carolina Press.

———. 1975. *The Portable Thomas Jefferson*. Edited by Merrill D. Peterson. New York: Viking.

Jenkins, Craig J. 1985. *The Politics of Insurgency: The Farm Worker Movement in the 1960s*. New York: Columbia University Press.

Jenkins, Craig J., and Charles Perrow. 1977. "Insurgency of the Powerless: Farm Worker Movements (1946–1972)." *American Sociological Review* 42 (2): 249–68.

Jensen, Richard J., and John C. Hammerback, eds. 2002. "The Plan of Delano." In *The Words of César Chávez*, 16–20. College Station: Texas A & M University Press.

Jiménez Moreno, Wigberto, José Miranda, and María Teresa Fernández. 1963. *Historia de México*. Mexico City: Editorial ECLALSA / Editorial Porrúa.

Johannsen, Robert W. 1997. Introduction to *Manifest Destiny and Empire: American Antebellum Expansionism*, edited by Sam W. Haynes and Christopher Morris, 3–6. College Station: Texas A & M University Press.

Johnston, Francis. 1981. *The Wonder of Guadalupe: The Origin of and Cult of the Miraculous Image of the Blessed Virgin in Mexico*. Deven, UK: Augustine Publishing Company.

Kapferer, Bruce, and Angela Hobart. 2005. "Introduction: The Aesthetics of Symbolic Construction and Experience." In *Aesthetics in Performance: Formations of Symbolic Construction and Experience*, edited by Angela Hobart and Bruce Kapferer, 1–22. New York: Berghahn Books.

Katz, Friedrich. 1980. *La servidumbre agraria en México en la época porfiriana*. Mexico City: Era.

Katz, Michael B., Michael J. Doucet, and Mark J. Stern. 1982. *The Social Organization of Early Industrial Capitalism*. Cambridge, MA: Harvard University Press.

Katzenellenbogen, Adolf. 1959. *The Sculptural Programs of Chartres Cathedral*. Baltimore: Johns Hopkins University Press.

Knight, Alan. 1998. "The United States and the Mexican Peasantry, circa 1880–1940." In *Rural Revolt in Mexico: U.S. Intervention and the Domain of*

Subaltern Politics, edited by Daniel Nugent, 25–63. Durham, NC: Duke University Press.

Knights, Peter R. 1971. *The Plain People of Boston, 1830–1860: A Study in City Growth*. New York: Oxford University Press.

Kristeva, Julia. 1976. *Desire in Language*. Translated by Thomas Gora, Alice Jardine, and Leon S. Roudiez. New York: Columbia University Press.

———. 1982. *Powers of Horror: An Essay on Abjection*. Translated by Leon S. Roudiez. New York: Columbia University Press.

Kurath, Gertrude Prokosch. 1949. "Mexican Moriscas: A Problem in Dance Acculturation." *Journal of American Folklore* 62 (244): 87–106.

Lacan, Jacques. 1977. *Écrits: A Selection*. Translated by Alan Sheridan. New York: Norton.

Lafaye, Jacques. 1976. *Quetzalcóatl and Guadalupe: The Formation of Mexican National Consciousness, 1531–1813*. Translated by Benjamin Keen. Chicago: University of Chicago Press.

Lamb, Ursula. 1956. "Religious Conflicts in the Conquest of Mexico." *Journal of the History of Ideas* 17 (4): 526–39.

Langer, Susanne K. 1953. *Feeling and Form: A Theory of Art*. New York: Charles Scribner's Sons.

———. 1957. *Philosophy in a New Key: A Study in the Symbolism of Reason, Rite, and Art*. Cambridge, MA: Harvard University Press.

Lázaro Salinas, José. 1955. *La emigración de braceros: Una vision de un problema mexicano*. Mexico City: Cuauhtémoc.

Leatham, Miguel. 1989. "Indigenista Hermeneutics and the Historical Meaning of Our Lady of Guadalupe of Mexico." *Folklore Forum* 22 (1–2): 27–39.

Lebbe, Dom Bede, OSB. 1949. *The Mass: A Historical Commentary*. Westminster: Newman Press.

León, Luis D. 1999. "The Poetic Uses of Religion in *The Miraculous Day of Amalia Gómez*." *Religion and American Culture* 19 (2): 205–31.

———. 2004. *La Llorona's Children: Religion, Life, and Death in the U.S.–Mexican Borderlands*. Berkeley and Los Angeles: University of California Press.

León-Portilla, Miguel. 1963. *Aztec Thought and Culture: A Study of the Ancient Nahuatl Mind*. Translated by Jack Emory Davis. Norman: University of Oklahoma Press.

Lévi-Strauss, Claude. 1951. "Language and the Analysis of Social Laws." *American Anthropologist* 52 (2): 155–163.

———. 1966. *The Savage Mind*. Chicago: University of Chicago Press.

Lewis, Oscar. 1961. *The Children of Sanchez: Autobiography of a Mexican Family*. New York: Random House.

Lewis, Richard W. B. 1955. *The American Adam: Innocence, Tragedy and Tradition in the Nineteenth Century*. Chicago: University of Chicago Press.

Leyerle, John. 1977. "The Rose-Wheel Design and Dante's *Paradiso*." *University of Toronto Quarterly* 46 (3): 280–308.

Limón, José E. 1992. *Mexican Ballads, Chicano Poems: History and Influence in Mexican-American Social Poetry.* Berkeley and Los Angeles: University of California Press.

———. 1994. *Dancing with the Devil: Society and Cultural Poetics in Mexican-American South Texas.* Madison: University of Wisconsin Press.

———. 2007. "Américo Paredes: Ballad Scholar." Phillips Barry Lecture, 2004. *Journal of American Folklore* 120 (475): 3–18.

———. 2012. *Américo Paredes: Culture and Critique.* Austin: University of Texas Press.

Lloyd-Moffett, Stephen R. 2008. "The Mysticism and Social Action of César Chávez." In *Latino Religions and Civic Activism in the United States*, edited by Gastón Espinosa, Virgilio Elizondo, and Jesse Miranda, 35–51. Oxford: Oxford University Press.

Locke, John. [1690] 1988. *Two Treatises of Government.* Cambridge: Cambridge University Press.

Longe, Jacqueline L., and Deirdre S. Blanchfield, eds. 2002. *The Gale Encyclopedia of Medicine.* 2nd edition. Detroit: Gale Group.

Lopez, Elias S. 1995. *Education and Integration Prospects by Agricultural Regions of California.* San Luis Obispo: California State University at San Luis Obispo, Ethnic Studies Department.

Lynd, Robert S., and Helen Merrell Lynd. 1929. *Middletown: A Study in Contemporary American Culture.* New York: Harcourt, Brace and Company.

———. 1937. *Middletown in Transition: A Study in Cultural Conflicts.* New York: Harcourt, Brace and Company.

Mahoney, John J., and Charles M. Herlihy. 1918. *First Steps in Americanization: A Handbook for Teachers.* Boston: Houghton Mifflin.

Majka, Theo J., and Linda C. Majka. 1982. *Farm Workers, Agribusiness and the State.* Philadelphia: Temple University Press.

Marie, Sister Joseph, IHM. 1948. "The Role of the Church and the Folk in the Development of the Early Drama in New Mexico." PhD diss., University of Pennsylvania.

Martin, Joann. 1990. "Motherhood and Power: The Production of a Women's Culture of Politics in a Mexican Community." *American Ethnologist* 17 (3): 470–90.

Martin, Philip L. 1990. "Harvest of Confusion: Immigration Reform and California Agriculture." *International Migration Review* 24 (1): 69–95.

Marx, Karl. [1967] 1987. *Capital: A Critique of Political Economy.* Translated by Samuel Moore and Edward Aveling. 3 vols. New York: International Publishers.

Mason, Bert, Andrew Alvarado, and Robert Palacio. 1996. *Fresno in Transition: Urban Impacts of Rural Migration.* East Lansing: Julian Samora Research Institute, Michigan State University.

Massey, Douglas S. 1999. "International Migration at the Dawn of the Twenty-First Century: The Role of the State." *Population and Development Review* 25 (2): 303–22.

Matovina, Timothy. 2005. *Guadalupe and Her Faithful: Latino Catholics in San Antonio, from Colonial Origins to the Present.* Baltimore: Johns Hopkins University Press.

Matthiessen, Peter. 1993. "Postscript, Cesar Chavez." *New Yorker* 17 (May): 82.

McDowell, John H. 1981. "The Corrido of Greater Mexico as Discourse, Music, and Event." In *And Other Neighborly Names*, edited by Richard Bauman and Roger D. Abrahams, 44–75. Austin: University of Texas Press.

McWilliams, Carey. 1990. *North from Mexico: The Spanish-Speaking People of the United States.* New York: Praeger.

Menchaca, Martha. 1993. "Chicano Indianism: A Historical Account of Racial Repression in the United States."*American Ethnologist* 20 (3): 583–603.

Merleau-Ponty, Maurice. 1962. *Phenomenology of Perception.* Translated by Colin Smith. London: Routledge.

Mines, Richard, and Douglas S. Massey. 1985. "Patterns of Migration to the United States from Two Mexican Communities." *Latin American Research Review* 20 (2): 104–23.

Miyares, Ines M. 1997. "Changing Perceptions of Space and Place as Measures of Hmong Acculturation." *Professional Geographer* 49 (2): 214–24.

Monroy, Douglas. 1990. *Thrown among Strangers: The Making of Mexican Culture in Frontier California.* Berkeley and Los Angeles: University of California Press.

Monsiváis, Carlos. 1976. "Notas sobre la cultura Mexicana en el siglo XX." In *Historia General de México,* 4:303–476. Mexico City: El Colegio de México.

Montejano, David. 1987. *Anglos and Mexicans in the Making of Texas, 1836–1986.* Austin: University of Texas Press.

Monto, Alexander. 1994. *The Roots of Mexican Labor Migration.* Westport, CT: Praeger.

Mooney, Patrick H., and Theo J. Majka. 1995. *Farmers' and Farm Workers' Movements: Social Protest in American Agriculture.* New York: Twayne Publishers.

Moraga, Cherríe, and Gloria Anzaldúa, eds. 1981. *This Bridge Called My Back: Writings by Radical Women of Color.* Watertown, MA: Persephone Press.

Morrisey, Richard J. 1951. "The Northward Expansion of Cattle Ranching in New Spain, 1550–1600." *Agricultural History* 25 (3): 115–21.

Moses, Marion. 1993. "Farmworkers and Pesticides." In *Confronting Environmental Racism: Voices from the Grassroots*, edited by Robert D. Bullard, 161–78. Boston: South End Press.

———. 1998. "Pesticides." In *Public Health & Preventative Medicine*, 14th ed., edited by Robert B. Wallace, MD, MSc, 593–606. Stamford, CT: Appelton & Lange.

Nabhan-Warren, Kristy. 2005. *The Virgin of El Barrio: Marian Apparitions, Catholic Evangelizing, and Mexican American Activism*. New York: New York University Press.

Nájera-Ramírez, Olga. 1994. "Engendering Nationalism: Identity, Discourse, and the Mexican Charro." *Anthropological Quarterly* 67 (1): 1–14.

Namba, Tatsuji, Carl T. Nolte, Jerald Jackrel, and David Grob. 1971. "Poisoning Due to Organophosphate Insecticides: Acute and Chronic Manifestations." In *The American Journal of Medicine* 50 (4): 475–92.

Nether, Andrew. 1996. "Labor Republicanism, Race, and Popular Patriotism in the Era of Empire, 1890–1914." In *Bonds of Affection: Americans Define Their Patriotism*, edited by John Bodnar, 82–101. Princeton: Princeton University Press.

Nugent, Walter. 1999. *Into the West: The Story of Its People*. New York: Alfred A. Knopf.

Nunis, Doyce B., Jr. 1997. "Alta California's Trojan Horse: Foreign Immigration." *California History* 76 (2–3): 299–330.

Nutini, Hugo G., and Betty Bell. 1980. *Parentesco ritual*. México City: Fondo de Cultura Económica.

Obeyesekere, Gananath. 1992. *The Apotheosis of Captain Cook: European Mythmaking in the Pacific*. Princeton: Princeton University Press.

Oliver, Kelly. 1993. *Reading Kristeva: Unraveling the Double-Bind*. Bloomington: Indiana University Press.

Ortner, Sherry B. 1973. "On Key Symbols." *American Anthropologist* 75 (5): 1338–46.

Ovid. 1993. *Metamorphoses*. Translated by Allen Mandelbaum. San Diego: Harcourt, Inc.

Pagden, Anthony. 1982. *The Fall of Natural Man: The American Indian and the Origins of Comparative Ethnology*. Cambridge: Cambridge University Press.

———. 1987. *The Languages of Political Theory in Early-Modern Europe*. London: Cambridge University Press.

Paine, Thomas. [1791] 1984. *Rights of Man*. New York: Penguin.

———. [1776] 1986. *Common Sense*. New York: Penguin.

Paredes, Américo. 1958. *"With His Pistol in His Hand": A Border Ballad and Its Hero*. Austin: University of Texas Press.

Paredes, Américo, and María Herrera-Sobek. 2012. "The Corrido: An Invited Lecture at the 'Music in Culture' Public Lecture Series." *Journal of American Folklore* 125 (495): 23–44.

Parenti, Christian. 1999. *Lockdown America: Police and Prisons in the Age of Crisis*. London: Verso.

Park, Robert E., and Herbert A. Miller. 1921. *Old World Traits Transplanted*. New York: Harper & Brothers Publishers.

Parsons, Elsie C. 1929. *The Social Organization of the Tewa of New Mexico*. Menasha, WI: American Anthropological Association.

Paz, Octavio. 1985. *The Labyrinth of Solitude*. Translated by Lysander Kemp, Yara Milos, and Rachel Phillips Belash. New York: Grove Press.

Peirce, Charles S. 1940. *The Philosophy of Peirce: Selected Writings*. Edited by Justus Buchler. New York: Dover Press.

———. 1998. *The Essential Peirce: Selected Philosophical Writings*. Edited by the Peirce Edition Project. 2 vols. Bloomington: Indiana University Press.

Peña, Elaine A. 2011. *Performing Piety: Making Space Sacred with the Virgin of Guadalupe*. Berkeley: University of California Press.

Peninou, Ernest, and Sidney Greenleaf. 1954. *Winemaking in California*. Vol. 3, *The California Wine Association*. San Francisco: Porpoise Bookshop.

Pepper, Stephen P. 1942. *World Hypothesis: A Study in Evidence*. Berkeley and Los Angeles: University of California Press.

Perin, Constance. 1977. *Everything in Its Place: Social Order and Land Use in America*. Princeton: Princeton University Press.

Pitt, Leonard. 1971. *The Decline of the Californios: A Social History of the Spanish-Speaking Californians, 1846–1980*. Berkeley and Los Angeles: University of California Press.

Pius IX. 1980. *Egregiis suis*, 3 December 1869. In *The Holy Rosary*, translated by Paul J. Oligny, OFM, 37. Boston: St. Paul Editions.

Plato. 1961. *The Collected Dialogues of Plato*. Edited by Edith Hamilton and Huntington Cairns. Bollingen Series 71: Princeton University Press.

Plummer, William. 1988. "Cesar Chavez Breaks His Longest Fast as His Followers Pray for an End to the Grapes of Wrath." *People Weekly* 30 (September): 52.

Poole, C. M. Stafford. 1995. *Our Lady of Guadalupe: The Origins and Sources of a Mexican National Symbol, 1531–1797*. Tucson: University of Arizona Press.

———. 2006. *The Guadalupan Controversies in Mexico*. Stanford: Stanford University Press.

Proceedings: Americanization Conference. 1919. Washington, DC: Government Printing Office.

Quiñones, Juan Gómez. 1990. *Chicano Politics: Reality and Promise, 1940–1990*. Albuquerque: University of New Mexico Press.

Radcliffe-Brown, A.R. 1948. *The Andaman Islands*. Glencoe, IL: Free Press.

———. 1952. *Structure and Function in Primitive Society*. London: Cohen & West LTD.

Rappaport, Roy A. 1999. *Ritual and Religion in the Making of Humanity*. Cambridge: Cambridge University Press.

Rhodes, Lorna A. 1998. "Panoptical Intimacies." *Public Culture* 10 (2): 285–311.

Ricard, Robert. 1966. *The Spiritual Conquest of Mexico: An Essay on the Apostolate and the Evangelizing Methods of the Mendicant Orders in New Spain, 1532–1572.* Translated by Lesley Byrd Simpson. Berkeley and Los Angeles: University of California Press.

Ricoeur, Paul. 1987. "Energetics and Hermeneutics in *The Interpretation of Dreams.*" In *Modern Critical Interpretations: Sigmund Freud's "The Interpretation of Dreams,"* edited by Harold Bloom, 67–76. New York: Chelsea House.

Rivera-Batiz, Francisco L., Selig L. Sechzer, and Ira N. Gang. 1991. *U.S. Immigration Policy Reform in the 1980s.* New York: Praeger.

Robb, J. D. 1961. "The Matachines Dance—A Ritual Folk Dance." *Western Folklore* 20 (2): 87–100.

Rodriguez, Jeanette. 1994. *Our Lady of Guadalupe: Faith and Empowerment among Mexican-American Women.* Austin: University of Texas Press.

Rodriguez, Sylvia. 1991. "The Taos Pueblo Matachines: Ritual Symbolism and Interethnic Relations." *American Ethnologist* 18 (2): 234–56.

———. 1994. "Defended Boundaries, Precarious Elites: The Arroyo Seco Matachines Dance." *Journal of American Folklore* 107 (424): 248–67.

———. 1996. *The Matachines Dance: Ritual Symbolism and Interethnic Relations in the Upper Río Grande Valley.* Albuquerque: University of New Mexico Press.

Rojas Sánchez, Mario, and J. Hernández Illescas. 1983. *Las estrellas del manto de la Virgen de Guadalupe.* México City: Francisco Méndez Oteo.

Rosaldo, Renato. 1989. *Culture & Truth: The Remaking of Social Analysis.* Boston: Beacon Press.

Roseberry, William. 1995. "Latin American Peasant Studies in a 'Postcolonial' Era." *Journal of Latin American Anthropology* 1(1): 150–77.

Rosenus, Alan. 1995. *General M. G. Vallejo and the Advent of the Americans.* Albuquerque: University of New Mexico Press.

Rossi, Peter H. 1955. *Why Families Move: A Study in the Social Psychology of Urban Residential Mobility.* Glencoe, IL: Free Press.

Rossi, Peter H., and Anne B. Shlay. 1982. "Residential Mobility and Public Policy Issues: 'Why Families Move' Revisited." *Journal of Social Issues* 38 (3): 21–34.

Ruiz, Vicki L. 1996. "'Star Struck': Acculturation, Adolescence, and the Mexican-American Woman, 1920–1950." In *Between Two Worlds: Mexican Immigrants in the United States,* edited by David G. Gutiérrez, 125–47. Wilmington: Jaguar Books on Latin America.

Sagarena, Roberto Lint. 2002. "Building California's Past: Mission Revival Architecture and Regional Identity." *Journal of Urban History* 28 (4): 429–44.

Sahagún, Fray Bernardino de. 1969. *Historia general de las cosas de Nueva España.* 4 vols. Mexico City: Editorial Porrua, S. A.

———. [1590] 1975. *Florentine Codex: General History of the Things of New Spain.* Edited by Charles E. Dibble and Arthur J. O. Anderson. 12 books. Santa Fe: School of American Research.

———. 1976. *A History of Ancient Mexico.* Translated by Fanny R. Bandelier. Glorieta, NM: Rio Grande Press, Inc.

Sahlins, Marshal D. 1981. *Historical Metaphors and Mythical Realities: Structures in the Early History of the Sandwich Islands Kingdom.* Ann Arbor: University of Michigan Press.

Salley, H. E. 1977. *History of California Post Offices, 1949–1976.* La Mesa, CA: Postal History Associations, Inc.

Sampson, Robert D. 2003. *John L. O'Sullivan and His Times.* Kent, OH: Kent State University Press.

Sánchez, George. 1993. *Becoming Mexican American: Ethnicity, Culture and Identity in Chicano Los Angeles, 1900–1945.* New York: Oxford University Press.

Sánchez, Rosaura. 1995. *Telling Identities: The Californio Testimonies.* Minneapolis: University of Minnesota Press.

Sandell, David P. 2014. "Mexican Retablos." *Journal of Folklore Research* 51 (1): 13–47.

Sandos, James A. 1998. "Historic Preservation and Historical Facts: Helen Hunt Jackson, Rancho Comulos, and Ramonana." *California History* 77 (3): 168–85.

Schieffelin, Edward L. 1985. "Performance and the Cultural Construction of Reality." *American Ethnologist* 12 (4): 707–24.

Segal, Aaron. 1993. *An Atlas of International Migration.* London: Hans Zell Publishers.

Sharlip, William, and Albert A. Owens. 1925. *Adult Immigrant Education: Its Scope, Content, and Methods.* New York: Macmillan.

Sheridan, Alan. 1977. Translator's note to *Écrits: A Selection*, by Jacques Lacan, viii–xi. Translated by Alan Sheridan. New York: W. W. Norton.

Shorter, Edward. 1975. *The Making of the Modern Family.* New York: Basic Books.

Skeat, Walter W., ed. 1881. *Aelfric's Lives of Saints.* London: N. Trübner & Co.

Slotkin, Richard. 1992. *Gunfighter Nation: The Myth of the Frontier in Twentieth-Century America.* New York: Maxwell Macmillan International.

Smith, Henry Nash. 1950. *Virgin Land: The American West as Symbol and Myth.* Cambridge, MA: Harvard University Press.

Smith, Jody Brant. 1984. *The Image of Guadalupe: Myth or Miracle?* New York: Doubleday / Image Books.

Smith, Jonathan. 1980. "The Bare Facts of Ritual." *History of Religions* 20 (1–2): 112–27.

———. 1987. *To Take Place: Toward a Theory in Ritual.* Chicago: University of Chicago Press.

Southern, Richard William. 1953. *The Making of the Middle Ages.* New Haven: Yale University Press.

Spicer, Edward H. 1962. *Cycles of Conquest: The Impact of Spain, Mexico, and the United States on the Indians of the Southwest, 1533–1960.* Tucson: University of Arizona Press.

Srinivas, M. N. 1952. *Religion and Society among the Coorgs of South India.* Oxford: Oxford University Press.

Steinbeck, John. 1939. *The Grapes of Wrath.* New York: Viking.

Steiner, Michael. 1995. "From Frontier to Region: Frederick Jackson Turner and the New Western History." *Pacific Historical Review* 64 (4): 479–501.

Stevens-Arroyo, Anthony M. 2002. *The National Survey of Leadership in Latino Parishes and Congregations.* The PARAL Study. Brooklyn: Brooklyn College Print Works.

Stevens-Arroyo, Anthony M., and Gilbert R. Cadena, eds. 1995. *Old Masks, New Faces: Religion and Latino Identities.* New York: Bildner Center for Western Hemisphere Studies.

Stevens-Arroyo, Anthony M., and Ana María Díaz-Stevens, eds. 1994. *An Enduring Flame: Studies on Latino Religiosity.* New York: Bildner Center for Western Hemisphere Studies.

Sticca, Sandro. 1972. "The Literary Genesis of the Latin Passion Play and the *Planctus Mariae*: A New Christocentric and Marian Theology." In *The Medieval Drama*, edited by Sandro Sticca, 39–68. Albany: State University of New York Press.

Tambiah, Stanley J. 1985. *Culture, Thought, and Social Action: An Anthropological Perspective.* Cambridge, MA: Harvard University Press.

Taussig, Michael. 1992. *The Nervous System.* New York: Routledge.

Taylor, J. Edward, Philip L. Martin, and Michael Fix. 1997. *Poverty amid Prosperity: Immigration and the Changing Face of Rural California.* Washington, DC: Urban Institute.

Taylor, Paul S. 1983. *On the Ground in the Thirties.* Salt Lake City: Peregrine Smith Books.

Taylor, William B. 1987. "The Virgin of Guadalupe in New Spain: An Inquiry into the Social History of Marian Devotion." *American Ethnologist* 14 (1): 9–33.

Tedlock, Dennis, and Bruce Mannheim. 1995. Introduction to *The Dialogic Emergence of Culture*, edited by Dennis Tedlock and Bruce Mannheim, 1–32. Urbana: University of Illinois Press.

Thernstrom, Stephan. 1964. *Poverty and Progress: Social Mobility in a Nineteenth-Century City.* Cambridge, MA: Harvard University Press.

Thernstrom, Stephan, and Richard Sennett, eds. 1969. *Nineteenth-Century Cities: Essays in the New Urban History.* New Haven: Yale University Press.

Thickens, Virginia Emily. 1939. "Pioneer Colonies of Fresno County." Master's thesis, University of California, Berkeley. CSUF Library.

Thompson, Waddy. 1846. *Recollections of Mexico.* New York: Wiley and Putnam.

Tobey, Ronald, Charles Wetherell, and Jay Brigham. 1990. "Moving Out and Settling In: Residential Mobility, Home Owning, and the Public Enframing of Citizenship, 1921–1950." *American Historical Review* 94 (5): 1395–1422.

Toor, Frances. 1947. *A Treasury of Mexican Folkways.* Mexico City: Mexico Press.

Torre Villar, Ernesto de la, and Ramiro Navarro de Anda. 1982. *Testimonios históricos Guadalupanos.* México City: Fondo de Cultura Económica.

Treadwell, Edward. 1931. *The Cattle King: A Dramatized Biography.* New York: Macmillan.

Treviño, Adrian, and Barbara Gilles. 1994. "A History of the Matachines Dance." *New Mexico Historical Review* 69 (2): 105–25.

Treviño, Roberto R. 2006. *The Church in the Barrio.* Chapel Hill: University of North Carolina Press.

Trexler, Richard C. 2003. *Reliving Golgotha: The Passion Play of Iztapalapa.* Cambridge, MA: Harvard University Press.

Turner, Edith. 2006. "Advances in the Study of Spirit Experience: Drawing Together Many Threads." *Anthropology of Consciousness* 17 (2): 33–61.

Turner, Frederick Jackson. 1920. *The Frontier in American History.* New York: Henry Holt and Company.

Turner, Victor W. 1962. *Chihamba, the White Spirit: A Ritual Drama of the Ndembu.* Manchester: Manchester University Press.

——. 1967. "A Ndembu Doctor in Practice." In *The Forest of Symbols*, 359–94. Ithaca, NY: Cornell University Press.

——. 1974. *Dramas, Fields, and Metaphors: Symbolic Action in Human Society.* Ithaca, NY: Cornell University Press.

United States Department of Labor, Office of Policy Planning and Research. 1965. *The Negro Family: The Case for National Action.* Washington, DC: U.S. Government Printing Office.

Valdez, Luis. 1971. "The Tale of la Raza." In *The Chicanos: Mexican-American Voices*, edited by Ludwig Santibáñez and James Santibáñez, 95–100. Baltimore: Penguin Books.

Vallejo, Mariano G. n.d. *Historical and Personal Memoirs Relating to Alta California.* Translated by Earle E. Hewitt. 5 vols. Berkeley: Bancroft Library, University of California at Berkeley.

Vanderwood, Paul J. 1992. *Disorder and Progress: Bandits, Police, and Mexican Development.* Wilmington: SR Books.

Vandor, Paul E. 1919. *History of Fresno County with Biographical Sketches.* Los Angeles: Historic Record Company.

Van Nuys, Frank. 2002. *Americanizing the West: Race, Immigrants, and Citizenship, 1890–1930.* Lawrence: University of Kansas Press.

Vauchez, André, ed. 2000. *Encyclopedia of the Middle Ages.* Translated by Adrian Walford. Chicago: Fitzroy Dearborn Publishers.

Vélez-Ibáñez, Carlos G. 1996. *Border Visions: Mexican Cultures of the Southwest United States.* Tucson: University of Arizona Press.

Verdier, Paul. 1933. *History of Wine: How and When to Drink It.* San Francisco: City of Paris.

Virgil. 1983. *The Aeneid.* Translated by Robert Fitzgerald. Toronto: Random House, Inc.

Wade, Peter. 1999. "Working Culture: Making Cultural Identities in Cali, Columbia." *Current Anthropology* 40 (4): 449–71.

Wagner, Henry Raup. 1944. *The Rise of Fernando Cortés.* Los Angeles: Cortés Society.

"Walkout in Albuquerque: The Chicano Movement Becomes Nationwide." 1972. In *Aztlan: An Anthology of Mexican American Literature*, edited by Luis Valdez and Stan Steiner, 211–14. New York: Vintage Books.

Warner, Michael. 1993. "The Mass Public and the Mass Subject." In *The Phantom Public Sphere*, edited by Bruce Robins, 234–56. Minneapolis: University of Minnesota Press.

Way of the Cross: The Passion of Christ in the Americas. Edited by Virgil Elizondo. Translated by John Drury. Maryknoll, NY: Orbis Books.

Webb, Walter Prescott. 1931. *The Great Plains.* New York: Grosset & Dunlap.

———. 1952. *The Great Frontier.* Boston: Houghton Mifflin.

Weber, David J. 1982. *The Mexican Frontier, 1821–1846: The American Southwest under Mexico.* Albuquerque: University of New Mexico Press.

Weber, Max. 1958. "Politics as a Vocation." In *From Max Weber: Essays in Sociology.* Translated by Hans H. Gerth and C. Wright Mills, 77–128. New York: Oxford University Press.

Weinberg, Albert K. 1935. *Manifest Destiny: A Study of Nationalist Expansionism in American History.* Baltimore: Johns Hopkins University Press.

Wells, Miriam J. 1981. "Social Conflict, Commodity Constraints, and Labor Market Structure in Agriculture." *Society for Comparative Study of Society and History* 23 (4): 679–704.

———. 1996. *Strawberry Fields: Politics, Class, and Work in California Agriculture.* Ithaca, NY: Cornell University Press.

———. 2000. "Politics, Locality, and Economic Restructuring: California's Central Coast Strawberry Industry in the Post–World War II Period." *Economic Geography* 76 (1): 28–49.

White, Franklin M. M., Fay G. Cohen, Greg Sherman, and Ross McCurdy. 1988. "Chemicals, Birth Defects and Stillbirths in New Brunswick: Associations with Agriculture Activity." *Canadian Medical Association* 138 (2): 117–24.

Whitman, Walt. [1867] 1921. *"Leaves of Grass" and Selected Prose.* New York: Modern Library.

Williams, Raymond. 1977. *Marxism and Literature.* Oxford: Oxford University Press.

Willis, Roy G. 1999. *Some Spirits Heal, Others Only Dance: Journey into Human Selfhood in an African Village.* Oxford: Berg.

Wilson, Tamar Diana. 1993. "Theoretical Approaches to Mexican Wage Labor Migration." *Latin American Perspectives* 20 (3): 98–129.

Winston-Allen, Anne. 1998. *Stories of the Rose: The Making of the Rosary in the Middle Ages.* University Park: Pennsylvania State University Press.

Wolf, Eric R. 1958. "The Virgin of Guadalupe: A Mexican National Symbol." *Journal of American Folklore* 71 (279): 34–39.

Womack, John, Jr. 1970. *Zapata and the Mexican Revolution.* New York: Vintage Books.

Wrobel, David M. 1996. "Beyond the Frontier-Region Dichotomy." *Pacific Historical Review* 65 (3): 401–29.

INDEX

DAVID P. SANDELL

is associate professor of anthropology at Texas Christian University.